Conversations With California's New Winemakers

VINTAGE TALK

CONVERSATIONS WITH
CALIFORNIA'S NEW WINEMAKERS

VINTAGE TALK

DENNIS SCHAEFER

CAPRA PRESS
SANTA BARBARA

For Bud and Goldie,
who taught me moderation in all things.

PHOTO CREDITS:

Larry Brooks, courtesy Chalone, Inc.; Patrick Campbell, courtesy Laurel Glen Vineyard; Jim Clendenen, by Dennis Schaefer; Bruno D'Alfonso, by Dennis Schaefer; Jill Davis, by M.J. Wickham, courtesy Buena Vista Winery (cover); and by Fred Lyon, courtesy Buena Vista Winery (inside); Steve Doerner, courtesy Steve Doerner; Randy Dunn, by Dennis Schaefer; Bill Dyer, courtesy Sterling Vineyards; Dawnine Dyer, courtesy Domaine Chandon; Randall Grahm, by Dennis Schaefer; David Graves and Richard Ward, by Dennis Schaefer; Scott Harvey, by Dennis Schaefer; Dan Lee, by Dennis Schaefer; Bob Lindquist, by Dennis Schaefer; Zelma Long, by David Buchholz, courtesy of Simi Winery; Tim Mondavi, courtesy of Robert Mondavi Winery; Joel Peterson, by Jean Marie Simonet, courtesy of Ravenswood; David Ramey, courtesy of Chalk Hill Winery; Adam Tolmach, by Dennis Schaefer; Nils Venge, by Dennis Schaefer.

Library of Congress Cataloging-in-Publication Data

Schaefer, Dennis.
Vintage Talk: Conversations with California's New Winemakers/Dennis Schaefer.
p.   cm.
ISBN 0-88496-360-8
1. Wine and winemaking—California. I. Title.
TP557.S27 1994
641.2'2'09794—dc20

93-44347
CIP

CAPRA PRESS
P.O. Box 2068, Santa Barbara, CA 93102

CONTENTS

INTRODUCTION

"I do not make the wines," an aging patriarch of California winemaking once said, "Nature makes the wines and I am just the caretaker." As much as that seems to devalue the role of the winemaker, those pioneer immigrants who attempted to adapt European viticultural and fermentation methods in California were basically content to accept what nature gave them. But in many cases their old-world knowledge was out of context in the soils, climates and grape varieties of the New World. Uprooted from their native land and without the support of centuries-old cultural traditions, they did the best they could under the circumstances. The human contribution to winemaking was sometimes little more than educated guessing based on previous vintages. For many winemakers, their only training came informally at the side of their fathers. In essence, with a little nudge from the hand of man, the wines did indeed make themselves.

This passive approach to winemaking gained California a mediocre reputation for most of its wines in the first half of this century. Prohibition, of course, didn't help matters either. Even as late as the 1950s, much California wine was sold off in tank car lots to wholesalers and retailers who plastered their own brand name on the wine and labeled it "Chablis," or "Burgundy." Wines that were actually bottled and sold by the wineries had a limited market and sold for a pittance. Consequently, there was no commitment to excellence and little reason to search for the components that contributed to world-class wine. The wine of that era was unquestionably inferior to its European counterparts, an image that has taken California wine nearly three decades to overcome.

1966, however, ushered in the modern era of California winemaking. That was the year Robert Mondavi established his own winery, determined to set high standards for wines that carried his name. Other skillful and iconoclastic winemakers, like Andre Tchelistcheff and Martin Ray, had come before him but they had labored on a smaller scale, appealing to a cult of connoisseurs. Mondavi was the first to back up his beliefs on such a large scale. From the modern Mission-architecture winery design by Cliff May to the expensive French barrels and all the high tech equipment money could buy, Mondavi let it be known that he intended to set the standards for those who came after him.

Mondavi had no aversion to new methodology or technology, as his forebears did. Unfortunately, with Mondavi leading the way, the pendulum swung to the opposite extreme, where the use of technology in winemaking was so overemphasized that many wines made under these technological regimes tasted sterile and lifeless. Consequently, some of his experimentation led to dead ends and Mondavi wines sometimes reflected that. But Mondavi was not afraid to take risks if they might bring better wines. One thing was sure: he was no longer a "caretaker" of the wines. He became an active participant searching for the keys to producing the finest wines in California.

Paradoxically his "technological innovations" had exactly the opposite effect on a number of smaller, artisan wineries: many of these winemakers redoubled their efforts to take a long look back at traditional European methods and properly adapt them to California's climate and soil.

Just to put things in perspective and to see how far we've come in a little over twenty-five years, Mondavi was the first major winery established in the Napa Valley since Prohibition. It was only the twenty-third winery in the valley; today there are more than two hundred in Napa Valley alone, with over eight hundred wineries in California.

* * *

During the wine boom seventies, many fledgling wineries based their viticultural and enological methods on their neighbor's vineyards or on what someone in the next county was successfully doing. Some of the business people behind the wineries believed winemaking was akin to mathematics: plug the variables into the winemaking equation and get a salable wine product. Many vintners didn't even acknowledge that different grape varietals demanded different handling and winemaking regimes. They had one formula for red wine and another for white. The terrible reputation of Pinot Noir in California is partly attributable to winemakers who ran Pinot Noir through the red wine formula and treated it just as they would Cabernet Sauvignon. This procedure would be laughed at today but such blanket winemaking "recipes" had wide credence then. Moreover, many winemakers didn't understand that the terroir, the various differences in soil, climate and exposure, also required different methodologies.

Coupled with this confusion was the fact that wineries and grape growers were still planting specific grape varietals according to the highest price paid per ton, disregarding the fact that the climate and soil might be inappropriate for that particular varietal. Cabernet Sauvignon was widely planted in Monterey and Santa Barbara counties, where the cool climate made it difficult to ripen these grapes; Pinot Noir was planted in Calistoga, where the climate was altogether too hot. From a viticultural standpoint of planting the best varietals in the best soil and the best climate, this was ridiculous, but top dollar was being paid for these grapes.

Ironically, the recent onslaught of dreaded phylloxera has a silver lining. This root louse nematode attacks individual vine roots, eventually destroying the grapevine. Today vast vineyards, principally in Napa and Somona, have varying degrees of phylloxera; it will cost untold millions to replant the vineyards using disease resistant rootstocks. But when these vineyards are replanted, the grape variety most suited to the soil and climate will be planted. A sad and expensive viticultural lesson but perhaps a blessing in disguise for the future of California wine.

Another disturbing factor was the practice of larger wineries paying growers a bonus for every extra degree of ripeness in the harvested grapes they bought. In theory, this practice insured the winery of getting ripe grapes. In practice, many growers, tantalized by that extra cash bonus, let the grapes hang until they were overripe. In the bottle, this translated roughly to 13.5 to 14 percent alcohol in wines that had little finesse or style; the high alcohol content made the resulting wines harsh, unpleasant and, in retrospect, poor candidates for extended aging.

In spite of, and perhaps because of these factors, California wine was considered to have come of age in 1976, when, at a much publicized blind tasting in Paris, several California wines were clear winners over much more renowned French wines. When it was revealed that the distinguished French judges had awarded first place to a Cabernet Sauvignon from Stag's Leap and a Chardonnay from Chateau Montelena, the American media seized on these facts with a vengeance, much to the delight of the California wine industry.

Unfortunately, this "winning" development was probably one of the most detrimental things to happen to California wines. At that time, the prevailing winemaking wisdom was to harvest overripe grapes resulting in a high degree of alcohol. This type of wine had great power and intensity. In a blind tasting, they naturally steamrolled the competition. These high alcohol wines were big and brawny, without more important characteristics like structure, balance, elegance and finesse. In addition, these wines were so overpowering and alcoholic that they rarely matched up well with food. The first glass rarely invited a second. The final disappointment was that these wines were so poorly structured that they did not age well like classic European wines; they were best when consumed young and did not gain much complexity with time in the bottle.

But the 1976 Paris tasting sent a message to California winemakers to continue pursuing this style. Consequently, progress in California winemaking stalled at this level as many of the larger wineries stumbled over each other in a rush to emulate these award-winning wines. This is not meant to paint an overly pessimistic picture of California winemaking in the seventies. In the premium wine category, some small wineries were turning out exceedingly good and age-worthy wines, but they were the exception. While Europeans continued to make world-class wines, California vintners struggled to attain a track record of consistency, both in style and quality, from year to year.

However, during the last fifteen years, things have changed dramatically. California wines have taken such a tremendous leap in quality that it is no longer complimentary simply to compare them en bloc to their French counterparts. While comparisons are still inevitable, contemporary California wines are not necessarily better or worse than European wines from some abstract quality standpoint; they are just different.

California wines have different nuances from European wines due to the obvious differences in soil and climate. The new wave of California winemakers do not wish to slavishly imitate the best French or Italian wines; instead they wish to utilize whatever methods will produce balanced, flavorful and delicious wines from California soil. They are beginning to find their own voice; the way best to express themselves. Their wines are good enough to be judged on their own merits rather than some arbitrary benchmark.

This increase in quality is attributable to a number of factors: better viticultural practices, proper utilization of soil and climate and more appropriate enological techniques. But the greatest factor is the human element—the emergence of knowledgeable winemakers who, through their deep involvement in all aspects of managing winemaking variables, have demonstrated their firm commitment to producing fine wines.

These young, contemporary winemakers are at the forefront of the evolution to higher quality at California wineries. While they are well-schooled in classical winemaking procedures, they are not afraid to experiment and utilize new techniques or resurrect ancient ones when it produces a better wine. They are part of a movement to emphasize the intensity of flavor that is the birthright of California, owing to its sunny Mediterranean climate and rich soils. They are refining their techniques to preserve the innate characteristics of the fruit while at the same time building in more complexity to enhance both drinkability and longevity. They are eliminating distracting and disparate elements from their wines in favor of creating a harmonious balance where no one element of the wine is dominate. In this way, a variety of complex aromas and flavors combine to bring a suppleness, delicacy and finesse that has heretofore been missing from many California wines.

*　　*　　*

If there is any one element these winemakers agree on it is that the basic raw ingredient, the grape, is the primary determining factor in the quality of the wine. Ancient and honorable tradition says that "wine is made in the vineyard." This new wave of winemakers, the second "active" generation of winemakers, believes this even more fervently than their predecessors. It is relatively easy, they say, to make great wine from great grapes; conversely, it is nearly impossible to make good wine from inferior grapes. These winemakers consistently utilize vineyards that combine the proper grape varietal with the appropriate climate and soil. Assured of access to quality grape sources, they feel confident they can lead the winemaking down the right paths. The emphasis on the grapes may seem to minimize the contribution of the winemaker but consider this: from the selection of the grape clone and planting it in the proper soil and climate, through the vagaries of nature and the harvest, through fermentation, cellaring, aging and bottling, there are a thousand potential paths that grapes and the resultant wine can follow. The winemaker, through training and past experience, must make a decision at each juncture, as to the correct path for the type and style of wine they intend to make.

California's climate may be relatively stable compared to Europe's, but nature is variable and grapes from different vineyards may be acquired each year, so every vintage is different here too. Each harvest presents a new set of variables for the winemaker. No intelligent winemaker makes wine by a strict formula or recipe. Recipes are great for insuring consistency when preparing chicken piccata or when making an industrial-grade food product like mayonnaise. Just as a stopped clock is right twice a day, so winemakers in the seventies who chose to make wine by a recipe found that the recipe meshed with the variables once or twice in the decade and occasionally they produced very good wines. Unfortunately, the other eight years out of the ten, the wines ranged from mediocre to downright poor. Ironically, the consistent application of a recipe bred inconsistency in the wines because no consideration was given to the changing variables that can affect grape and wine quality.

So many factors enter into the decision-making process for great wine that there are no simple directions for winemaking. What worked in the vineyards last year may not work this year, due to the variations in the growing season.

What seemed a good fermentation and cellar regime last year may not be appropriate this year because the winemaker may have picked the grapes earlier or later than last year. Winemaking procedures must always reflect what is happening in the vineyards and cellars this year; in fact, any number of procedures described herein may be modified or even totally dismissed next year because they might be inappropriate for that harvest.

Although it's true there are empirical measurements of sugar, acid and pH levels that give the winemaker an indication of the condition of the grapes and the resultant wine, winemakers can become overreliant on this type of methodology. This kind of winemaking has been criticized as "making wine by the numbers," resulting in what are cryptically termed "enological wines." These wines have all the right sugar, acid and pH ratios but seem to be put together by a lab technician whose only reference points are these numerical values. While these wines may be flawless, they really don't express the character of the grape; rather the character of the grape is subverted and neutralized in favor of the idea of a "technically correct" wine. These wines tend to be passionless and soulless, as though the winemaker didn't take the time to monitor and shepherd the wine to its fullest potential.

This winemaking philosophy gave rise to a fad of so-called "food wines." These were wines with little flavor or body, and by virtue of their being indistinct, were said to go better with food. Unfortunately, a lot of mediocre wines achieved some cachet by passing themselves off as such. The good news is that both winemakers and wine drinkers realized this notion was a marketing canard. Food wines in the eighties were just a new euphemism for the recipe winemaking prevalent in the seventies.

However easy winemaking may appear to the uninitiated—the first wine was probably made by bruising ripe grapes and letting them sit until fermentation began and the juice was transformed—it requires more than just a passing grasp of agriculture, plant science, chemistry, physics, philosophy and economics. Thousands of decisions must be made in a wine's lifetime which are multiplied by the many competing and sometimes conflicting variables. This is why knowledgeable winemakers will often be found on the cellar floor with their nose in a barrel, assessing the constant development of the wine. These winemaking decisions are made daily and are never made in a vacuum. There are always trade-offs; what is gained in one area for the wine is often lost in another area. For example, fining Cabernet Sauvignon will reduce its tannins and make it more palatable but some of the flavor components are also lost as a result. The impact of all the decisions are cumulative so that the bottle of wine finally represents a whole more complex than the sum of its parts.

This book is the first to focus on some of the new breed of California winemakers, the second generation of "active" winemakers. The patriarchs of California winemaking and their history are already well known. Their legacy will now be expanded into the future by this younger, more idealistic group of winemakers (and many others who could not be included here).

These winemakers are on the cutting edge of viticultural and enological knowledge and will be leading the progress of California wines into the next century. This period may well go down in history as the first "golden age" of California winemaking. Europeans have had centuries to perfect their winemaking craft; in California, we have absorbed and matured a great deal in only twenty-five years.

These interviews explore each individual's aspirations, techniques and philosophies, both in the vineyard and in the winery. They illustrate, in the winemakers' own words, exactly what it is they do, why they do it and what impact it has on the winemaking process and the finished product. It offers a thorough, first-hand knowledge of the winemaking process, emphasizing details that distinguish a good wine from a great one. It also attempts to spotlight the craft of winemaking and some of the individuals who have sought to extend its aesthetic parameters, providing the wine consumer with a wider variety of choices in the marketplace. This is not a "how to" book, although the technical aspects of winemaking will naturally be discussed. This is a "why" book, concerned, above all, with the individual winemakers' perspectives. It is a snapshot, a freeze of history, of how they felt toward their chosen calling at a certain place and time. Due to the ever-changing nature of winemaking, the focus of these conversations might very well be different tomorrow.

Most of these winemakers are about forty years old, have a college background, plus a hands-on winemaking apprenticeship. They are now in place as winemakers throughout the state and have established significant reputations. Some chose to become proprietors of small, artisan wineries, while others are committed to producing fine wine in large, corporate settings. Some are establishing new standards with mainstream varietals like Cabernet Sauvignon, Chardonnay and Pinot Noir, while others are leading the way in exploring lesser known varietals like Syrah, Marsanne, Viognier and Nebbiolo. Winemaking is more than just a job to them; it's a passion. Many came to winemaking as a second career, attracted by the life-style and the opportunity to be involved in a timeless craft both intellectually and sensually stimulating. Since they are relatively young, they will be making wine for the next thirty or forty years, influencing the variety and style of wine we drink far into the future. Taken collectively, they are representative of a new generation of winemakers who find new challenges with every vintage. It is an exciting time to be a winemaker in California and, by extension, a rewarding era for the wine consumer.

The achievements of the winemakers included here, individually and collectively, are extremely impressive. The proof, as they say, is "in the bottle." The end product of their efforts is available to complement and augment the pleasures of the dining table. Certainly, many other winemakers in California (as well as in Oregon, Washington, Texas and New York) are making contributions to the general body of winemaking knowledge that bode well for the future of quality wine. The process of choosing twenty winemakers for this book was extremely difficult; obviously the judgment was subjective, as judging wine itself is. However, this book is a result of twenty years of traveling up and down the dusty wine trails and back roads of California wine country. In the process, many opinions were gathered from winemakers, vintners, grape growers, barrel brokers, wholesalers, retailers, wine writers and finally, wine consumers. This book, and the winemakers who have their say here, represents a cross section of the great diversity of types and styles prevalent in California winemaking today. Every effort was made to include a wide range of backgrounds and perspectives.

During these conversations, I came to truly appreciate the winemakers' innovative approaches to their work and I was impressed with the seemingly boundless energy they displayed for their craft. Without exception, I found them to be hardworking, down-to-earth, articulate individuals whose range of knowledge and interests extends far beyond winemaking into philosophy, art, music, literature, medicine, science and, of course, the culinary arts. I am grateful to them all for generously making their time available to me, and through the book that follows, I am most happy to share their insights and observations with readers in the hope of fostering a greater understanding of California winemaking. The new generation of winemakers are charting an innovative and exciting course for California wines.

Larry Brooks
ACACIA WINERY

"If I had to pick my ten best wine experiences, nine of them would probably be Pinot Noir of one type or another."

Larry Brooks' entry into winemaking was a matter of being in the right place at the right time. He happened to be at a party where he met Mike Richmond and Jerry Goldstein who were starting up Acacia Winery for a group of investors. He signed on at Acacia in 1979 and learned cellar management and winemaking from the ground up. With a background in plant pathology and microbiology, his skills were put to good use. He took his wine production cues from Richmond and augmented his practical experience with university winemaking courses and independent study. By 1981, Brooks had become winemaker and was making the day-to-day decisions in the winery.

Acacia was one of the first wineries to establish itself in Carneros, concentrating solely on Pinot Noir and Chardonnay. Now over two dozen wineries either own vineyards in the area or buy grapes from Carneros growers. Brooks was a leader in keeping individual vineyard lots from Carneros separate in the winery, then releasing them with a specific vineyard designation on the label. The Madonna, St. Clair, Lee and Iund Vineyards, while located in the same area (sometimes just a road's width apart), produce distinctly different wines because each vineyard has a different combination of slope, exposure, soil composition, clone and farming practices. Rather than homogenizing the differences by blending all the lots together, he prefers to recognize the differences by bottling them separately to accentuate the nuance of each vineyard.

In 1986, Chalone, Inc., a publicly held company that owns and operates several individual wineries (Chalone, Carmenet and Edna Valley Vineyards), acquired Acacia. Among the positive changes that corporate ownership has brought is a mandate to expand the winery. Production is presently in the 36,000 case range. In addition to his responsibilities as winemaker, Brooks is also general manager of the operation. He approaches each new vintage with enthusiasm, always challenged by the potential he sees in the vineyards.

What were your impressions of your first harvest?

I remember clearly the moment when I knew I was going to be a winemaker. We were pressing the first Pinot Noir and I thought, "This is it. I'm doing this for the rest of my life." I didn't have the imagination to intellectually or abstractly figure out that I should be a winemaker. But as soon as I started doing it, I had the ability to recognize that this was better than anything else I'd ever done. It suited me perfectly.

What I realized was that it's an activity that could engage me both sensually and intellectually. I think a professional musician might have the same access to those two things. I want to live in the world of the senses with something that challenges me intellectually at the same time. Wine does both. That's what makes it unique for me.

By 1981, you were the winemaker at Acacia. You had two year's experience. Were you confident in your ability at that time?

Yes and no. I've always been a quick study. If you're paying attention, you can grasp almost anything in a year or two. In California, there is a real community of knowledge. You can call people and ask for their help. If someone called me right now, I'd tell them everything I know. There's not this type of proprietary knowledge where you're trying to protect something that's yours.

I'd rather see everybody's wine be extremely delicious. It's a shame when you have something less than that. At the minimum, a wine should be delicious. I mean, it's easy to do; this is a peasant occupation. It's easy to make wine. It always mystifies me to a certain extent when I taste bad wine because I think, "This is stupid. If they were paying attention, it didn't have to taste this way." You could drop me in any grape growing area in the world and, within a year, I'm sure I could be making delicious wine there. Anybody with experience could do that. You're not going to make sublime wine there for ten or twenty years but you should be able to make a good wine after a year or two.

Tell me about the vineyards here. Did you plant the Marina vineyards?

This vineyard was planted in 1974. When we bought it in 1979, it was probably thirty percent misses. It was in terrible shape and that's why we were able to afford it. From 1979 through 1984, we finally had it mostly replanted. It's difficult to interplant because there's light and root competition from the existing vines. It's so important to do it right in the first place. It's very frustrating to go back and try to redo it. Not only was it poorly planted and cared for but it was a poor choice of clone material and rootstock combination. We really liked the 1985 Marina, so it took six years for us to bring the vineyard to a point where we were really happy with it. The best Chardonnays we made in 1986 and 1988.

Before, I said it should take about two years to learn anything. Well, vines are an exception to that. You can learn the techniques in that time but in terms of moving a vineyard forward, it's like trying to push an elephant. It can take a generation or more to accomplish the flavor you want in the vineyard. The big problem all along, as is typical in California vineyards, is that it's too vigorous and we tend to have vegetative flavors. A hint of those flavors is nice, like the smell of dry hay that lingers in the background. It would be a shame to completely lose that. But when the vegetative flavors are dominant and you're getting this tiny fruit crop, it's not good. It's economics too because if the vine is all in leaf, there's not much fruit there. When the bare land is $25,000 an acre, you've got to get some fruit off of it.

The nice thing about a white wine vineyard is that you get your results fast. With a Pinot Noir vineyard, it has to be twelve to fifteen years old before it can even show you what it is capable of. Think about that. I'm forty years old; that means I wouldn't get to make the first wines that really meant anything until I'm fifty-five. Then you have to watch them in the bottle for ten or twelve years, so just about the time I'm ready to die I'll have a good idea of what's going on in that vineyard, whether I did it right. So it's a twenty or thirty year process.

People talk about their vineyard experiments and all the conclusions they're getting but all that's hogwash unless they've been watching them for twenty years. Now in white wine, you can make super wine from five or six year old vineyards. And a typical white wine goes through its evolution in five to ten years.

What about the surrounding vineyards here where you get grapes? Are these vineyards on long-term contracts?

I guess you could say that. We have a dozen people we buy grapes from. Again, the people that run the financial end of the corporation would love to see all long-term contracts. But some of these growers don't want to sign contracts. One of our best vineyards has been on a handshake basis from the beginning. Sometimes you sit and worry that someone is going to steal that from you but other times you think it's a pretty lousy world if you've been doing business with this guy for ten years and suddenly he's gone. It's a source of anxiety. The stablest operation is to own everything yourself. Only then can you control the farming, and you don't have to worry about someone coming in and stealing the fruit from you.

If you owned the vineyards, the costs of production would probably be cheaper too?

Yes and no. It depends on when you bought the land and what you had to pay for it. This winery was structured to buy fruit and so we're profitable doing that. If we tried to acquire and develop vineyards, we'd lose our profitability for a decade or more because the raw land is more than $20,000 an acre and the development costs are $15,000 an acre. It would take you about seven or eight years to get even on the investment, at which point, you would be making a profit and saving money because you can farm less expensively than you can buy. Napa may be at the point of prestige now where it's like Burgundy or Champagne vineyards and they are priceless. They really don't make agricultural or investment sense. But they have such prestige that people will pay any price for them just to own them.

How do you control the quality of the fruit that you get from your growers?

Who you choose to buy from is your first decision. We came into this area because we tasted some good Pinot Noirs from the area. They weren't exactly what we would have done but we saw a potential for it. This is the largest planting of fine Pinot Noir in this country, within five miles of where we sit. That's what brought us to this area. Then it was a choice of who's got the size holdings we want and who were the first people planting here. All of our Pinot Noir vineyards, with one exception, are nearly twenty years old. I think that's a real advantage to us since we got in early here and started doing business with these growers.

With Chardonnay production, it's more of who has the clones you want and what crop levels they have. The minimum size we can move through the winery is about ten to twelve tons. So when we're looking at a vineyard, we'll buy that amount and follow it through. We'll try fermenting in tanks and fermenting in barrels and with or without malolactic. So we'll buy small quantities for several years before we'll make a commitment to buy substantial quantities. We also get a better idea of what clones and what crop levels will give the type of wine we want. Every winery is aiming for different things and different grapes suit different house styles. I think a fairly small clustered, moderate yielding clone works for us. We're willing to pay more for that because obviously, in terms of return per acre, that's not something the grower is real happy about farming. So those are the considerations we look for in choosing a vineyard.

What is it about Carneros, in terms of the soil and the climate here, that make it conducive to making good Pinot Noir?

Climate. Carneros has far from ideal soil. There's a common misperception that I think is based on the French idea of terroir, which people believe means the dirt or the soil. Actually it means mesoclimate, the site. Terroir really means site and site is a combination of everything: exposure, soil and climate. Climate you can't change; you can modify everything else. It's slow work modifying the soil but it can be done. You can change planting densities but you can't change the site in the sense of exposure. The ideal site is something that is a mild southeasterly slope. The ideal climate for Pinot Noir is something that's cool, in California terms. Carneros is cooler than the rest of Napa County by a long shot; it's also warmer during the winter. The San Pablo Bay influences the climate here; it keeps the temperature moderate. If there weren't rolling hills down here, you couldn't grow grapes. In the flats the soil is too heavy. There's too much water and the vines won't survive with wet roots. The very first records of viticulture indicate you should plant the vines in the hills. If you just look out the window here, you'll see that the vines stop as the terrain gets flat. To me, climate is paramount because you can't change it. It's the typical farmer's lament, "You can't do anything about the weather." Well it can also be positive. In other words, go to a climate that suits what you want to do.

The Burgundians come over here and wonder how we can grow Pinot Noir here. It's widely held that you need calcareous soil. I think the calcium, which tends to keep the pH high in the soil, makes a nice wine. You can do the same thing by liming your vineyard regularly. You can fight the negative influence of the acidic nature of the clay soil. In a truly Mediterranean climate, which is what we have here as opposed to the Continental climate of Burgundy, clay soil is nice because it holds a lot of water. The past three years have been really dry and that's been a lifesaver. Many of the vineyards we buy grapes from are dry farmed so the clay soil is a real help. Clay also has a lot of metallic elements. I think the reason that Carneros Pinot Noirs are darker than some of the others is that there's lots of iron in the soil here. Those metal ions have a real influence on the color development.

Explain to me the differences between the three vineyard designated Pinot Noirs. Why does a Pinot Noir from the other side of the road here taste different from a Pinot Noir on this side of the road?

There are many factors. If everything were the same as far as soil, slope and viticultural practices, then you could start talking about clonal differences. Clone has a big influence. Pinot Noir, as a grape, is prone to clones. It's genetically unstable for one reason or another. In the St. Clair Vineyard, the grower has shown me two vines right next to each other that he knows came off the same stick of budwood. In theory, they're genetically identical. But morphologically, their overall look is completely different. You could go into any Pinot Noir vineyard and find twenty different clones by gross morphology.

Rootstock, training, crop level, water reserves, vine age and wind exposure are all important. It's very difficult to separate out any one thing but I did talk about clone first. That's important. Farming practices are equally important, particularly how the vines are trained and how they're cropped. Not only that, but probably in our very early wines, you could taste the raw nature of the vineyards more so than now. Over a decade of working with them, we learned how to finesse the handling of the fruit into our perception of what the ideal tastes like. We don't simply let vineyard flavors dominate. We don't treat all the fruit the same when we get it here. We treat the fruit differently in order to push it toward what we conceive of as the ideal. There're so many threads that go into it; like weaving a carpet. How did that carpet get the way it is? It's not any one little piece that made it what it is.

Would you term Acacia a Burgundian winery?

In Pinot Noir production, very much so. Burgundy is the home of Pinot Noir. For me and most of the people in this area, Pinot Noir is the best wine. Our little joke is that we say, "If you don't like Pinot Noir best, you're not paying attention. You need to drink some more Pinot Noir until you figure it out!" We're not saying that from a narrow viewpoint. We taste other wines all the time. But if I had to pick my ten best wine experiences, nine of them would probably be Pinot Noir of one type or another. In a certain sense, Burgundy defines Pinot Noir. So if somebody says they're not Burgundian, I'm suspicious that they don't understand Pinot Noir.

What's the ideal yield from your Pinot Noir vineyards?

There isn't one. But if you had to average it out, it would be in the three to four tons per acre range. One of our best vineyards is consistently the highest yield, which kind of puts the lie, to a certain extent, to the theory of low yield making the best wine. Some of the best vintages from that vineyard have been ones where there is a little less fruit too. It's just a mark of the vineyard's strength that it can carry a little more fruit. Our Marina Vineyard would be a much better wine if we could get fifty percent more fruit from it. It's under cropped. We've been working for years to bring the crop level up and make the flavor better. So it really works from both directions. There's still a widespread misconception that a low crop makes better wine. That's not true. A crop appropriate to that vineyard makes better wine. Growers generally want a higher yield so there is a certain wisdom in trying to moderate the crop level.

You seem to be more interested in Pinot Noir than in Chardonnay?

It's because white wine is so much easier to make. Any idiot can make white wine; you really can. Because you're separating the juice out so early in the process, you're just doing juice processing. It's very straightforward compared to doing skin processing with Pinot Noir, where any little flaw in the grapes is going to show up in the wine. In fact, one of the best Chardonnay vintages was 1983, where there was a lot of rain and hail; it was also one of the worst Pinot Noir vintages we ever had. The white wine was unbelievably good because that little bit of rot and damage to the Chardonnay added some interest that wasn't normally there.

Tell me about your fermentation practices for Chardonnay.

When we started making Chardonnay, there were good benchmarks in California. So we were trying to make something that did taste Californian, with abundant fruit in it. We wanted a big wine, with high alcohol, lots of new wood flavor and no malolactic. It was definitely slanted toward a California palate. At that time, we macerated the skins (skin contact, as it was called then) overnight, pressed and barrel fermented fifty percent in new wood and fifty percent in stainless steel tanks. Then we swapped the lots four or five months into the vintage.

What purpose did that serve?

In tank fermentation, it's our thinking that you get something that's fruitier and more floral. In barrel fermentation, you get the new wood, barrel flavors, which are thought of as Burgundian. We wanted both. White wines tend to be simple so we took sort of a spice cabinet approach, if you will, by making it in different ways. We still do that. Before we started doing any blending this year, we had over fifty separate lots of Chardonnay that ended up in only two bottlings. A dozen of those lots were from our own Marina Vineyard and the other forty were from the ten other Chardonnay vineyards we buy from. We artificially create different flavors by using different yeasts, fermenting at different temperatures and all kinds of things to try to create more interest in what is essentially pretty simple. I'm talking about flavor interest here.

We always fermented warmer than what was common in California and we still do. Our tank fermentations were in the 60F degrees range instead of 50F degrees. Barrel fermentations, unless you keep your cellar extremely cold, will peak up in the 70F degrees to 80F degrees range. The very nature of barrel fermentation is that it is warmer than tank fermentation. It's one of the biggest factors and not discussed very much. With the 1983 harvest, we started to make some changes because the 1983 fruit was maybe twenty percent rotted and we didn't want any skin contact with that. So we pressed it as quickly as we could. In 1984, we had a very hot vintage and so we didn't do any skin contact again. You don't want to be too definite about what you will and you won't do because the raw material is changing all the time according to the vintage. You don't carve your recipe in stone. You want to stay really light on your feet. We had seen what the 1983s and 1984s were like with no skin contact and we thought we liked them better. In 1985, the 1979 Chardonnays were six years old and we didn't like the way they were evolving in the bottle. They were browning and showing aged characters too quickly. In doing library research, talking to other winemakers and based on some research done in Germany, we started consciously modifying what had started as a subconscious reaction to vintage conditions that became, by 1985, a conscious desire to get away from skin contact and the early use of sulfites. If you go back and taste the library of our Chardonnays, you will see an evolution between 1983 and 1985. Since 1985, we've used similar methods, which involve no skin contact and pressing right away. We don't use sulfites so a lot of the phenolic, brown compounds in the white wines are dropped out as juice because there's no antioxidant in there to keep them in solution. In winemaking there's always a trade off. What you give up is grape tannin flavor and so there's a certain richness in the middle, a certain fresh fruitiness and youthful appeal. If someone asked me to make a Chardonnay that would peak in two years, I could do that. Right now, we're making Chardonnays that I think will peak when they are about six or seven years old. So we've given up a little bit of early lusciousness in the wine for better structure and flavor in the longer term. Curiously, with the next harvest, we'll probably integrate back in a bit of skin contact, maybe twenty percent or so. We've grown to such a size now that we're getting ready for a restructuring of our processing equipment. I don't know anybody else who has decided to go back to skin contact after moving away from it. When you've done a lot blending of different lots, you realize what percentage you can use as subliminal influence. I think with fifteen percent to twenty percent skin contact, we can put some very interesting flavors back into the wine and still keep the long-term aging potential.

We've dropped the percentage of new oak down a little bit. We've been averaging thirty-five percent to forty percent new wood for Chardonnay. The problem is you really don't know how a vintage is going to take wood and the 1988 vintage is a good example. Both the Estate and the Carneros went into the same percentage of new wood and you can't taste it in the Carneros. Whereas with the Estate, the wood is perfect. They're both about the same alcohol and the same acid. That's a mystery to me. But the fact is you have to order the barrels a year before the vintage. So you make an arbitrary decision and you set up your cellar for a certain percentage of barrel fermentation to where it works most of the time. Sometimes you have to finesse it. We're bottling the Estate first because it took the wood well; we're leaving the Carneros in the barrel longer in hopes that it will pick up more wood. But it loses fruit the whole time it's in those barrels. That can skew your style; how much fruit and floral flavors are you willing to lose to pick up the wood character? Those are the kind of things that you're fighting all the time. We've come to an accommodation with it but I don't feel like we've figured it out.

One hundred percent barrel fermentation is really not your style because you want that fruit component?

You get fruit in barrel fermented wines but you always lose the floral component. Fruit blossom is more of what I'm looking for. They're all grape flavors; that's obvious. If you walk out right now in this vineyard that's in full bloom, you will find a floral smell there. I want some of that in the wine.

You're walking a fine line here. You want your Chardonnay to taste good to the wine writers and consumers on its initial release, but you also want to have built in those characteristics for longer aging.

Those same wine writers, when they taste your wine five years from now and it's fallen apart because you've made it for luscious, early consumption, they're going to ding you anyhow. They're going to say, "An expensive wine like this should hold up better." So you're damned if you do and damned if you don't. There's an old Italian saying that "You can't have a full barrel and a drunk wife." And it's very difficult to have a wine that's luscious in its youth and ages well. That's the rarest wine; less than half of one percent of the wine made. Once a decade you get wines like our 1986 Pinot Noirs; they just taste super from the minute they come out of the press and you know they'll age as long as the cork holds. Those are gifts; those are not the normal materials you're working with. Now our recent Chardonnays are starting to taste good six months after their release. You've got to have about six or eight months of patience before you start getting into the sweet spot and then they improve for probably another three or four years. But they really are pretty clumsy in the first six or seven months. So it's a matter of reducing that clunkiness, if you will. You need to put in some stuff that will hide the rough edges until it settles down. The great temptation is to add a little sugar because that takes all the edges off. But that's like Frankenstein; you think you're making a life but when you start messing with it at that level, you're making a monster. You really outsmart yourself. If you really like wine and if you have an ethical sense toward it, you get to like it best when it's messed with least.

For example, our ideal now is no fining whatsoever. Because the biggest intrusion you can ever make in a wine's life is when you add fining material to it. When we do all these fining, tasting trials, we always keep gravitating to the control wine. These tastings are blind. But we all keep gravitating toward the control because we all recognize and know it's the control because we prefer it. It tastes like the wine we've been living with all year. It tastes like the vineyards. It may not have the smoothest structure or the most appeal; it may have a few rough edges but it tastes like real wine. It tastes the most vinous. That's what you're constantly battling, but the consumer doesn't know what it's supposed to taste like! That's a really tough aspect of winemaking: how much you're willing to modify the basic flavor and structure of the wine to make it fit into the market. The only business of the company, Chalone, is fine wine. So we're lucky that way. They don't allow too much of the tail wagging the dog business. The marketing really is the tail; the thing itself is the wine.

Has there been an evolution here in the style of Pinot Noir, similar to that of Chardonnay?

Yes, but it's been more subtle. From the beginning, we wanted to make intensely colored wines and we wanted to make wines with apparent fruit. Plus we wanted to make fine wine out of Pinot Noir. In California, there was a self-fulfilling prophecy that Pinot Noir doesn't make fine wines, so you used the worst barrels, you didn't monitor the fermentation and gave no thought to it. Of course with that attitude, California made lousy Pinot Noirs. We wanted to make a wine that tasted typical too, a wine that tasted like Pinot Noir. Most

California Pinot Noirs just tasted like red wine. You might think it was nice red wine but you wouldn't guess it was Pinot Noir. Whereas most Burgundies taste like Pinot Noir. That was our intent. Toward that end we used warm fermentation and we still do. I think the warmer the better. You can't always get it but I think a hot fermentation is crucial to Pinot Noir.

What temperature?

Say 90F degrees in the juice and 100F degrees in the cap. We're talking very hot. A minimum for a successful Pinot Noir is 85F degrees in the juice and above 90F degrees in the cap. You really have to get heat for two reasons. One is to extract color because Pinot Noir tends to be light colored and, two and more importantly, to drive off the false fruit. In Pinot Noir, there is a Beaujolais like fruit that is gross. It's a very grapey fruit and the high temperature tends to drive that off. It's a fermentation fruit, the flavor of Beaujolais. People always jump on me when I say this but Beaujolais is a clone of Pinot Noir basically. It's maybe not a brother but it's a close first cousin. The best Beaujolais taste like good Pinot Noir and the worst Pinot Noirs taste like Beaujolais, to my mind.

Color peaks in fermentations are usually about three to five days out. Pinot Noir is a ready fermenter so it's usually dry in six or seven days. We opted to press at dryness in the first few years because the color was more intense then and we knew that there would be a diminution of color with more time in the fermenter. What we didn't realize, at that time, was that we would then have to fight a battle with these bitter flavors. The intense colors and bright colors are small molecules and taste bitter. So now we let it sit in the fermenter longer and get more oxygenated. There are a lot of other things going on in the fermenter too. The little finings, if you will, with the solids and yeast that's in there. But what's really going on is that those smaller phenolics, the brightly colored ones, are linking up and making stuff that isn't as brightly colored or as densely colored (you lose both brightness and absolute density of color with time in any red wine fermentation) but you get something that tastes softer in its phenolic structure and more complete. Whereas when you press early, you get something bitter; the phenolics, which are perceived as bitterness, are all there but they're in the back. In fact, when pressing early, there are less phenolics absolutely, but the ones there attack you in a point that your mouth doesn't like.

So we evolved, over the years, to longer maceration. That comes back to the same subject I was talking about in terms of stressed (both water and heat) versus less stressed vintages. In a hotter vintage, you can shorten your maceration. In a vintage like 1984, your average maceration might be eight days. In a vintage like 1986, it might be fifteen days. Again, flexibility is paramount.

We don't use any stems. Early on we used about ten percent whole clusters so that meant ten percent stems. But fruit added as whole clusters is different than stems added back. A lot of people add stems back, which is disgusting. We've even given up adding whole clusters because we don't want any stem flavor in our wine. Stem flavor is green, it's a very rough tannin and it doesn't go away. Skin tannins and seed tannins will integrate into the wine and evolve over time. Stem tannins just hang in there. I can't believe anybody does it. It's beyond me.

We press by hand in the sense that we use a pneumatic press but it's hand controlled. Many of the more modern presses are computerized in that you program in a press cycle and then the press just does it. You just load it, push the button and go do something else for two hours while it presses. I think that's a real mistake with Pinot Noir. You need to taste every fraction that comes out of the press. It's not that you can't do that with an automatic press, it's just that the temptation is too high to walk away and do something else. When you actually have to operate the cycle by hand, then you might as well taste because you're there. Even with fruit from the same vineyard, two fermenters can have very different cut off points in terms of what's the acceptable amount of press wine. With Pinot Noir, making those tannin judgements is hard. It's a more lightly structured wine than other great red wines and you've got to get it just right. And you've got to get it early; at the maceration and press. Because if you get a wine that is grossly unbalanced at the press, you'll never bring it back into balance. Well maybe not never, but it will be ten or more years. If the fruit, acid and structure is there to carry it to ten or twelve years in the bottle, then the tannins will eventually resolve. But usually there isn't that depth of fruit and Pinot Noir tends to be a high pH variety so you have lots of things working against you if you're betting on it to come around in the bottle. I think it's important to strike a balance as early as you can. Toward that end, there are ways to modify it. You give it more maceration, you give it more oxygen early which tends to speed up the linking of these phenolics. From very early on, we felt people weren't putting enough new wood on their Pinot Noir and they were putting the wrong kind of wood. When we went to Burgundy, almost all the wines we liked were in Francois Frere barrels. So from the beginning, we used Francois Frere barrels and we told them we wanted a Burgundy toast. In the early eighties a lot of people were worried about infections in their wine. When you toast a barrel, it tends to blister a bit and so it'll trap yeast and therefore it's not as "sanitary" as a more lightly toasted barrel. But the flavor of Pinot Noir as a grape, once it ferments, has this kind of roasted, burnt aroma. So you want a barrel that augments that. When we order our barrels, we ask for a medium toast, and if they make a mistake, we tell them to make it on the dark side. That's if we're trying a new barrel. With Francois Frere, we just tell them to do the barrels the way we like them.

Depending on the wine, we usually settle it for a couple of days before it goes into barrels. So it goes in pretty dirty. We'll get the malolactic fermentation in the barrel. We like a drawn out malolactic, and that is a little riskier and goes contrary to current trends, which are simultaneous malolactic and primary fermentation.

The minimum of new oak for Pinot Noir is thirty percent. We use fifty percent on our best wines. Our style leans toward a lot of new wood. In the best years of the St. Clair and Madonna Vineyards, they've probably had sixty percent to sixty-five percent new wood. Pinot Noir eats up good wood; it loves it. I was at a seminar with Rob Davis of Jordan and we were talking about wood aging. We did a tasting of wines that he'd brought up in wood and others that had less wood influence. The conclusion I came to is that wood isn't so important in a young wine in a bottle because the fruit is so important. But fruit fades in the bottle after a few years. After three or four years, most of the fruitiness is gone. Then for the flavors that are left, the evolved fruit flavors and evolved tannin flavors, the wood serves as kind of a container for them. If the wood isn't there to hold those flavors, the wine just disperses. It was a real revelation to taste that experiment of these wines brought up without the wood, a fascinating demonstration.

We go for a slow malolactic fermentation and we like it to finish around Christmas time or so. Then we rack them and add a little SO_2 at that point, which if they were healthy grapes would have been the first SO_2 they would have seen. If they were really in poor condition, they would have gotten some SO_2 at the fermenter. Typically, the longer you can hold off adding SO_2, the better. Then they go back into barrels. The lesser wines will be pulled out of the barrel and bottled right before the next vintage; so they'll get ten or eleven months in barrel. If we've got a vintage in a wine that we think is something special, we'll hold it over through the vintage and bottle it in October or November. One of the big problems we perceived early in red Burgundies, and I still think it's a big problem, is that many Pinot Noir are left in barrel too long and dry out. The fruit is the sexy part of Pinot Noir and you will dry them out if you're not careful. People who go eighteen or twenty months in barrel with Pinot Noir are making a mistake, I think.

Conventional wisdom is that Pinot Noir is so delicate that you want to leave it alone or do as little to it as possible.

I'd agree with that, by and large. That's especially true of a very good Pinot Noir. But if you're having a problem, as we did with one vineyard in 1988, we tried everything we could and we finally racked it and it shaped up. It's a last resort measure for us. More and more, unless it's a perfect vintage, we'll sterile filter. If I could guarantee how the wines were going to be stored, I would probably polish filter, just for minimum acceptable clarity. Mainly, not because I feel it damages the flavor but because I lose wine when I do it. We only have 1,000 or 1,500 cases of some of these wines. And when you do the filtration right, you might lose twenty or thirty cases of wine in the filtration. It just breaks your heart to see that going down the drain, after you've worked with it all year. From a practical point of view, I'd love to have the type of vintages where you didn't have to filter. We've had vintages where we haven't filtered at all. It's one of those questions where it's kind of up to the wine. The thing with Pinot Noir is it's the wine that's probably least appropriate to not filter most of the time. If you have any doubt about it, filter your Pinot Noir because it tends toward high pH and low phenolics. Now low pH and high phenolics are what keep wine sound and free from subsequent bacterial infections. There's a myth that malolactic fermentation makes wines microbiologically stable. It's not true. You can get secondary and tertiary full populations of bacteria after malolactic. And, if that happens in the bottle, you've got a spoiled wine. It's just as likely to happen in the bottle as anywhere else. Yeast infection in the bottle is unusual unless there's residual sugar. Pinot Noir being a ready fermenter, the chances of substantial sugars are low. But most people don't understand bacterial ecology in wine very well. There's misconceptions about what's going on with bacteria in wine. It hasn't been well disseminated, yet the information has been known for seven or eight years at least. So generally we'll filter and we look at the history of the vineyard in conjunction with that. With some of the vineyards, we know we should sterile filter. I don't care if it's a 3.2 pH and black as ink. As soon as you put in into the bottle, if you haven't sterile filtered, it's going to get active and get fizzy and stinky. If you don't sterile filter, it's a big risk. If you're dealing with only a hundred cases of wine, it's one thing. But if you're dealing with the livelihoods of dozens of people and millions of dollars, it's not a smart risk. You can see a whole year's work spoiled.

What are the characteristics of a great Pinot Noir in California, from a sensory point of view?

The same as anywhere. We were blind tasting some 1985 Oregon Pinot Noirs and we threw in a 1985 Burgundy as a ringer. I got my favorite Oregon wine and the Burgundy mixed up. I had brought the Burgundy and I knew it real well but I still confused it with this Oregon wine. In fact, I actually preferred the Oregon wine. In my notes on both these wines, I had, "What can you say?" It leaves you speechless. It's one of those things that whatever you say about it diminishes it, in that the best wine is not an intellectual experience. It's an emotional one, from the heart. It's as if someone asked you, "Why do you love your wife?" You don't go into it because it's inappropriate to go into a detailed description of it. It's one of those exercises where people want you to talk about the wine and tell them what it tastes like. You ultimately say, "It tastes like itself." That's why it's so good; it expresses the vineyard, the vintage and the type perfectly. It's typical. The greatest compliment is, "It's typical. It tastes like Pinot Noir. Very Pinot." That's the highest praise here. What's Pinot Noir? It's a very complex fruit, spice and floral amalgam. Pinot Noir smells like everything; not any given glass of Pinot Noir. But over a lifetime of drinking Pinot Noir, you will taste and smell every flavor that exists within that wine. Because there's mineral, petrochemical, fecal, feral, fruit and floral. It's all there. They're not all the result just of the fruit; many of them are the result of the microbial processes and the aging processes. But it really is a microcosmos, if you will. It should be so complex that you can't describe it. I think that the essence of Pinot Noir is that it's complex and delicate at the same time. That's something that throws people off. You get into big arguments about it because some people think Cabernet is more complex. Well, it's just the contrary. Cabernet is bigger but it's not more complex. In a certain sense, Pinot Noir is quieter but more complex. An interesting phenomena.

Patrick Campbell
LAUREL GLEN VINEYARD

"You have to keep an open mind when you're working in a medium that changes from year to year. If you ever get into a rut, start making wine by formula and stop asking questions, then you might as well give up."

Retuning to the San Francisco Bay Area from a Harvard education of philosophy and religion, Patrick Campbell planned to pursue a career as a violinist. He happened to move into a Zen commune just down the road from Sonoma Mountain. At night he played music; during the day he tended the commune's vineyards. In short order, he was taking vineyard management courses at the local college.

In 1976, he was ready to strike out on his own; he and his wife, Faith, bought the Laurel Glen Vineyard high in the rugged Sonoma Mountains, where recommended access is by four wheel drive vehicle. Three and a half acres were already planted; subsequently he expanded to thirty-eight, primarily consisting of Cabernet Sauvignon and Cabernet Franc. At first he sold the grapes to locals like Chateau St. Jean and Kenwood, but by 1981 he had constructed a winery on the property in time for his first vintage. Campbell's Cabernets have received rave reviews ever since.

Despite the acreage, yields are so low that, in a good vintage, only 3,000 to 4,000 cases of Cabernet are produced. In a year the weather is problematic, only 1,200 cases are made. In addition, wine that does not meet Campbell's exacting specifications ends up in a second label, Counterpoint, which nevertheless would put many other California Cabernets to shame. In recent years, he has also purchased grapes from select Napa County vineyards and bottled the wine under the Terra Rosa label.

Campbell is a sort of renaissance man among winemakers, who is equally at ease giving a toast at a formal dinner or applying a well chosen wrench to a recalcitrant tractor engine in the vineyard. Thoroughly dedicated to his craft, he gets his hands dirty everyday, overseeing all aspects of the vineyard and winery.

In the early seventies, you became a vineyard manager at a Zen Buddhist commune. What was that experience like? What did you discover about Zen and the art of grape growing?

Well it was a lay community and fairly casual, at least so far as Zen groups go; it wasn't a monastery and I wasn't a hermit. I would play my music jobs at night and tend the vineyard by day. We had a period of meditation for a couple hours during the morning and evening. It worked out to be quite a nice day. After a while I started taking the professional vineyard manager course at Santa Rosa Junior College, which is probably the best practical, hands-on type of class in the state. Then, three years later, I decided it was time to move on. What can I tell you about Zen and the art of grape growing? I wish I could tell you there was some connection, or that I am an enlightened grape grower or some such thing. But really I just started farming there and I continue being a farmer to this day.

What are the soil conditions here on the mountain?

Geologically this is known as the Sonoma Mountain Volcanics soils type; it's a tremendously complex soil, tremendously diverse. It's close to the margin of two soil areas: it's where the Petaluma formation and the Sonoma Mountain Volcanic area join. There are a few heavy clay soils, unusual for the mountains, but by far, our predominant soil is of volcanic origin. It doesn't get terribly hot or cool. I think that the narrow temperature band gives a distinct quality to the grapes here; the wines have much softer tannins.

What's the climate like here on Sonoma Mountain?

We have an interesting climate that's different from a lot of places as our vineyards are inclined toward the northeast. The significance is they're inclined toward the morning sun. So we warm up fairly early, relative to the rest of the area. We're inclined away from the afternoon sun so we don't get the intense heat of the afternoon. Being up in the mountains at about 1,000 feet, we are about 600 feet above the valley floor. We get the warm thermals rising at night. Consequently, we get a much narrower temperature band without extremes of highs and lows. In contrast, the west facing hills warm up slowly and get an intense blast of heat in the afternoon. And at night, they might get the thermals if they're around our elevation; if they are significantly higher, the thermals will have dissipated. Given that, you can draw your own conclusions about the valley floor.

What does the narrow temperature band mean? I've done a lot of testing of this and I really think it's true. The west facing vineyards tend to have much higher tannin levels than we have on the east facing side. The reason is that the west facing vineyards are much hotter in the afternoon and the vines compensate by getting a much thicker skin on them. That's the only explanation I can come up with. The fact is, however, the west facing vineyards are more tannic than the east facing and there's very little dispute about that. That's not necessarily good or bad. To me it's negative, but then I'm pleading my own case here. You can get a coarse wine from the western side and I like a more supple wine. For what it's worth, the Medoc are inclined toward the northeast. It's a way of making the best of an otherwise rather warm climate that we have here in California. It tends to make the natural heat not quite as strong, by being inclined toward the northeast. Now whether that's good or bad, I'm not going to say. I prefer it; I think most people prefer a more supple wine.

I do think a more narrow temperature range, that is devoid of extremes, is probably going to be better. The common line in California is that we have cool evenings and warm days, and that cool evenings help to retain the acid. You know, there are so many explanations that just tend to rationalize the situation you already have. I suppose that's alright. But the Bordeaux vineyards have warmer nights with relatively cooler days. They too have a narrow temperature band. Again, whether that's better or worse, I don't know; but I do believe that it's going to make a more supple wine, if you don't have those extremes.

California is not France, either.

Yes, let's not try to be France. I certainly maintain that. However, I don't think the clumsy, terribly extracted and very tannic California wines of the late seventies are the sort of wines I want to make.

Do you think our vines in California are too vigorous and our soils too rich, compared to the French model? That really doesn't apply to your vineyards here on Sonoma Mountain.

That certainly doesn't apply to me here because we have, at best, twenty-four inches of top soil and often, closer to twelve inches. The vines don't grow vigorously here, even though we are planted on St. George, a very vigorous rootstock.

Which is good, in your situation here.

Yes, I think it is good although it's a hotly debated issue these days. It's the age old question. We're fooling around with closer planting spacing to make the vines work a little harder. But I have a feeling that the soil is naturally limiting anyway. Maybe, in the mountain soils, you want to be spaced further apart, because here the soil is already such a limiting factor. In the valley, you don't have the soil as a limiting factor; so you might want to crowd the vines together more so that the vines themselves compete. In the valley soils, your neighboring vines rather than the soil would provide the limiting factor, so to speak. I'm not saying that the vines should be stressed but equally and in the opposite extreme, they should not be given luxuriant growing conditions. Grapevines are a tremendous scavenger of nitrogen, meaning if nitrogen is excessive, the vines will use an enormous amount and grow big and lush, sometimes not setting much fruit. Excess nitrogen is a principal cause of "shatter" in the vineyard. So you do have to be careful about deep soil. I think there are very few people who honestly would not maintain that mountain grapes tend to be more intense than valley grapes, all other things being equal. I think the reason for this is mountain vines tend to have a smaller crop. First of all, you have an extensive root system spread out through the thin soil, feeding a relatively small amount of fruit. The grapes themselves are usually smaller because of less available soil moisture, so they have more intensity. You have less aqueous solution, presumably for the same amount of flavor components.

I am working with a lot of different trellising systems and have been for years. I've found that while trellising is very important, I'm not sure that spacing has that much to do with quality. Some of the first growth vineyards in Bordeaux are planted about one meter by one meter, which is very close, about nine or ten square feet per vine. Traditional California spacing is eight by twelve feet or ninety-six square feet, almost ten times fewer vines per unit of ground space. But the current research coming out of Bordeaux recommends much wider spacing than traditional and using the trellising systems to position the shoots. California is going to closer spacing, emulating old Bordeaux, while Bordeaux is going to wider spacing, emulating California. So I'm not yet sure that the spacing is as important as either soil depth and structure or trellising.

You are obviously doing something right here. How is it that you can consistently produce this quality of wine?

My response to that is, "Let's try to make the wine even better." Maybe by just sheer luck we selected a very good place for vineyards. And I do mean luck really, or at least nothing more than intuition because there was certainly no science involved. I think our wines since 1984 have been much better than before. That's because I think I've learned something, not only in the winery but also out in the vineyard. Since 1984, we have been doing a lot of leaf stripping, meaning we expose the fruit a lot more. We're now using trellising systems that naturally tend to expose the fruit more. We don't want to get our fruit out into the direct sun, which I think is a big mistake. You need to get light into the vine and onto the fruit; that's light as opposed to direct sunlight.

What does that do for the fruit?

One of the major factors is it reduces rot because you get air circulation through the vines. That's an important factor. If there were no other reason to do it, that would be enough in itself. It seems to have the potential of raising tannin levels, which is something I don't particularly want to do, but it also raises the color and intensity of the fruit. It reduces the vegetative flavors of the Cabernet, which naturally tends to be a very vegetative varietal. And it brings out the fruit flavors to yield a wine which is much more my style Cabernet. It does all those good things.

But, once again, it's a trade off. The problem is that it's an expensive way to grow the fruit, if you're going to strip the leaves and retrofit the trellising system. And we do summer pruning a couple of times, which means we take off every single shoot that wasn't planned, about twenty-five percent of them.

That's pretty severe.

Yes, that's pretty severe. We use pruning as our guideline for what we eventually want, taking off anything else that's extraneous. Pruning is the single most important factor in winemaking. During the growing season, the vine pushes out nonbearing shoots (known as "adventitious growth") from all over the vine in addition to shoots which come from buds selected by pruning. The adventitious growth is removed in spring and summer. It's an expensive way to grow grapes. Hopefully, the vertical, movable wire trellising system, which we're putting in for about $2,000 an acre, will save a lot of that labor.

What constitutes ripeness in Cabernet?

Between 23 and 24 degrees brix. We usually pick around 23.3; somewhere between 23 to 24, although we are tending more toward higher sugars these days.

Do you go by the numbers or are there other things you look for?

I go by total acidity, pH and sugar. The main criterion is taste. My feeling is, at least in our vineyard, sugar and taste correspond pretty well. So I'm less concerned about the acid and the pH than I am with the sugar. I think a lot of people try to get a balance of all three. But if the flavor isn't there, if the sugar isn't there, why bother? You can't add flavor. You can add acid; generally, we don't and we haven't done it for years and we tolerate much higher pHs than we used to tolerate. I think a lot of people are overly concerned about the balance of the three; although in striving for that balance, they can often short-change the flavor component by picking too early. It's wonderful when they all come into balance but what are you going to do when they don't, as is usually the case? You have to make a choice at that point and I'll opt in favor of sugar and flavor.

Generally, what is the yield on these mountain vineyards?

Two to two and a half tons per acre. That's quite low; it's an expensive place to farm, unfortunately. Everything costs much more. For example, we put in a bunch of tall metal stakes this year for the vertical trellising system. Ideally, they are pushed into the ground with a hydraulic ram on a big tractor. One out of every three stakes hit a rock and wouldn't go in, so we had to go back and pound them in by hand. We almost might as well have done it by hand to begin with rather than hiring a specialized tractor. Rocks tear up tractors and disks. Side slopes cause equipment to drift downhill. You have to be aware of erosion. Crawlers rather than wheel tractors are the norm here. Rows of vines can lean downhill over time. "Tractor blight" results in vine loss and so on. It's a very expensive way to farm.

Do you drip irrigate?

We do when we're establishing a new vineyard block but we don't generally use drip irrigation on what goes into the Laurel Glen because those vines are well established and generally older.

Some people crow proudly that they dry farm their vineyard. I don't believe in a stressed vineyard; you've got to have enough water in the vineyard to keep the vines happy. You've got to keep them growing because, if they stop growing toward the end of the season, you "ripen" by dehydration. The vine cannibalizes its fruit to stay alive. In 1977, in the second year of the drought, I saw a block of vineyard turn shriveled overnight because it had gotten to the point where there was not enough moisture in the soil to keep the vine alive. Apparently the vine sucked the water back out of the berries.

At harvest, what type of containers do you use and how do you convey the grapes to the winery?

Instead of taking the grapes to the winery, we, in effect, take the winery to the grapes. We have a portable crushing unit that has a stemmer/crusher mounted right behind the tractor. It has a 1,000 gallon tank on the back, roughly equivalent to five tons of grapes. The pickers are instructed not to pick anything that is damaged, bruised, mildewed, shriveled or has bad color. We pay by the hour, so they don't have any incentive to pick lousy fruit, as they would if they were paid by weight. I also have a crew that's been working for me long enough to know what my standards are.

But you're right there next to the crusher, inspecting the fruit.

That's exactly right. So we have a two part selection process out in the vineyard: the pickers themselves and myself or my foreman at the crusher. This idea only works for a fairly small operation; you can't do it on large acreage because it's just too slow. But you select the grapes out in the vineyard and they're put to bed immediately. They're crushed into the tank, so they don't just sit around.

What happens then?

As soon as the tank is full, we bring it over to the winery and pump it into a fermenter. We have six 2,000 gallon stainless steel fermenters, which hold about seven or eight tons of grapes each. They are open top fermenters, so we get up on top and punch the cap down. We try to keep the fermentation temperature under 30C degrees, in the range of 85F degrees to 92F degrees. I like a hot fermentation because it yields more intense flavors, but I don't want to see the temperature go much above 30C degrees and risk a stuck fermentation. We have water jackets on the fermenters, to cool them. But we don't have high tech, computerized glycol tanks. Even if we did, I'm not entirely sure what temperature we would shoot for. You hear people say, "We keep our fermentation at the optimum of 86F degrees." Well, bullshit, who knows what the optimum is? Even if 86F degrees was last year's optimum temperature, it doesn't necessarily follow that 86F degrees is perfect for this year's vintage. You have to work within ranges. You know that if you get too hot, you can kill the yeast and you don't want to do that. If it's too cool, you might not extract as much flavor as you would if it were hotter. By experience, you work within a range you know or hope will work for the grapes that year. The wine business is full of people who are quick to pontificate about optimum temperatures, sugar levels, pruning techniques, vine spacings and so on. It's crazy to be dogmatic in this business because it is ultimately not a science. Each vintage and growing site is different. It makes no sense to be dogmatic about a set of conditions which has few constants

Is it a fairly fast fermentation?

It's just about complete in ten days. We don't add any SO_2 until all fermentations are completely done.

Do you do extended skin contact after it has gone dry?

That's currently in vogue in California. Everybody wants to leave their Cabernet on the skins for extended maceration. I don't do it. My feeling is that it doesn't work well with our grapes and perhaps with mountain grapes in general. I do have one fermenter that I turned into a closed top tank and have done extended maceration with certain lots for the past two years. I have not been satisfied with the results and they have all gone into the second label. So it seems like I'm throwing money away by doing it. Extended maceration is logistically a pain. You have to pump the wine over, which for quality reasons I don't like to do at that stage. You tie up a lot of fermentation space and have to be very attentive to excessive volatile acidity. I find the flavors are not as good, at least with my fruit. So I go for a ten to fifteen day fermentation, based on flavor criteria.

After fermentation, you take them out of the tanks...

We take them out of the tank and press them. We have an automatic press but we don't utilize its automatic feature. We do it manually and press them gently. We taste the pressed wine as we press to avoid excess tannins and thin flavors. The Laurel Glen is mostly all free run juice and very little press juice. The wine then goes into barrels right away; it's pressed directly into barrels. It's racked maybe after the first week or two; we splash it around a lot in the first rackings, trying to get air into it. This regime seems to help the wine develop quicker. Certainly we don't go in for intentional yeast autolysis, leaving it on the lees, or any of that business.

We generally rack the wine eight or nine times during its life. It's kept in barrels for twenty-two months or so and then it's bottled. We don't do much fining, if any. Generally I don't feel fining accomplishes much for our wines. If you're stripping away tannin, you're probably stripping away flavor as well. That's been my experience anyhow. So I do very little fining; occasionally we'll do half an egg white per barrel.

Fining is just going to take away things from the wine?

Yes, that's the whole point. That's why we try to reduce the tannin at all the other levels, including in the vineyard: so we don't have to do much fining at the end. Color is a protein and tannin is a protein. Fining works on proteins, so if you're stripping out tannins, you can strip color as well. Winemaking is a series of trade-offs. I've generally found that fining, when we do it, works well by combining a fined lot with an unfined lot. Then we get something better than either part individually. We do fining trials every year just to make sure that fining might not be appropriate for the vintage. But generally we haven't fined much.

Do you filter the wine?

Currently there is lots of talk about the perceived virtues of unfiltered wines. Most of the rhetoric follows the logic that filtering "strips" the wine. Well, obviously filtering does strip something out of the wine; that's why you do it. But that's not necessarily bad. There's little doubt that a heavy-handed regime of excessive manipulation of any wine can hurt it. The market abounds with sterile wines devoid of flavor. But it doesn't follow from this that a carefully considered and executed filtration will harm the wine. I would venture to guess that there are far more wines ruined by lack of filtration than by filtration. The market also abounds with yeast and bacteria laden wines which can and occasionally do turn cloudy and funky in the bottle. Remember that wine is a food and, unlike most foods, it has a shelf life of perhaps decades. We don't leave fresh food out on the table for days, to say nothing of decades, and expect it to be palatable. Is it all that much different for wines? So a minimum filtration can be a prophylaxis.

Additionally, I truly feel that a conscientiously filtered wine often has cleaner and truer flavors; that's the case with Laurel Glen. The rhetoric usually fails to mention that much of what is filtered out of the wine naturally falls to the bottom of the bottle over time. So much of what is being "stripped out" is never really part of the eventual wine in any case. And if all the solids that fall to the bottom taste so good, why don't we shake up the older bottle when we serve it rather than carefully separating the liquid from the sludge? Once again, there are no simple answers in winemaking and anyone who attempts to be doctrinaire about winemaking and pontificate mightily is usually full of it.

What type of barrels do you use and what percentage is new every year?

It depends on the vintage. I shoot for about fifty percent to seventy percent new barrels for the Laurel Glen. I don't like a lot of oak flavors, so I use the new barrels more for the smoothness and freshness that they impart than for the shot of vanillin and oak. I find most wines, including Bordeaux, way too oaky for my taste. It's a very meretricious sort of flavor. I think it can often cover up the fruit so that eventually you get a much harder wine. I think there are few wines, if any at all, that can handle one hundred percent new oak. We soda ash the new barrels to get the really harsh tannins out and generally, we've been putting the Counterpoint in the brand new barrels and letting it get a hit of new oak while tempering the raw oak flavor for the Laurel Glen lots. Then we'll put the Laurel Glen in those barrels. All that's to say that, even with the new barrels, we try to temper them flavor wise as much as we possibly can.

During the twenty-two months the wine spends in barrels, you rack it eight or nine times? And you splash it around quite a bit to give it some aeration?

We splash it around at first, later not so much. I think we do more racking than most people. But I think this regime helps develop a more supple and softer wine. The racking tends to aid in that process. I find many wines have reduced flavors, meaning that they have not had the benefit of oxygenation. They have tanky, musty, slightly sulfury smells. I try to keep away from that end of the spectrum. We're dealing with such intense fruit here that I want to stress the fresh fruit flavors the vineyard naturally gives. I do, however, think the aeration tends to help complexify the flavors; we are not trying to make a simple fruity wine here.

Could you tell me about the different vintages?

Normally we'll make about 4,000 cases of Laurel Glen; in 1988, we made 1,500 cases. Obviously we were way down in quantity. This vintage certainly puts to lie the theory that a lower tonnage per acre makes a richer, higher quality wine. We relegated half our crop that year to the second label. So even though we had less fruit per vine the overall vintage was not exceptional in its intensity. Of course, the other extreme, a huge crop, perhaps may reduce quality also. Balance is the key.

We've never really had an enormous vintage here. Certainly we had much more good fruit in 1985 and 1986. I can't tell you why a certain year is very good. You can often see why a year is bad. In 1983 we had a lot of rain at harvest; so that's pretty obvious. 1986 was potentially a difficult year. The grapes were not ripe and a big storm was ready to come in. The grapes were almost ready to pick. I had to decide whether to pick before the rains and play it safe but maybe sacrifice some quality, or pick after the rains and go for greater ripeness but lose the crop. My feeling was it was better to wait until after the rains because I wasn't satisfied with the quality we had. We got a tremendous amount of rain. Luckily the heavens cleared, the sun shone and we had some beautiful weather. It was the best harvest we've ever had. But that's the sort of gamble you often have to take when high quality is the goal.

But I didn't worry that much I guess. There's no point in having second quality wine. It just doesn't pay off. So I think the growers that did wait to pick did better than the growers who picked right away. Those are examples of extreme situations, but I couldn't tell you why 1985 was a better year than 1984, although I think 1985 was an exceptionally good year in general. You can look at the temperature charts; you can look at the number of fog days. I keep records of all these things, but I look at them at the end of the year and I can't make any correlation out of the data. Frankly, I don't know why I bother to keep track of it. I suppose if I was really into the science of winemaking, I'd feed fifty different variables into the computer each day; maybe then I could make some sense out of it. But the fact is, even if you were to know the reasons for a good vintage, you couldn't duplicate it so it's sort of useless knowledge. I mean, you can't make the sun shine more brightly in June, if, for example, you have determined that's one of the common quality themes of a great year.

How has your winemaking style and philosophy evolved since 1982?

I think the main thing we've done since 1982 is establish a second label, called Counterpoint. I've never liked the idea of a "reserve" wine because I think the Laurel Glen should speak for itself. It should be the best wine that we can make. Parenthetically, it's very easy to achieve a high profile wine by making fifty cases of something super special. I mean, you can always pick out something in the cellar that's really terrific and offer it up to an enthusiastic press. But I think that's a chicken way of getting ink. Your whole line should be good; you shouldn't try to put a little superstar out there and expect it to carry your whole line. You know, your whole line will be that much worse for selecting out some terrific part that otherwise would have gone into a regular part of your line.

But, in a effort to make the Laurel Glen, our main focus, as good as we can, we decided to relegate some younger vineyards and those that didn't do as well in any given year to a second label. If the wine was no good at all, we wouldn't sell it, however. Frankly, I've never had that happen. Counterpoint is a very good wine but generally it just doesn't have the intensity and length of the Laurel Glen. But it's also half the price. So I think we're trying to be as fair as we can by making as good a wine as possible and then relegating the rest to what I and a lot of other people think is a very good wine. It's just not up to Laurel Glen's standards.

That's the main and very significant change that we've had and that came into effect in 1985. Frankly, I think the quality of the Laurel Glen since 1985 has been much better than the quality of the wine previous to that. That's a direct effect of lot selection, in addition to the improvements in the vineyard we have already discussed.

Any other changes that evolved over the years?

The Zen teachers say that the best knowledge comes slowly, by osmosis, almost without perception. It's the difference between going out in the fog and being soaked through gradually or going out in the heavy rain and being soaked through very quickly. I've certainly gone out in the fog and been soaked through after a number of years. So we've had a very gradual, subtle change that you don't notice so much.

Do you think it helps to have just one focus rather than being concerned about many different varietals?

Absolutely. I think wineries are going to come to realize that you can't be all things to all people, at least in the very high quality end. I think the whole wine business, especially the small producers, is full of home winemakers run amuck. They just want to try everything that comes along. And that's fine. Randall Grahm has done a wonderful job that way and he's paved the way for a lot of other people. His approach and my approach are dramatically different, as much as I respect him, and I do respect him enormously. He has virtually no vineyards, he buys just about every variety he can possibly buy, he tries it all out, he does a hundred different styles and he comes up with some real winners and also probably some real dogs that we don't see. I control all my vineyards, just do one thing and try to do as well as I can in expressing the vineyard. In a poor year, maybe we won't have such a good wine but that's the way it goes when you've made a commitment to estate winemaking.

As far as the future of California winemaking, I think the wineries that don't control their vineyards are going to have a very tough time. Land prices are going way up and it's going to be very difficult to buy more land. I'm priced out of land around here; I simply can't afford anymore. You'll also find that if a grower controls a piece of land that grows very good grapes, generally he'll start a winery and thereby effectively take those grapes off the market. That's what I did, after all. Following this thought, those growers that find their vines admirably suited to their area will establish a record that their area is admirably suited to a certain varietal and his neighbors will see his success with that variety and the area will become known more by the varietal than the wineries that are in the area.

What is your feeling about "Meritage," the label designation for premium wines utilizing a blend of Bordeaux grape varieties?

The name "Meritage" is a dumb solution to what many perceive as a real problem. The problem is that the U.S. wine industry has chosen to designate wine by its varietal content and the BATF (Bureau of Alcohol, Tax and Firearms) has therefore stipulated that a wine called by its varietal name must contain at least seventy-five percent of the designated grape. So what does one call a blended wine that contains, for example, fifty percent Merlot, twenty-five percent Cabernet Sauvignon and twenty-five percent Cabernet Franc? Until recently it could only be called red table wine. But now it can be called Meritage. Red table wine, according to the wine snobs, has a pejorative connotation, whereas Meritage has the requisite snob appeal, with its French sounding name and perceived traditional, as in heritage, implications. Over and above the pomposity of the name, I'm not sure that it will accomplish its goal in the long run. What's to keep a blended bulk wine or, for that matter, a pretentious but lousy blended wine from being called Meritage and thereby vitiating the name. Meritage, as I understand it, applies only to Bordeaux types of wines, both white and red. Where would this leave Laurel Glen if, for example, we decided to add twenty-six percent Syrah? Either we could call it red table wine, which is precisely what it is and seems alright to me; or we could leave any further descriptor entirely off the label and simply call the wine Laurel Glen. The latter is the best solution and one we will very likely utilize in the near future, even if our wine continues to have over seventy-five percent Cabernet Sauvignon. After all, it's not what the wine is called but who makes it and how it tastes. People don't buy Laurel Glen because it is red table wine, Meritage or Cabernet Sauvignon but hopefully because it is Laurel Glen.

Is winemaking an art, craft or science?

A craft. In art, you're dealing with a blank slate. You have true artistic expression when you have a blank canvas with which you can do anything you want. You aren't limited by your medium. There's no winemaker that can claim to be as wonderful as Mozart. If they do, they're ignorant. With Mozart, you're just dealing with a totally different level of artistic expression.

On the other hand, winemaking is a craft. You're given eighty percent of what you're ever going to have. You can change it to some extent; you can certainly ruin it. But you can't really do a heck of a lot with what you're given. It would be nice to think I'm some great "artiste" but that's not the case. I spent this afternoon fixing the gear box on the tractor, not working on arcane and artistic subtleties in the winery. You can't jimmy the wine around into some-thing that it isn't. You just can't do it.

In the greater realm of the universe, what is the winemaker's contribution?

The winemaker is a purveyor of pleasure, I think. Ultimately, you're trying to give to the world something that will bring greater happiness and pleasure. There's nothing wrong with that. To augment the pleasures of daily dining is, I think, a wonderful thing. Everybody eats, and if you can make that facet of everybody's day a little more pleasurable, then that's fine. If I had been good enough in music, I would have become a professional musician. I tried but I wasn't good enough. So perhaps I'm a winemaker by default. However, I enjoy winemaking most likely much more than I ever would have enjoyed performing.

Let me tell you one more thing that I think is interesting. I taste with a number of winemakers who I feel have a common perspective of Cabernet winemaking. We all respect each others' winemaking and we taste together once a month. Of the twelve people in the group, five of them have either undergraduate and/or graduate degrees in philosophy, including myself. I think that's rather interesting. I'd be interested in seeing how many people from a philosophy background are involved in winemaking. I'm not quite sure what it tells you. But I think it indicates that you've got a type of person that is intrinsically rather analytical but who has come to a rather skeptical view of the world. Skeptical is the opposite of doctrinaire. A skeptic keeps an open mind. You have to keep an open mind when you're working in a medium that changes from year to year. If you ever get into a rut, start making wine by a formula and stop asking questions, then you might as well give up.

A person who is attracted to philosophy is looking for truth. He goes through a search for truth and then often comes to realize he's never going to find it. He holds a skeptical view because he realizes the limitations that he has to work with. I think philosophy is a good training for a winemaker because you constantly have to work with limitations. Because eighty percent of what you're given initially is the grape source and you can't do a heck of a lot more to it; you learn to bear with what you're given.

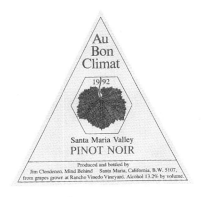

Au Bon Climat

1992

Santa Maria Valley
PINOT NOIR

Produced and bottled by
Jim Clendenen, Mind Behind   Santa Maria, California, B.W. 5107,
from grapes grown at Rancho Vinedo Vineyard. Alcohol 13.2% by volume.

Jim Clendenen

AU BON CLIMAT
IL PODERE DELL OLIVOS

"That's the rule of the game: to express, with traditional winemaking, the flavors indigenous to the vineyards you are working with."

Sometimes known as "the wild man of the Central Coast," Jim Clendenen is one winemaker who doesn't dangle participles or mince words. He has a considered opinion on just about everything, which he will relay to you with a charming directness, a somewhat refreshing quirk in an industry where winemakers often take the middle road so as to offend the least amount of people. Possessed of a keen mind and sharp wit, he was set to attend law school when he got waylaid by the food and wine he discovered on trips to France.

In 1978, without any formal training, he signed on at the then fledgling Zaca Mesa Winery, where he soon became assistant winemaker and also met his future partner, Adam Tolmach, who joined the staff a year later as enologist.

Three years later, Clendenen left to work in the Australian wine industry, followed by a harvest in Burgundy, where he was reunited with Tolmach.

Their Burgundian experiences reaffirmed their traditional winemaking philosophy and, upon their return, they began making Pinot Noir and Chardonnay in 1982 as Au Bon Climat (roughly translated as "to the good climate"). From the beginning, ABC (as it's often called) placed the emphasis on making small, artisan, hand-crafted lots of Burgundian varietals. In a decade's time, they have continued to refine the details and the wines have reflected that evolution.

Recently, Tolmach left to pursue his interest in Ojai Vineyards and Clendenen became the sole proprietor of ABC. In addition, he is involved with Bob Lindquist of Qupé in producing Bordeaux style varietals on the Central Coast under the Vita Nova (literally, new life) label. As if that were not enough (between annual trips to the wine producing regions of France, Italy and Germany), Clendenen, with his wife, artist Sarah Chamberlin, started a new label, Il Podere dell´ Olivos, specializing in Italian varietals.

After three years as assistant winemaker at Zaca Mesa and some time spent in production winemaking in Australia, you then went to work the harvest in Burgundy? What kind of experience was that?

It was clearly a confirmation of what I wanted to do. I was able to learn precisely what a small Burgundian vintner would do with grapes of certain flavors, tastes and chemical components. All experimentation aside, from what I was doing in Australia, this was a complete in-depth, hands-on exposure to what is about ninety-five percent of the winemaking I do here.

It continues to be the main influence on you today?

Yes, it's the rules of the game. If you don't know the rules, you can't play the game. Most people in California, who try to make what they consider to be Burgundian wine styles, just flat out don't know the rules of the game. They've never been exposed to it.

You would consider yourself a traditionalist winemaker?

Completely. Even more traditional than the bulk of people working in Burgundy.

When you established your own winery, Au Bon Climat, with Adam Tolmach, why did you think you would succeed?

Self-hypnosis! Seriously, here is the way I envisioned things. And this is something that has been an axiom of my life; that is, if something looks, tastes, feels and smells the same, there's a large likelihood that it's going to be the same. Rather than looking at something and saying, "That's over there, we're over here. That's foreign; that can't possibly be right." I've traveled extensively and I think traveling extensively, on this planet anyway, has allowed me to compare and contrast different situations in a quick and easy fashion. I can go over and taste ground nut stew in Senegal; it's made with chicken, peanuts and what they have indigenously as cream. It's blended up in a certain fashion and it gets a certain texture, consistency and flavor. As long as I can isolate those flavors, then I can come back and make the same thing here. Chicken is not inherently different in Senegal, nor are peanuts, so why not do it over here? Well, the same thing happened in Burgundy. We were looking at grapes that tasted and felt very similar to coastal California grapes, both in Chardonnay and Pinot Noir. So we didn't have any doubt that we could, by using this traditional framework, interpret the grapes in Los Alamos in such a way that they would have similar structure, that is, texture, acid and things that are constituents of wine, while having different flavors. The wine would have the flavors of the vineyards in Los Alamos or in the Santa Ynez Valley. That's the rule of the game: to express, with traditional winemaking, the flavors indigenous to the vineyards you are working with. We knew we could do that but the idea of being able to make a financial go of it was a different thing all together. That was really a dim flame of entrepreneurial spirit, blind faith and a whole lot of sheets of penciled out cash flow prognosis that were erased and diminished.

It was rough financially for the first couple years?

We started with a capitalization that wouldn't buy a press for most wineries. I'm talking about just a press, without a building, without barrels, without vineyards. Our entire capitalization was a press; we leased our facilities and we bought our grapes. There was just no other way we could start the operation.

But you were sure of your own talent?

We're winemakers. Most operations that start up in California have vineyards, buildings and someone who has never made wine before. That's like starting up a restaurant with a concept and then hiring a kid from the local university to sauté your scallops. You know, it's great. It's a fern bar, it's got nice tables, it looks pretty. And there's this kid in the kitchen who's never sauteed scallops before. That's how formula restaurants are started. Wineries are started the same way. They bring in a winemaker as an afterthought. Someone has land, someone plants grapes, someone invests in a building and then someone hires a kid who has never made wine, has no track record and has no style.

To quote you, on a previous occasion, you said, "What we make is California wine with European elements of style." Could you amplify on that?

There's nothing I find more insulting than somebody in California who follows no winemaking regime from France and then declares the grape variety he makes to be in a certain style. Let's talk Burgundy, for example. The grapes are grown in California, the winemaking is purely Californian, purely high technology. The winemaker doesn't have a clue to what's going on in France and he makes a wine and declares it to be Burgundian because he, with his limited palate information, decides that what he's made reminds him in some way of something that he's had from France. I am asked that question more often by people who are touring the winery and tasting the wines. They say, "Aren't your wines Burgundian?" What I have to emphasize more than anything is that the wines are made in a traditional, rigorous, attention-to-detail fashion that only the most return-to-roots winemakers in Burgundy are doing right now. Not large negotiant houses, not people who really don't care about the quality of their wine but merely the money they're getting in the market-place; but people who understand what they're doing from an enological stand-point. They've been to enology school so they understand what can go right and what can go wrong. And then they have decided that the best way to inter-pret their grapes is to utilize traditional picking, pressing, fermenting and bar-rel aging methodology. We do that as attentively as we possibly can but with California fruit. Now if you declare something is Burgundian to me, then you have to demonstrate, through geographical and palate knowledge, that you can determine the difference between a Santenay from a premier cru vineyard ver-sus a Santenay from the commune. You have to be able to do this all the way up to the great wines of the Cote de Nuits. You have flavors with the Santenay that tend toward a raisiny, coal-like character that are quite ripe and that bear no relationship to the elegance of the interior spice that you find in a Cote de Nuits. But there is consistency of winemaking to express the fruit flavors. And that's what we do. We make California wines that, we hope, have the texture, the length, the structure of things that you would expect to find in France. While recognizing completely that they can't be Burgundian because the grapes are grown in California.

Since you don't own vineyards, how do you control the quality of your fruit?

There are many ways to answer that. One is something I always like to say to prove how far out on a limb Au Bon Climat is in its winemaking philosophy. The grapes we work with are merely the raw materials, the blank canvas that we imprint or stylize. The grapes have to be a certain way numerically. We've found vineyards in Santa Barbara County that will give us natural acidity and a low enough pH with a sufficient ripeness to allow us to interpret our style. We also believe that there are seven or eight different vineyard sources that we could use in the county the same way. This is a unique area, especially when we first got involved in 1982, in that a large quantity of grapes had been planted in the previous five to seven years. They were not being utilized by anyone in the county; they had a reputation for being unappreciated in the remainder of the state. The grapes were inexpensive relative to Napa Valley grape prices and, for the style of wine we were trying to make, far superior in quality. When you consider that presently the wineries in the county only utilize four percent of the grapes grown here, you realize that the idea of planting a vineyard, which was impossible for Adam and I, was foolhardy and would have been just another example of wasting cash rather than trying to make good wine. Now as the world catches up, and who knows how fast this is going to be, as we get into a situation where the grapes that are planted are being utilized and become more difficult for us to obtain, then the situation would change dramatically.

We like the quality of the fruit that we've utilized in the past. We've been lucky enough to work with a number of vineyards and we'd love to own them but we're not in that position. We make suggestions and the vineyards cooperate as well as they can. I also don't believe that it's a handicap. I believe that, within the present constraints of the California wine industry, it's something we can live with comfortably.

Why do you concentrate on just two varietals, Chardonnay and Pinot Noir, other than the fact that they are Burgundian?

It's not an "other than the fact" thing. That's the fact of the matter; that's the essence of it right there. I enjoy the life-style of the small winemaker in Burgundy and that includes their attitude toward life, their philosophy, their demeanor and their behavior at the table. After working in Burgundy, we wanted to come back and set up a cellar that a Burgundian winemaker would walk into and smell, feel, see and believe that they could be back in Burgundy. That's the level of technology we have. It transcends merely the winemaking. Obviously Pinot Noir and Chardonnay are popular grapes and grow well in close proximity. I think the more you deal with things that don't do that, the more you try to have Cabernet and Chardonnay or Syrah and Chenin Blanc, grapes that for fairly traditional reasons have proven they don't coexist well in a vineyard with the same exposure, then the less sense you are making. So we have complimentary grapes that grow well in similar vineyard areas. The production techniques they require are very similar in the way that we make wine. We don't need a series of machines for one that you don't use for the other. We have small, portable, open top fermenters for the reds, which is the only thing we don't use for both the varietals.

In your experience, what are the characteristics of a great Pinot Noir from this area? Or from California?

From this area, the things to look for are vineyard character, that is, more like the Pinot Noirs that I'm interested in from France rather than most of them grown any place in California. Those characters descriptively are spice, in the sense that you can smell cinnamon, nutmeg or sandalwood. You can get strawberry, tawny Pinot Noir type fruit rather than getting bing cherry flavors that I would associate more with Zinfandel or very ripe grapes from the south of France than I would with Burgundy. Length and texture are things we get in Santa Barbara County that I don't think you get elsewhere in California. I'll hedge a little by saying that while I think, for instance, the area that Calera is working in has just got to be too warm for Pinot Noir, the sensible winemaking that Josh and Steve employ on their grapes makes a wine that has much of the same character that Santa Barbara coastal Pinot Noir has. That has to do with the barrels they use, the stem inclusion, the wild yeast fermentations. That winemaking technique can steer the process in the right direction. But when I go up to the Carneros region, knowing the winemaking technique is totally different, I haven't found wines there that speak to me with the same texture, structure and length, while having individual vineyard characters highlighted that I find from Calera.

Technically, what's so difficult about making Pinot Noir in California? Let me run down the various theories and have you respond. One theory is that we have the climate but we don't have the soil?

I disagree. Soil is certainly a component. You have to have soil that's well drained and that has a proper exposure to the sun. California winemakers are still arguing over the rules of the game and they don't really know how to vinify the stuff. So you have to understand that once winemakers in Burgundy have figured out how to vinify the stuff, they have to find other things to argue about. One of the things they argue about is why one vineyard plot, separated from another plot by a path, sells its wine for $14 while the original plot sells its wine for $170. Why is that? If you're looking at given things, then you've got to create a complex explanation for it and that usually is, in France, soil. Then when they go through and define it and find out exactly what's in the soil, they may find limestone, clay and trace chemicals. But usually they can't find great differences so they try to fractionalize it even more. They think that a small trace amount of something in the soil is going to be a real big difference. Frankly, what you usually find is that one farmer has more money than the other farmer, buys better barrels, harvests at the right time and tends not to get drunk, go carousing and hunting when he should be pruning the vines. What it comes down to is that he's just not as good at it as the other person. That explains it quite a bit more than just soil.

Calera Winery attributes the distinct characteristics of their Pinot Noir to the limestone soil.

So if we find limestone in the Atlas mountains of Morocco, are we going to go over there and plant Pinot Noir? And if we are, wouldn't the French already have done that around Algeria. That's my "perfect world" argument. If it was a perfect world, and the only difference between Hollister (Calera) and Santa Barbara County was the soil, and Josh Jensen found this type of soil up there, then that might give him a benefit. People really tend to get lost in the short term of the California industry. They look at small facets of the business that have little to do with the large picture. In Josh's case, from a marketing standpoint, he's done a big thing with limestone and I think that's important for him. More important than that, I think he's made real good Pinot Noir since 1982. I think that's the most important thing. All the limestone in the world didn't mean very much to me when I tasted his first wines. It didn't speak to me as the type of Pinot that I'd be interested in vinifying. So then he would have picked the wrong place, even though he had his limestone.

In Santa Barbara County, the Benedict Vineyard has soil with fractured monterey shale and limestone. We were lucky enough to get some fruit from that vineyard in 1987. I think that Pinot Noir is far and away superior to anything else in this county that I've tasted.

So now we're getting somewhere in the "perfect world" program. Working with the Los Alamos fruit gives us one wine; working with the Benedict fruit, for whatever reason, the soil being one of those reasons, gives us a better wine. Okay then, that's the direction we want to look in. But to start off without knowing and plant an area like the Hollister hills (Calera) that are quite warm and well away from the coast, shows that Josh has a pioneering spirit. But that's my argument once again: if I find a nice outcropping of limestone in Bakersfield, would I be foolhardy enough to plant in Bakersfield and base my winery's future on that because of the soil there. No. But if I happen to own the vineyard at Romanee Conti or La Tache and the vineyard up the hill from me can get only one-tenth the price for their wine that I get for my wine, then, at that point, you start looking for answers that will be different.

In California, winemakers get lost when choosing yeasts to ferment their Chardonnay! You'll talk to them and they'll give you sixty reasons why they've experimented with six different kinds of yeasts and how they've focused on using one particular yeast. The fun thing of it is when you taste a Chardonnay that has no personality at all, one that is just fruit juice overlaid with oak, and then have the winemaker tell you he went through a rigorous yeast selection. I just say, "Wow, you spent that much time worrying about yeasts and this is all you've got?" So there you are; someone who loses sight of the big picture.

Another criticism of Pinot Noir in California is that we don't have the proper clonal variety here.

I'm not much interested in clones, but most people are. I'll give you a short personal anecdote that convinced me. Michael Benedict at Sanford and Benedict Winery planted and dry farmed three different clones, including Gamay Beaujolais, the most prolific of Pinot Noir clones and one that's often used as one of the three clones they plant in Oregon. He made wines from the three and found little difference the first two years. He also found little yield difference because the vineyard itself was the regulator, with dry farming and the difficulty in achieving any kind of vigor. The vines just didn't want to produce. So there you have the proper vineyard situation, that is, not planting on successful agricultural soil and not planting on a river bottom. If you plant in a situation where anything will grow to its most ultimate abundance, then you damn well better worry about your clone because you're going to have to regulate the amount of vigor, regulate the amount of crop produced and do other things to keep the vine from overproducing. But if you plant a good clone in a self-regulating vineyard, it's not that important.

Another Pinot Noir criticism is that we don't get the proper yield in California. In Burgundy, the yield is one to two and a half tons per acre. We generally plant Pinot for higher yields.

Yield is important. One thing that I use as a rule of thumb is something Dale Hampton, the local farmer and vineyard consultant, uses. That is, balance your vines. Understand from experience what the vine can take because to have a vigorous vine and to thin it back to one ton per acre yield is stupid. Because you're going to get unbalanced grapes anyway. To have a vine that can handle four tons per acre that will ripen and vinify properly will give you a far better wine than a vine that can handle four tons and gets pruned down to one ton. We've gotten grapes from a vineyard that has a south and east exposure, has very dark soil and ripens early. We've discovered that at a three tons per acre yield, it has absolutely no character at all. In 1986, it had a half ton per acre and the wine is dark and spectacular. At three tons, the wine was light and insignificant. I have seen good Pinot Noir made from vineyards with a four ton yield. I think yield has to be considered on an individual vineyard basis.

In Burgundy, they may add sugar to the wines. We aren't allowed to do that here, the argument goes, so we'll never produce great wines like they have.

The point of making wine from balanced grapes can not be overstated, whether the grapes are grown on limestone soil or sandy, well drained soil. But the problem in California has been that a lot of winemaking decisions are made after the fermentation is finished. So what you've done essentially is fermented without balanced grapes. You've fermented with the grapes you got naturally and then decided, after the fermentation, that the wine doesn't have nearly enough acid. So you correct the acid. But you're only taking action after the fermentation. What the French have discovered through chapitalization (adding sugar) is something that corrects the wine as it is fermenting. They've also discovered in the last few years when they've introduced systemic vineyard treatments that they can have more healthy leaves per vine and less rot, mold and mildew. And they're finding with the grapes staying on the vines longer, they need to add acid rather than sugar. The grapes can actually ripen longer because the vines are becoming little invulnerable plants out there in the same inclement weather they've had in the past. So rather than watching the whole thing die early on and having to chapitalize, they're picking a lot later and have to chapitalize less but have to add acid as we do in California. That's a big change for them. It's illegal in California to add sugar but it's legal to add acid. In France you can add sugar but you couldn't add acid until very recently. But you can't add sugar and acid at the same time. All of which are stupid rules. The whole point is to have balanced grapes. If you have to add sugar and acid because you're losing your acid balance and the grapes still aren't ripening fast enough, in Burgundy or California, you've got to do it and you have to do it while you have the raw materials, the fermenting grapes. You can't do it afterwards to the wine. As long as we know what the numbers are, that is, the sugars, the acids, the pH, then we can try to predict what we are going to get after fermentation. You chapitalize to prolong fermentations; we can duplicate that in California. One of the ways is to add more grapes later on in the fermentation; so you add riper grapes later in the picking season and this prolongs fermentation.

What you have to understand is the difference between the orientation toward harvest. In California, the orientation has been one of waiting for perfection. The wait for perfection has been traditionally based on sugar amounts without any reference to acid at all. Now, there's a big reference to acid and a smaller reference to sugar. Things that have been ignored altogether are flavor, that is, whether a grape tastes ripe and tastes good. Instead you've got these manipulated numbers. You've got farmers adding water all the time. They're keeping their grapes healthy on the vine; they're getting up to 24 or 24.5 brix and they taste like asparagus in the case of Cabernet or some Pinot. They're so herbaceous that they don't taste like grapes any longer. Because they've been farmed, they've been induced to conform to certain numbers that bear no relationship to ripeness or good flavors. They're still altogether wrong.

In France, the harvest is usually a movement to get the grapes off the vine before disaster strikes. If it rained on Monday, you've got Tuesday clear and there's a feeling it's going to rain like hell on Wednesday, then you get in and get off the grapes in healthy condition. If you feel like it's not going to rain on Wednesday, then you wait and you can just push it to the outer limits of what's going to happen. Now, with better mildicides and fungicides in the vineyard, they can wait a little bit longer because the amount of rain that would induce mold and rot quickly in the past doesn't have the same effect. So they can stretch out the harvest a bit.

In California, we can stretch out the harvest over a two or three month period. People believe that if it rains for two weeks in August, it's still going to dry out in September. If it rains all of September and most of October, well it can't continue, can it? So you see people waiting and waiting for these higher sugar levels while the acids are falling out and the flavors may not ever be coming into balance anyway. Then you have to worry about correcting all these things. In France, they worry about correcting right before a disaster hits. They've got to add sugar if they've picked under-ripe grapes. Even if they don't pick under ripe, some silly French winemakers are adding sugar anyway because even though they pick ripe, that's what they are used to doing. And they end up with fifteen percent alcohol wines!

Some critics say Pinot Noir doesn't complete malolactic fermentation easily.

We have real good strains of malolactic bacteria. In fact, we no longer inoculate the Pinot Noir for malolactic; it just goes by itself. The Chardonnay is always inoculated because it has problems with browning color change. We don't put SO_2 in at the crusher. We don't put SO_2 in until the wine has finished both primary and malolactic fermentation. So the wine is unprotected for a long period of time. There are arguments as to why we do that. It may seem to be radical when compared to techniques used by other people. I don't find that radical at all. They were doing research in Germany when I was first starting to get into the wine business that said no SO_2 before fermentation was better as an anti browning program than if you put SO_2 in. So I think we're actually doing something positive by doing this. You just have to be really careful to make sure you don't jeopardize the wine after the fermentations have finished, both primary and secondary, by not getting SO_2 in when there's no longer CO_2 being generated to protect the wine.

Some North Coast winemakers say that Chardonnay is too delicate to put through malolactic fermentation. Possibly with the fruit that they're working with, maybe that's true. You wouldn't agree with that?

No. This is the discussion we were just having about letting the fruit come through in the wine. Unfortunately the technique used most often in California is cold fermentation in stainless steel tanks, then transferring into barrels when the wine is already clean, so the wine tends to have high alcohol and lots of SO_2. The combination of the ripe, clean wine with high alcohol and SO_2, most commonly put into new French barrels, elicits a combination of fruit and oak that's just disgusting. It makes for short, bitter, hard wines. If that's their idea of letting the fruit show through, then more power to them.

And that's the reason that barrel fermented, malolactic styles of Chardonnay from the Central Coast are becoming the wines of choice for anybody who pays real money to drink Chardonnay. The same reason they do it in France. The opposite for us. We have no SO_2, we have wines with a whole lot of suspended solids in them because we don't settle out the fermentation lees. They're all in the barrel. We have low pHs, high acids, low alcohols. The barrels we use are the heaviest toasted barrels you can get in France. We leave the wine in the barrels longer. They just can't put wines through malolactic in the North Coast because the numbers just aren't right. They don't really seem to understand that, when you have ripe grapes, malolactic fermentation is a completion of the wine style. If you don't put it through malolactic, you haven't completed your wine style. If you can't put it through malolactic, you're already working from a different game. Now, in Bordeaux, they're not putting the majority of the Sauvignon Blanc grown there through malolactic because they found that the wines were just too soft when they did. So they're going to much more sterile winemaking and changing the whole style of the wine. And if the public likes that style, then it will be successful. The same thing was going on in Alsace the last time I was there. I couldn't believe what winemakers were doing in Alsace. They were filtering their wines in November after the October harvest. As far as I was concerned, the wine was dead at that point. The wine no longer had anything to grow in it to benefit it. So they could bottle it up right then if they wanted instead of holding it any longer. That was their choice. If the wines find favor with the public, then more power to them.

I'm not arguing against a California style of Chardonnay production for the Napa or Sonoma. For me, and the type of Chardonnay I want to make, those areas are not suitable for Chardonnay and I would recommend they plant other grapes. For the style of Chardonnay that was popularized in the mid-seventies by Sterling, Freemark Abbey, Chateau Montelena, Grgich and Mondavi, that style of Chardonnay is a valid California style. You'll only get me to start speaking up about driving through with a tractor and plowing all the Chardonnay vines over, when they start saying, "Aren't our Chardonnays Burgundian? Our Chardonnays beat the Burgundians in the 1976 tasting." Because they are comparing apples and oranges. They're not comparing wines that have understood the rules of the game and have been effectively completed along that line; they are comparing wines that are fresh and fruity versus wines that are complete and complex. Or they're comparing wines that will mature "better" but become completely different. I think when you're really looking for the great wine styles and then you try to compete against them without doing similar things, you are just deluding yourself thinking that you are better. You certainly wouldn't find anyone in Napa Valley not putting their Cabernet through malolactic. They do things along the same vein for red wines but they don't do it for white wines. Explain to me why? Because they're handicapped with the raw materials to start with and they're trying to find a way to circumvent the methodology.

But the crux of the situation is that while many Chardonnays are fresh and fruity, that's not what you're looking for?

I think it's important that people gradually begin to recognize that what they like, as far as flavors, come from a certain winemaking direction. There are people who don't like our Chardonnays because they don't like the idea of the fruit being masked, when they taste the wine, and not the theoretical idea that because we put it through malolactic it must be different. Our wines, particularly when young, are as apparently fruity, fresh and vibrant as any wines on the market. I don't drink our wines often when they're first released. I wait four to five years, after our wines have gotten better in the bottle. Most so-called fresh and fruity Chardonnays from the North Coast will not improve in the bottle; they're already at their peak. I've tasted ten year old Chateau St. Jean Chardonnays that haven't gone bad but they haven't appreciably changed either. They didn't get richer; they didn't change in the way great Burgundies change, that is, softening their acid or having a bigger texture in the mouth.

What's the difference between your regular Chardonnay and your reserve Chardonnay?

We have a reserve program for Chardonnay for the obvious reason that the majority of the Chardonnay we produce is consumed early. It's drunk in restaurants by the glass, it's drunk at home when the wine is less than eighteen months old. With that in mind, we make a Chardonnay that is more appealing for early consumption. The grapes are picked progressively over a three or four week period. We get fruit that is ripe to our palates. It has flavors that show no greenery, no balance toward too much acid. The grapes are ripe but not too ripe; certainly they're not ripe by the numbers that people use in California. Then we amplify that with fruit with riper numbers. We start picking around 20.5 or 21 brix and we end up at 23.5 or 24 brix. That combination, of putting riper fruit at the end, softens the wine and makes it more accessible for early drinking. We leave it for nine to eleven months in barrels that are twenty percent new ranging to twenty percent that are four years old. We filter the wine as a method of achieving clarity because we recognize that we can't rely on careful cellar techniques in that short period of time. So we release our regular Chardonnay and people drink it at a fair price.

The reserve program is a different beast. We made a Chardonnay in 1983 that was picked at 21.5 brix from a new vineyard. The material was so immutable when you tasted it as a barely fermented wine—it was minerally, incredibly citric and hard—that we knew it needed new oak and lots of time in the barrel to structure it, to soften and round it out. Bottled without filtration, the wine was well received. So we set out in 1985 to find the best parts of the vineyard that would allow us to do similar things to an immutable just fermented wine that would end up being just as interesting with cellar and aging time. So now we're doing extended barrel aging, fourteen to eighteen months, depending on the vintage. We pick once and we pick as soon as it has ripish flavors but that will be the highest acid, lowest pH grapes that we'll bring into the winery. Then we work with the material and we call that our reserve. That means that we believe the wine will benefit greatly from extended cellaring. We don't consider it something to be consumed in its first eighteen months.

You've make a number of different Pinot Noirs but the Benedict Vineyard designated one seems to be your favorite.

We think we've found something very close to that ultimate quality in Benedict Vineyard. That roughly corresponds to "grand cru" status here at Au Bon Climat. It's a vineyard that has quite a combination of things that other vineyards don't have. So far I can't see which element has the most impact on the quality of the grapes. The vineyard is dry farmed, which obviously would tend to give higher quality, more intense fruit. Because of the dry farming and the inclement area, the vineyard sets ludicrously small crops. They're not commercially successful. So if the vineyard ever made itself a commercial proposition, it would probably grow a lot more grapes, which would undermine the quality but that's not the case right now. The vines are planted on gently sloping, fractured shale type soil which is well drained. It has wonderful nobleness of Pinot Noir fruit character.

*You recently started to release wines under a new label, Il Podere dell'
Olivos. I understand the label will concentrate on Italian varietals. What are
your plans for it?*

Il Podere dell' Olivos is the name that my wife, Sarah Chamberlin, and I
have chosen for what will hopefully turn into a vineyard in the area. We plan to
plant varieties like Sangiovese, Nebbiolo, Cannaiolo, Malvasia, Trebbiano and
probably Chardonnay. We should be making wines from those grapes by the
late 1990s. In leading up to that we've produced some wines under the Il Podere
label from grapes grown elsewhere.

What interests you about the Italian grape varieties in California?

First of all, the name of the little town we live in, Los Olivos, to me has
always connoted something that's reminiscent of Tuscany in Italy. If you look
at the rolling hills, the soft rock formations, the olive trees, the benign climate
that tends to grow herbs and gardens well along with the combination of benign grape climate and cows, it speaks to me of Tuscany. We've always thought
it might end up providing a good setting for those Italian varieties.

Bruno D'Alfonso

SANFORD WINERY

"I'm a traditional winemaker but I interpret the data I get in a modern way. I look at wine as an equilibrium of chemicals, compounds and substances. I don't read romance or mysticism into it."

An outdoorsman at heart, Bruno D'Alfonso was thinking of a career with the Forest Service when he was a student at Cal Poly in San Luis Obispo. But a summer in their employ convinced him that their near-military regimentation didn't agree with him. With a background in soil science and agriculture, he thought winemaking might be a way to utilize his training and challenge his senses. After a false start in the graduate program at UC Davis, he took some time off, then returned to get his advanced degree.

He got a job right out of school, as assistant winemaker at Edna Valley Vineyards, where he was exposed to many traditional winemaking techniques. Richard Sanford, proprietor of Sanford Winery, was also making his wine under the same roof, in space leased from Edna Valley Vineyards. Sanford and D'Alfonso soon discovered they had similar winemaking philosophies.

Sanford tapped D'Alfonso to be winemaker at Sanford Winery in 1983 and he has been there ever since. D'Alfonso is best known for Pinot Noir and Chardonnay made from cool climate grapes from choice vineyards in the Santa Ynez Valley. Other varietals include Sauvignon Blanc and a dry, barrel fermented Vin Gris. Production is presently around 30,000 cases.

All D'Alfonso's wines are big, bold, challenging and draw immediate attention to themselves. They very much reflect the personality of the winemaker himself. You may not always agree with his style but you can't argue with his skill of inducing the utmost of flavor into his wines.

What did you learn at UC Davis?

I learned discipline and theory. I learned that it matters if you have the degree but it doesn't matter if you have the learning behind the degree. I got to where I had to get by virtue of my personality. It was just something I fell into and all of the sudden, I really liked it. All the things I learned about the wines I make, I learned on the job. As a matter of fact, Davis is more geared toward a larger winery operations where everything is pretty much a safe bet. You would always go the safe route rather than doing something like barrel fermentation or malolactic fermentation.

As assistant winemaker at Edna Valley Vineyards, you got daily, hands-on, winemaking experience?

Yes, I was exposed to lees contact, stirring the lees, use of new oak, etc. I didn't make many decisions but sometimes I influenced decisions by subtlety suggesting things. In a position like that, you sometimes won't get credit when that idea works out; the winemaker will. You try to keep your ego out of it and take personal pride in the fact you made something good happen.

How do you perceive your role as winemaker at Sanford?

It's determining the style of the wines and how to achieve that style. I do some light and personable marketing and I'm generally a good envoy for the winery. I'm involved in the day-to-day operation of the winery. I crush the fruit and determine how it's handled, with the final goal being a certain style and taste. One thing often overlooked is that, as winemaker, you have to talk to the public and create good public relations.

What I hear you saying is that the public relations aspect is almost as important as the technical, winemaking aspect?

It's important in relating technical information to them, not necessarily to sell them that bottle of wine; but to make them understand, for example, that the Chardonnay in this area is the finest they'll find in the whole country. You should be able to do that without getting technical, without alienating them or insulting their intelligence.

Richard Sanford is the proprietor here; how do you interact with him on the winemaking philosophy and goals of the winery?

The main reason he hired me was because our philosophy of winemaking is similar. In 1981 and 1982, he was making his wines at Edna Valley and I processed a lot of his fruit. He was making decisions and I was executing them. But our pathways were the same; pretty much parallel. I think I hold on to the idea of quality above all else, even more than he does.

But you probably don't consult much with him on the day-to-day operation? You both set a philosophy early on and then it's up to you how it gets implemented?

Right, exactly. Where I get influenced is on the availability of new oak because of money constraints. That can have an effect on style a little bit. Sometimes he feels a need to release a wine in order to keep the marketing pipeline full, while I would rather let the wine age longer. And I can appreciate his predicament.

Whose decision is it to concentrate only on a few varietals?

That's Richard's decision. I would enjoy making Pinot Blanc; I don't like to make Merlot. I like to make Burgundian varieties, not necessarily because I'm hooked on them but because I like to make the varieties that make the best wine in the area where we get our fruit. I don't want to make popular wines; if I did, I'd be making White Zinfandel.

Do you consider yourself a specialist because you have a fairly narrow varietal focus?

Sure, you have to be. You have to be a specialist because those varieties show best in our area and the desire is to make the finest wine from what does best here. I dislike making Cabernet or Merlot from this area because they don't grow well here and the consistency is not there.

Sanford Winery owns no vineyards, so how do you control the quality of the fruit?

Well, the whole concept of estate fruit is overdone. It's in the grape growers' best interest to produce the best fruit possible. That is, not to overcrop, not to overwater. So the growers work with you. I think the estate concept is a little overblown. It does protect you, in this marketing climate, from fluctuations in grape prices. But we've contracted out for our fruit and we've received firm commitments.

Do you see yourself as a winemaker in the traditionalist style?

Coincidentally, the traditional method produces the best Chardonnay. Barrel fermentation is traditional. You can't make the best Chardonnay without getting grapes from a cool climate, with high acid, high sugar, high alcohol and low pH. You can't make the best Chardonnay without barrel fermenting and putting it through malolactic fermentation. All these things feed the best Chardonnay. It just so happens that those things are traditional. So I'm a traditional winemaker but I interpret the data I get in a modern way. I look at wine as an equilibrium of chemicals, compounds and substances. I don't read romance or mysticism into it. What I am is a chemist, a wine chemist.

So how much of winemaking is art and how much is science?

Personally, none of it is art. Most of it is science and some of it is craft. I don't want to make myself seem to be above others or to be on a certain level because of what I do. I want people to understand what wine is. It tastes good, it gives you pleasure and it accompanies food. It's all positive in those ways. And it's not a big deal to make, if you know what you're doing. But being a winemaker doesn't confer on me any special insight. It's just that I've made enough mistakes to know how to prevent them, so I won't make them again.

My impression is that it's fairly easy to make wine; the hard part is making good or even great wine.

That's where, all of a sudden, style comes into play. You have good wine all starting at the same level; it could be in the style of Napa Valley, it could be in the style of the Central Coast. Those styles are different. But if it's the style of this area, then it's fat, rich, full-blown and extracted. All these things are just beating on your senses and you're influenced by that. You like that. That's the thing that gets people going. What really gets to them immediately is how they smell and taste and that sets them off. As opposed to having to read something into it or being told to by a wine writer. Consequently, you read, "This wine is overblown; you should look for elegance." So now everyone goes out and looks for an elegant wine because that's what you're supposed to do. Rather than just sitting down at the table and trusting your own instincts to like what you like and to believe what you like. Our wines are always overblown on one end of the spectrum. People are impressed with them immediately; some are even startled by them.

I've seen your Chardonnay reviewed in the press as "a very stylistic Chardonnay." The implication is it's really not the type of Chardonnay we're used to and we don't quite know what to make of it. What do you read into that?

A backhanded compliment. I read that it's not a mainstream Chardonnay. It's a Chardonnay that makes a statement. Now this country is not geared to making statements. If you make a statement, you are going to alienate some people but others will also join your camp. If you don't make a statement, and be a politician about it, people won't love you or hate you, they just tolerate you. So I would much rather have some people dislike me and my wines and other people like me, than to be in the middle. I don't want to be all things to all people. You can dislike the Sauvignon Blanc for its aggressiveness and you can dislike the Pinot Noir for its herbaceous qualities. That's fine; there are others who like them.

Another important point here is the notion of finding and creating a market, not just supplying a market that has already been created. The Vin Gris is a very good example. It took us about eight years to create that market and now we're finally selling out of that. Initially, nobody was ready for a barrel fermented, dry, blanc de noir. Now we're running out of it every year and that's what I like. It's a statement making wine. Accept it, reject it; I don't care. But it's a statement.

How do you handle your Pinot Noir in the winery?

The first thing about Pinot Noir is that, genetically, it's not like any other red grape. As a result, it needs to be handled a certain way or it becomes subject to certain pitfalls, which are all associated with chemistry. The main thing is pH; that's where the success or failure of Pinot Noir is determined. You must have a low pH. The way I make Pinot Noir is to acidulate on a regular basis throughout the fermentation process to hold it to a pH around 3.2 or 3.25. That preserves the color, flavors, aromas and microbiological stability. Once the fermentation is finished, it sits on the skins to finish malolactic and is pressed off. The important part here is to incorporate, on its way into barrel, as much of the solids as possible. Don't rack it clean into barrel; keep all the sediment suspended. Let the aging of the wine involve autolysis from the yeast and everything that goes in there.

It gives it complexity and softens the oak. It's a very easy variety to make; once you know how to structure the pH, it's extremely simple. The majority of winemakers don't make Pinot Noir well because they approach it the same as Cabernet or Zinfandel. They just put it through the standard red wine process. On the other hand, there are these fashionable things to do, like stem addition or pitch back, which are totally ludicrous.

You don't destem the Pinot Noir fruit, do you?

We destem fifty percent and retain fifty percent. We do that rather than add back stems. But retaining the stems and adding them back later are two totally different things. With stem retention, you have whole clusters with the stems intact, carbonic maceration involved and you don't have split stems. With stem addition, you have split stems, which leach out a lot of bitterness in the wine.

Isn't that fairly traditional winemaking?

You want it to be earthy. You want it to be like the forest floor. You want it to be decomposing organic materials, you know, that rich, soily aroma. As a fruit, you want it to taste like dark, black cherries, cherries and raspberries. You don't want it to taste candied or sweet.

How long do you leave it on the skins?

About two to three weeks. You try to get the malolactic about eighty percent complete before you put it in barrel and then let it finish up in barrel.

Do you punch down the fermenters?

I punch down once a day. The extraction really comes with the fermentation. It's a hot fermentation, about 98F degrees. The punching down ruptures some of those intact clusters, releasing a little bit more sugar into the system, keeping the fermentation going. The heat stays at 98F degrees for quite a few days. After the peak of fermentation subsides, that heat is held in there just by sheer mass and there's where you're getting your extraction. But the proper color is held fast because of the pH. This Pinot Noir doesn't taste like a California Pinot Noir; it's not your Hanzell Pinot Noir, it's not your Calera Pinot Noir, it's a different Pinot Noir. The color of Pinot Noir has to be lighter than Cabernet or Zinfandel. It has to be garnet; it's not your deep, inky colored wine.

Let me get your reactions to what I've heard are the reasons we can't make great Pinot Noir in California. One reason is that we have the grapes and the climate, but we don't have the soil.

The whole soil thing is the biggest crock I've ever heard. There's one thing that anybody has to learn about wine appreciation or winemaking and that is that the soil doesn't mean anything from the level of its influence on the whole spectrum. In other words, it could influence the wine by one half of one percent, if that much.

It's said we don't have the proper clonal variety?

Pinot Noir, by fact, mutates in the vineyard on the vine. It's not going to be the same thing a few years from now. So who cares what clonal variety you have, unless you're talking about some real radical departure.

We don't have the low yielding vineyards, one to one and a half tons an acre, like they do in Burgundy.

The only reason why their yields are low is because their climate is lousy. No, you can make good wine out of three to three and a half tons per acre.

We can't add sugar like they do in Burgundy.

That's not important. The only reason to add sugar is to increase microbiological stability. No other reason than that. Although alcohol does add texture and viscosity to a wine. What you miss when you add sugar to a low brix must is all the complexity that comes with high brix fruit. That's why I hate working with anything below 22.5 brix, because I know the wines are going to be insipid.

We don't ferment with one hundred percent of the stems.

That just indicates a hard core, traditionalist who believes that tradition is going to carry him rather than understanding the grape.

They say you shouldn't fine or filter Pinot Noir.

I feel that I have a good understanding of Pinot Noir now. If all things are maintained properly, on a chemical level, in the fermenter, you can filter it and you can pump it, but not excessively. But you can process it properly to a higher quality standard than you could in the past. I used to believe that an unfiltered Pinot Noir was the best. But when you don't filter something and then bottle it, you still have bacteria working in that wine. And in three years, that wine you bottled will not be the same wine. The change in the wine is going to be in a microbiological as well as in a chemical nature. The direction I'm moving in is to structure the wine early on, and make it processable so the wine will be the best it can be. I don't want to leave a lot of things up in the air as far as the directions the wine is going.

Without sacrificing quality?

Right. If I felt I was sacrificing quality, I would not filter it or anything else that was detrimental. The primary reason for all this is to make the best wine possible.

Do you add acid?

Always. With Pinot Noir, it's vital.

How much?

I don't know, I don't care. There's a sixth sense involved here. I add thirty pounds immediately and then feed it a few handfuls everyday. People ask me, "What's your total acid?" I don't do a total acid so I don't know. What I do want to know is whether the wine tastes good, whether it's balanced and well structured. There comes a point where I don't want to know numbers anymore. But I know those numbers are important. Levels are important. To know the numbers, that's important initially. But the problem with relying on numbers is that you start using them as a barometer of your success or failure. You use them as an excuse if you fail. So instead of telling yourself that you made a mistake, you say, "The numbers said I should be doing this." I don't buy that. You have to know what you're doing and why you're doing it.

If you taste through the past vintages, you will get a sharper, more clearly defined image of a big style. You're constantly carving away fat, whittling it down to what you want. Take a clay form, for example. In that form there could be The Pieta, The Thinker or anything; it's just a matter of wasting away the form and finally getting down to what you want.

Tell me about the Sauvignon Blanc grapes growing here.

The Sauvignon Blanc fruit that comes from this area is really intense. It's herbal, grassy, peppery, weedy; all those things associated with green plants. The cool climate preserves all these esters in the berry. In hotter climates, they volatilize out because esters are so fragile. You'll find that Sauvignon Blanc from the Central Valley tastes pretty innocuous. The idea of any wine, as far as I'm concerned, is to smell like something, taste like something. It should, quite simply, smell like what it is and taste like what it is. Sauvignon Blanc does that well. Again, it's a wine that will put some people off and enchant others. In the early seventies, Sauvignon Blanc used to get beat up because it made a wine that was too herbaceous for wine writers' tastes. So they really jumped on it and, in a sense, forced the winemakers to change their style so that the wine became less of everything that is was supposed to be in the first place.

Once again, the idea with our Sauvignon Blanc is not to make the wine for a fixed market, but to create and develop the market for the wine. It goes with a narrow range of foods but it does go with herb dishes, spicy dishes and peppery dishes better than any other wine. That's what this wine is all about: to enhance the pleasure of the moment at the table. You have to look at the whole concept of wine and food. We're not looking at one wine to go with your whole meal. We're looking at the idealistic concept of having three or four courses and having that many wines to accompany your meal. That's why we do winemaker dinners: to show how these wines go with certain foods.

The Sauvignon Blanc is barrel fermented. It goes through malolactic fermentation, which is quite unusual. It's not lees infused as much only because it's settled extensively and inoculated with yeast. We use a combination of new French and American oak for fermentation and aging. The result is a leanly structured wine with herbal qualities.

All your Chardonnay is put through the secondary malolactic fermentation. In your experience, what does this do for the wine?

It gives the potential for the style we want to make. That is, extracted, rich, fat, flavorful, with texture and viscosity. That's starting with high ripeness of the fruit, meaning 23.5 brix and sometimes 24.0 to 25.0 brix. We crush, press, settle overnight to two days, depending on what the sulfur regimen was and how confident we feel with the grower. Then cool juice is inoculated with a strain of Montrachet yeast in the barrel, not the tank. We use thirty percent new oak and lees infusion for ten to twelve months. We don't use any sulfur at all until we rack out of barrel; then we fine, filter and bottle it.

What are the characteristics that malolactic fermentation contributes to the wine?

The desirable characteristics are the butteriness and the complexity. The reduction in acid is not that important. You need a high acid for this type of big structured wine. But your goal is not to reduce the acid vis-á-vis the malolactic fermentation; your goal is to make the wine even that much more complex, to the point where after a couple of years in the bottle, the wine loses fruit and does not seem to be Chardonnay any longer but appears to be simply an idea of a white wine.

You make a "reserve" Chardonnay bottling; how is that selected?

The "barrel select" Chardonnay, as we call it, is the type of wine which I would make if I owned my own winery and had unlimited funds to do anything I damn well pleased. Basically, this is a wine that gets extended barrel aging. There's a transformation that takes place, a point where the wine quits getting infused with oak. And all those extracts become oxidized and rounded as time goes on. The result is a wine of less obvious oak character because the oak has become a real part of the wine rather than a layering over it. We do this every year and we pick the ten or fifteen best barrels of wine and keep them aside. It stays in one hundred percent new oak with lees infusion until the twelfth month, it's racked out into a tank, blended, fined and put back in the same barrel until the fourteenth month. It's racked, blended and fined again; then it goes back into old oak and becomes polished in those barrels to the point where the wine is brilliantly clear. Again, it's no longer Chardonnay; it's an idea. If I had my way, I'd put 14,000 cases of that Chardonnay on the market. That's what can be done with Chardonnay. It's powerful; it makes a statement.

How many thousands of cases can you produce before the quality gets away from you. What's the threshold level where you begin to lose quality?

It's contingent on a lot of things. Primarily, it's determined by your source of fruit and the quality of that source. After that, it's the availability of barrels, which can be bought. Let's say there are no monetary constraints at all, then it all comes down to the quality of the fruit. That's it. Period. If you have the right fruit from the right region, you can make 100,000 cases of barrel select Chardonnay.

At that level, you can't have your hand in everything that's going on in the winery?

You have to give up certain things, but you know where your priorities are. You have to be in there every day and tasting the wines. If you're not going to be able to do those things, then you don't make 100,000 cases. But I would not have a problem doing that, not at all, all else being equal.

Jill Davis
BUENA VISTA WINERY

"From a winemaker's point of view, I like making all these wines. I'm able to keep my skills sharp. If I spent years not making a Gewurztraminer, how could I possibly understand the grape or the wine?"

If the Davis family hadn't tinkered with brewing a little homemade beer and sauerkraut in their garage, Jill Davis might never have thought of winemaking as a career. Their homemade efforts turned out better than what was commercially available and that intrigued her. One fall, when she was still in high school, her father was offered some Zinfandel grapes. They made wine but it wasn't as good as what they could buy at the stores; and that intrigued her too. She went through the requisite enology regime at UC Davis and, right out of school, signed on as winery lab technician at Beringer. After four years, she was ready for a change and came to Buena Vista Winery as assistant winemaker, quickly she became winemaker and then vice president of production. A. Racke & Co. of West Germany purchased Buena Vista in

1979 and made a major financial commitment to acquiring vineyards and improving the quality of the wines. Production exceeds 100,000 cases and a whole range of varietals are produced. The winery owns 1,700 acres of vineyards and the vast majority of its grapes are estate grown, giving them greater control over the viticultural practices. Davis has focused on utilizing their grape sources in Carneros to the best advantage of the wines. The application of her skills, coupled with the teamwork at the winery, have resulted in restoring the historic Buena Vista to its former glory. In 1988, Davis was named vice-president of the winery and, in addition to Buena Vista, oversees production at Racke owned wineries, Haywood and Robert Stemmler.

You came to Buena Vista as assistant winemaker, but suddenly you became the winemaker. You were twenty-seven years old and going to make 40,000 cases of wine for one of the largest wineries in Sonoma County. Were you quaking in your boots?

I was scared to death, no question about it. When you're the only one, there's nobody to fall back on. But I did have my safety net in Andre Tchelistcheff. I didn't know him then, but we got to know each other and became very good friends. I rely on him. You always need somebody else to tell you that you've got it right. I hope I never get to a point in my career when I think I know everything because that would be setting myself up for a fall. Andre really helped me through the first year. He tasted with me and was very honest with his opinions. He'll let you go out on a limb, do what you want, unless he absolutely believes it's the wrong thing. He uses young winemakers, to a certain extent, in that he learns from us. He's very open minded; he taught me a lot about not being afraid to change things.

The Buena Vista Carneros Winery was built in 1975; they purchased 1,700 acres here and started planting grapes. At that time, it was a bold move because there were not yet a lot of vineyards in Carneros.

It was quite unusual. Andre Tchelistcheff had a lot to do with that. He had been a proponent of Carneros since the fifties, I think. Buena Vista and the future of this winery is definitely tied into this region.

When the Racke family bought Buena Vista in 1979, what kind of shape was the winery in?

The facility was relatively new; the physical plant was in very good shape. The cellar was full. The vineyards were six to eight years old. The winemakers were still just learning how to deal with Carneros fruit. There hadn't been large quantities of it available before. The style of the winery and its wines needed developing. If you're in a region like this, everything is directly related to the fruit you work with. You could be a huge failure if you try to make the grapes into something they don't want to be. The wines were good but they were struggling a bit in trying to find an identity.

Anybody who's followed this winery's history agrees that Buena Vista has turned around from what it was fifteen years ago. While the Racke family and their access to additional capital was a direct influence, surely your abilities were an influence too.

I think that, as a team, we're a tremendous influence, more so than as individuals. I've made changes; they've made differences. In 1983, I became winemaker, Marcus Moller-Racke became president, and Anna Moller-Racke became director of vineyard operations. So you have to look at it more as a management group. We each take our own area of expertise and develop them together.

But fifteen years ago, one might not have given these wines a second look . . . or taste.

There's no question that the wine quality and the reputation and image of the winery have improved one thousand percent. We've defined ourselves. We finally know what we want to do and where we want to go. We're not floundering anymore. One big change came in 1983 when we took over marketing our own brand. And that meant infusion of capital and commitment; we needed that. In 1985, there was a big internal expansion of the production facilities. In 1984, we purchased an additional thousand acres in Carneros. Our sales were doing so well by then that if we were going to grow, we could either grow by buying grapes or growing our own. Our commitment was to be in control of our own destiny: you can only control the price of grapes if you control the source of your fruit.

Being in an estate grown situation gives you better control over all aspects of the winemaking process?

Much more. Just talk to anybody who's out there trying to buy grapes. That shows you the advantage right there.

You're making over 100,000 cases a year; it seems like a lot.

Yes, but it's easy to control because I came from a larger winery. So, to me, this is quite small. In 1983, we crushed only 900 tons and we've grown a lot since then. Each of our wines is very different. We don't just make a Cabernet and a Gamay Beaujolais to have two red wines. They're different wines and they have different personalities. Personally, from a winemaker's point of view, I like making all these wines. I'm able to keep my skills sharp. If I spent years not making a Gewurztraminer, how could I possibly understand the grape or the wine? When you make each varietal, it helps you in all aspects of winemaking.

You make so many varietals, doesn't your attention shift around from one varietal to the next, as need dictates?

We've narrowed our wines a bit since I've been here. All I can say is that I've always done this job with this variety of wines. I would be very sad to see any of the varietals we're making right now disappear.

But how do you keep your focus?

The focus is on the appellation. There's a similarity in all the wines because of where the grapes are grown. It makes focusing easy. You deal with one grape variety after another. Most of the grapes, in the same appellation, don't all get harvested and crushed at the same time. This is different from Napa where Chardonnay from Carneros and Cabernet might both come in at the same time. There is a natural progression at harvest so I do have the opportunity to focus on each wine, get it fermenting and go onto the next.

I see you have a flowchart on the wall. How do you keep track of everything: where each wine originates, where it's going and its stage of development?

There's no question that if you're not organized, you can't do this job on the breadth and scale of what we're doing. One thing I can safely say about myself is that I am organized and able to compartmentalize things. For example, some winemakers only taste the fermenting wines once a week. During harvest I taste every wine every day. That's the thing. If there's something going on with the wine, you know about it. When you taste the wines every day, you just don't lose track of them. But during harvest your whole life is your job, right here.

A number of people think that a large volume winery and high quality are incompatible. How do you respond to that?

I don't think that's necessarily the case at all. I think you have to have the commitment, the control system and the right staff. Most importantly, you have to know what you want to do. You have to have a commitment from your marketing and sales department to allow you to do what you want without cutting corners. I feel Buena Vista is in the small end of the medium sized wineries. I'm completely comfortable with the volume we're producing because each wine is different and handled differently. You get into trouble when you start doing things for cost-savings reasons. If you have good grapes you can make excellent wine on any scale as long as you don't cut corners. If you have all your controls in place and have a group of people that are really concerned about the quality of the wine, then you can do it. Usually all those things don't go together. Usually the bigger wineries are concerned about the bottom line. But here the Moller-Racke family has made a long-term commitment to this industry; they've been in the business in Germany for over 200 years. One nice thing about Europeans is they tend to take the long-term view over and against the short-term gain.

You can't sit back on your laurels and say, "Look at all those gold medals last year; I've got this pegged." Every year is different. You always have to be kind to the fruit. The minute you think you've got it figured out and you don't need to improve, that's the year you start sliding back. You can't ever relax. If you're going to be in the wine business for the long-term, you have to be ready to fight and struggle all the time.

In a winery of this size, it would be very easy for you to put the reds through a red wine formula and the white through a white wine formula. But you take a different approach to each varietal?

Each wine is different. I certainly have a general idea of what I'd like to do. I think I understand the grapes but I'm always open to changes. If I have weather problems I may have to do something different. I hand-make each wine. I look at the vineyards and the grapes before they come in. That's an advantage to having estate vineyards with the winery situated in the middle: you can actually go out and look at the fruit during the crush. Many winemakers don't get away from the winery during that time. I keep a pretty firm hand around here. We have a truly good staff and they understand what we're trying to do.

What's so special about Carneros. Tell me a bit about the climate, soil and the kind of fruit you get from the region.

To begin with, the soil is very different. The soil is a shallow and heavy clay. The vines tend to be small because they can't get their roots down very far. Three feet is about the maximum depth. Small vines, in general, mean small canopies and smaller clusters with smaller berries.

The ratio of skin to juice is higher, so you get more flavor intensity and fruit character. The climate is quite cool. It's cooler in the summer and warmer in the winter so we have a smaller range of temperature fluctuations, which means we have a long growing season. We bud out early because it's warmer in the winter; we have a very long ripening season because it's cooler during the summer. Again, this allows more fruit character to develop in the berries before you have to pick because of sugar. Nobody wants a fourteen percent alcohol wine. So our grapes tend to be physiologically mature before the sugar level is so high that you have to pick because of that. The cool climate tends to give us high acidity and low pH: well balanced wines. These wines will age well; most of our Chardonnays are better after a year in the bottle. Because of the wind we get off the San Pablo Bay, we have little mildew or mold problems. With the small foliage in the vines, even if it rains, the air keeps circulating preventing mold or mildew from growing. We have small yields, about two and a half tons per acre. I wish we could get four or five tons per acre but we just can't with standard vineyard spacing. But we do get a lot of fruit intensity because of the smaller yield.

UC Davis would consider Carneros a Region I?

This is a mid Region I. Chardonnay and Pinot Noir do very well here. Cabernet shouldn't grow here but the vineyard sites that we have it on are very good. We've sort of built our reputation on Cabernets from the Carneros. They are unique. They are one hundred percent varietal and they don't need Merlot blended in because the long ripening period allows the berry character, which can be part of Cabernet given time on the vine, to develop. I wouldn't hesitate to blend Merlot in it if I thought it made the wine better, but in most years, it's not necessary.

You would normally want to grow Cabernet in a warmer region?

It would be easier to get it ripe. We wait. We have a long season because we start early and still have Cabernet out here when all my friends are done picking grapes. I'm still working, waiting for the last Cabernet to come in. It's great fruit and well worth the wait.

What kind of fruit are you getting from Lake County for your Sauvignon Blanc?

In Lake County it's hot during the day and quite cold at night. These climatic conditions allow the Sauvignon Blanc character to become more fruity, more melony as opposed to herbaceous. This is what we're looking for in the style we're making. It's not everybody's style but I compare it more to Carneros style wines, which have a lot of fruit. This wine is a team effort. We did a lot of research and we tasted a lot of wines and found that a majority of wines in the style that I thought would be fun to make came from Lake County. So we went shopping for grapes. We started making it in 1985 and it's been highly successful. That's just one example of the open thinking that goes on here. Yes, we are an estate grown winery and until we made Lake County Sauvignon Blanc, we were almost totally estate grown. But making the best wine is our goal here. At this point, we're not sure that Carneros is the best place to grow Sauvignon Blanc.

How do you perceive the role of winemaker at Buena Vista?

I don't have to drag hoses around, that's one thing. But seriously, my first responsibility is the wine. My second responsibility are the people who work for me. Number three is the marketing aspect of the wine. I'm a leader here; that's one of my roles. I set the standard and maintain the standard. If I maintain the standard, everybody else does too. I feel very strongly about that.

Tell me a bit about your viticultural practices in Carneros?

We're on drip irrigation here, for a couple of reasons. One is that we don't have much water, so we're very conservation minded. Another reason is the heavy clay soil. You can waste water if you put it on fast; the ground soaks some up and the rest runs off. If you use drip irrigation, it gets used at the root zone and is fully utilized. Our yields are small because of the climate and the soil. We prune on a bilateral cordon to get two and half tons per acre. Any more than that and they wouldn't ripen.

We machine pick about eighty percent of what we grow. We pick at night when the fruit is cool. I am a big proponent of machine harvesting yet I know there are people violently opposed to it. I'm a big proponent of it because our vineyards are right around the winery. Twenty minutes after the grapes are off the vine, they're in the crusher at the winery. If you're hand picking into five ton gondolas, the bottom two tons are already squished up by the time they get to the winery, having bounced over the road for an hour. Our grapes are cool;

everything nasty that can happen to grapes, happens at a slower rate when they're cool. Oxidation, bacteria, wild yeast and extraction of phenolics all happen more slowly at cooler temperatures. I give myself more control, which is a key word to my style of winemaking.

You're a firm believer in fining and filtering?

Fining and filtration are necessary for a commercial winery. When you're only making 2,000 cases of wine, people don't really care if stuff falls out in the bottle. But if you're being distributed in every state of the nation, they will not accept heavy sediment in a new bottle of wine. So it's my job to make the wines stable, at least until they're five years old.

Does filtration strip wine of its flavor and character?

I do it as carefully as possible. I think, yes, you do lose something. In some cases, you do lose things you should lose. I think there is some truth in that but I tend to think it's overblown. I don't feel I am compromising when I filter the wines.

You like the fruit to really come through in your Chardonnay?

I like the fruitiness. That's the charm these grapes have that grapes from other areas don't. I want to enhance that quality and make these grapes be the best wine they can. I certainly don't want to lose that character.

Don't you sacrifice a bit of complexity by tending toward the more fruity spectrum in your Chardonnay?

Not necessarily. I don't want to make a wine like everybody else's. It's a matter of style and taste. And I'm certainly willing to experiment with it; we have found, over the years, that a small amount of malolactic in the blend adds complexity. But a wine that's eighty or one hundred percent malolactic is lacking fruit. So it's a matter of finding that balance. It's a matter of style. You definitely develop a winery palate.

Is there a Buena Vista style? How would you describe it?

Elegant and with lots of fruit character. The wines have good acidity so that they're crisp in your mouth. Mouth feel is very important; the wine should have a three-dimensional feeling on your tongue, not just lie flat. The wines should taste as good as they smell. There's nothing more disappointing than smelling a wine, thinking it's going to be great, but then you taste it and it just lays there. With both reds and whites, I keep the wood behind the fruit. I keep the fruit up front and use the wood as a structure. The first thing you smell is the fruit, the second thing is the wood. Not that you have to look for it necessarily, but wood is not the first thing you recognize. That's a very definite style. That's not something the grapes are doing, that's something I'm doing. I want wines to taste good, wines that people like, wines that go with the kinds of foods we eat now. As food and eating styles change and evolve over the next ten years, I predict my wine style will slowly evolve to match them. That's the value of traveling, doing winemaker dinners and listening to people's comments. People are eating lighter now; that's probably part of the reason people are turning to our wines, because our wines taste good with food. They don't overpower the food but instead are a nice complement to them. I'm not trying to say they're "food wines" because I think that term has been played to death. But Carneros area wines are quite naturally lower in alcohol, higher in acidity and more fruity than a lot of other regions. They just naturally tend to go with food a little better.

You designate "reserve" lots; how do you select them?

Sometimes I can tell in the vineyard if something looks really special. In that case, we take care to keep that vineyard lot separate. In the case of the red wines, sometimes it doesn't pop out at you until after fermentation. You get the wines cleaned up and you begin to notice that there's a richness, a lushness and a fruit character that's not in the rest of them. We earmark those wines as having reserve potential. We tend to put those wines in the best wood and coax them along. Our reserve isn't a reserve until it's sold. Even after it has been barrel aged, we make another evaluation. If we still think it has reserve potential, it's blended and finished as a reserve wine, which is lightly fined if at all. It's bottled in a reserve type package but with no label. It spends a year to two years aging in the bottle and we taste it every three months. Sometimes the wine takes a turn in the wrong direction; in that case it doesn't get a reserve label, it gets an estate label. About two months before the expected release date, we make the decision whether it will be a reserve wine or not. There is a lot of integrity in our reserve wine.

Do you feel that you are, in any way, a pioneer, that is, a relatively young woman heading up a major winery in a position that has been traditionally dominated by older males?

I don't know. I try not to look at it from that point of view. I don't think of myself so much as a pioneer because people like Zelma Long and Mary Ann Graf came ahead of me. They really broke the ground. I try not to think of myself as a woman winemaker. But it's still very much a novelty in other parts of the country. I'm young, yes, but I'm just part of the next generation of winemakers. We have a lot of new ideas. More is known now about where to grow grape varieties than has ever been known before. That's one of the biggest advantages we have. We are making wines from better grapes because grapes are planted in the right areas. We have better equipment and better technology. So far as pioneering, I think my generation are pioneers in a kind of a new way to make wine. But I was lucky; I worked with the old masters and they sort of tucked me under their wing and told me what they knew. I was like a sponge. I absorbed everything and performed all the tasks they handed me. That's where my organizational skills really started to pay off because I followed up on everything and became reliable. I've had some good breaks in my career but I was also prepared for them when they came.

CALERA
JENSEN
Mt. Harlan Pinot Noir
1991

GROWN, PRODUCED & BOTTLED
BY CALERA WINE COMPANY
HOLLISTER, CALIFORNIA
Table Wine

Steve Doerner
CALERA WINE COMPANY

*"To me, finesse is what Pinot Noir is all about. It's one of the few variet-
ies that matches power, richness and body with subtlety and finesse."*

Steve Doerner's entry into winemaking was a matter of lucky circumstance. He was a UC Davis senior, majoring in biochemistry, pondering
his career choices, when a request came in for a graduate to work in a
small, fledgling winery near Hollister in San Benito County. Josh Jensen,
founder and proprietor of Calera Wine Company, was looking for someone
with a good science background who could get a handle on fermentations and
microbial flora, but someone with no preconceived notions about winemaking
so he could train them in his style of winemaking.

His first harvest was a difficult transition for Doerner. He didn't understand
why it was "fun" to put in sixteen hours a day for two months straight. Gradually he began to settle in at the winery and, in 1981, when he went to Burgundy, he saw the traditions, observed the techniques and realized how much

wine was involved in the lives of the vintners. He found that winemaking wasn't just a job but a way of life.

The uniqueness of the Calera wines stem from the fact that, after an exhaustive search up and down the California coast, the vineyards were established 2,200 feet up in the Gavilan Mountains, an area that had no previous reputation for fine wines. But Jensen felt that limestone rich soil, combined with altitude and a cooling onshore breeze from the Pacific Ocean only thirty miles away, would provide the ideal elements for Pinot Noir vineyards. There are four designated vineyard releases: Reed, Selleck, Jensen and Mills. Chardonnay is also produced along with a minuscule amount of fickle Viognier. In a good vintage, production from these low yielding, estate vines is not much more than 5,000 cases. The same Calera pedigree can now be found in a more widely available Chardonnay and Pinot Noir, made from purchased grapes and bearing a Central Coast appellation.

Minimal intervention is how Doerner describes his approach to winemaking at Calera's gravity flow winery. His attention to detail, however, and his constant fine-tuning of the winemaking regime, is a big part of why the Calera wines seem to go from strength to strength with each successive vintage. In 1992, after sixteen years at Calera, Doerner has left to seek the Holy Grail of Pinot Noir in the vineyards of Oregon. The general winemaking techniques and style remain relatively unchanged from what he describes here. Josh Jensen, who was recently profiled in the book, *The Heartbreak Grape*, is still the guiding light and Sara Steiner is now the winemaker.

When you first came to Calera, I imagine Josh set the overriding tone.

I think he did that way before I got here. I like to think I've contributed a lot to the winery and it's winemaking talent that's helped. But, on the other hand, I really believe that it's the vineyards that make the wines. Wines are made in the vineyard.

But that kind of minimizes what you do?

It does. That's true. I believe it's easy to make great wine from great grapes. But it's really hard to make great wine from lousy grapes. Each vineyard has a certain potential that's given by nature and the winemaker's job is to try to preserve or realize as much of that potential as possible. You can't gain more than you began with. So a good winemaker has the ability to hang on to what nature has given him and not mess it up. It does minimize the winemaking. Certainly there's much that can go wrong in the winery, but you have to start with good grapes.

The most important thing Josh did to set things up for success was choosing these vineyards. He was a real maverick and went out on a limb by planting this unknown vineyard in the middle of nowhere on a hunch that the limestone in the soil was going to make a difference in his wines. My success is directly tied into the fact that I've had better grapes to work with than other people. That's where most of it lies. I bought that whole story because I was open minded and didn't have any preconceived biases.

What is it about the limestone in the soil that is important? Why, in your mind, is that the determining factor?

If you look at Burgundy, it's hard to explain major differences among vineyards strictly on climate. Two growers growing the same grapes in soil right next to each other get different wines. I mean, Roumier has three different plantings in Bonnes Mares, one in the middle and one on either end. But he bottles them all separately. And the wines are different. That's even within the same grand cru vineyard. He treats them much the same way in the cellar but he makes three wines out of them. Looking at the general climatic conditions, it's hard for me to imagine how a climate can vary within one hundred yards. Whereas you can find definite soil differences in that same hundred yards.

What does limestone do? Technically, I don't know. It's not so much that we are concerned with what it does but just that it does it. Not to belittle all other factors, but specifically for Pinot Noir, we feel the soil has proven that it does make a significant difference. A lot of people think you need a cool climate for Pinot Noir. Well, you do need a relatively cool climate. But I think if you ask most Burgundians, they would prefer a bit warmer climate than they have. You know, we tend to think that good Burgundies are made in spite of their climate, not because of their climate. It's not the climate that makes them great; they manage to make great wines even though they have such a cold climate and rainy seasons. Our climate situation here is warmer than what you might think is ideal for Pinot Noir but cooler than what you might think from our geographic location. The vineyards are up at 2200 feet elevation and only thirty miles from the coast. It's a more moderate climate than you would suspect.

You have several different vineyards of Pinot Noir and you obviously keep those lots separate.

Even some sub lots within each vineyard are kept separate until bottling because there are many different pickings of each vineyard. Everything is fermented separately. With the techniques we use they never get blended. Each fermenter is pressed individually and put directly into barrels. Because we don't move the wine around much, they go into barrels and don't have an opportunity to be blended. Obviously we could blend them if we wanted, but there's no need for it.

Viticulturally, and as far as the type of wine each produces, what are the differentiating characteristics of the Jensen, Selleck and Reed vineyards?

Generally speaking, I tend to prefer the Selleck vineyard. To me, it has a little extra dimension the others don't. It's hard to put a finger on it. It tends to have more cinnamony, spicy, cedary components that appealed to me when I first started tasting Burgundies. Selleck had a sweet cinnamony characteristic, more so in the early vintages, than the other vineyards. The other vineyards have somewhat caught up with that as far as they display some spiciness. But the Selleck seems like it has just another layer.

The Jensen tends to be the most tannic. Originally, we thought it was the slowest to develop but, in fact, in some vintages it develops the quickest. That's one of the other things about the Selleck. One of the reasons it's probably our favorite is it tends to develop sooner. We used to say Selleck was the more feminine and Jensen the more masculine. The Jensen tends to sometimes have a kind of leathery, green olive characteristic but, in recent vintages, it's had an awful lot of fruit.

The Reed vineyard is the lowest producer. The average yield for the Reed is a ton per acre. It's got coffee, tobacco, earthy, and musty components and it can be a little heavy.

Realistically, the wines are all very different but if you line them up together, they are probably more similar stylistically than they are different, especially to people who aren't familiar with Pinot Noir. So it is hard to always pick out which wine is which. They're not so distinctive that you can immediately identify a Jensen every time. But there are subtle differences; so we keep them separate because it's more interesting.

Your yield is generally less than two tons per acre?

Yes, in 1987, we got a two tons per acre average, the biggest we've ever had. We wouldn't mind trying to see what wine quality we would get with two and a half tons per acre, but so far we have not been able to achieve that.

So it's good the vines are stressed?

Yes, that's true. Whenever we give talks about the winery, we're always talking about trying to increase our yield and, of course, that's not considered to be a quality thing to do. So people are baffled by that. Then we explain we are trying to increase yield from one ton to two tons. Our average yield, over fifteen years, I would guess to be around one and a quarter tons.

But doesn't that contribute to the quality of the wine?

Yes, certainly. But I think one of our best vintages was 1987, which was our largest yield. We haven't yet felt that we had too much crop for the quality. From an economic standpoint, it would be nice to find out what two and a half or even three tons per acre would be like. But there's a definite quality correlation with yield and I've seen it in other varieties as well. So far we've been unable to find out how much crop the vineyard can carry without sacrificing quality. There's a lower limit too. I don't think you get increased quality when you get a yield lower than two tons, for example. I don't think a wine from a vineyard that yields one ton per acre is going to be twice as good as a wine from a vineyard that yields two tons per acre. It's not a linear relationship. I define a low yield as two tons per acre and anything below that is an extremely low yield without the quality getting necessarily better. I generally tend to complain a lot about the vineyards but, in reality, I couldn't be happier with the fruit. I just wish there were more of it.

In 1984, you had the opportunity to plant another twelve acres of Pinot Noir. From your and Josh's previous experience, did you do anything different as far as rootstock, clonal selection, spacing and trellising?

We kept the spacing pretty much the same. We're still conducting some experiments on the rootstocks but most of the vineyard is on its own roots. All the replants we did, even in the old vineyards, were planted on their own roots. Possibly they'll be more drought tolerant. Our vineyards are isolated, so we weren't too worried about phylloxera. We did use the bud wood from the Selleck Vineyard; we didn't choose to use the higher yielding one from the Jensen Vineyard.

What constitutes ripeness for Pinot Noir in your vineyards?

Originally, when I first came here, one of the things I really enjoyed about this winery was that we were supposedly completely hands-off; everything was natural and we didn't want to intervene. I liked that type of approach and I still like it. But from experience, I've changed my views to some extent. I think it's important to step in when needed. That's the difference between good and bad winemaking. You have to know when not to do things but that doesn't mean not doing anything. In the first vintages, we weren't adding any acid to the wines. I thought that adding acid was not natural. The pH was more a consideration earlier than it is now because I can adjust the pH. Before, I was afraid of adjusting the pH or I didn't want to, so I was more concerned about that than I am now. I think there's an industry-wide trend now to pick more for the acidity and picking less ripe than in the past. We're kind of going the other way. For the first few vintages, we felt like the intensity of the wine was diminishing; each year was a little bit lighter than the one previous. We were at yields of a half a ton per acre, so certainly the vines weren't overly stressed at those low yields. But we were wondering why we were having trouble getting some body in the wine from a half ton an acre. So we started to think that maybe we needed to pick a little later. Gradually we started picking at higher and higher sugars and found that we got more complexity, richness and flavor. In fact, we often do an early pick and late pick in every vineyard. We have the ability to blend them but we can also see what they're like in the barrel. We always find that the early pick is leaner, greener and not round and rich. So we tend to pick now between 24 and 25 degrees brix, which is pretty high. Also, I don't mind putting acid in the wine. We'd have to add acid if we picked at 21 degrees brix. So my justification is that if I have to add a little anyway, what's the difference if I add more. I don't have any moral problem with adding acid. Those sugar levels are where we get the most flavor; it's not just to get alcohol. In fact, for many years it was necessary to pick late because we were getting low conversions from sugar to alcohol. Even if we picked at 24 degrees brix, we were getting twelve percent alcohol wines, which is not what you would expect. I always thought it was due to the native yeasts, that some of them were fermenting the ethanol all the way to CO_2. So from an energy standpoint the yeasts were more efficient but from a winemaking standpoint, they were inefficient in the conversion to alcohol. But it's a season-to-season variable here.

In 1988, you picked a little earlier than usual?

Yes, we did, just a bit. Each year we've sort of been pushing the limit. Each year has been better than the last. The 1984 through the 1987 wines are similar as far as style, body and alcohol content. But each year the wine has been a little bit bigger than the previous one. There is, however, certainly a limit to that and we don't want to go over it. In 1987, some of the lots were over fourteen percent alcohol and they started to taste kind of heavy. To me, finesse is what Pinot Noir is all about. It's one of the few varieties that matches power, richness and body with subtlety and finesse. It's a paradox: you have a big, rich wine but yet you have all this flavor, complexity and elegance. It's really intriguing in that sense. I think once you get beyond a certain point, it just becomes weight, bigness and heaviness. It stops becoming Pinot Noir. So big isn't necessarily better. Our general style is that we like richer, more concentrated wines but we don't want to lose the best part of Pinot Noir, which is elegance. In 1988, we decided to pick around 24 to 24.5 degrees brix. We knew the yields were so low that we would get lots of concentration. We were getting a quarter ton an acre in 1988; so we're off seventy percent or so on our yields. Knowing that, we were afraid that the grapes would ripen quickly and get out of control. We didn't want to end up with three barrels of overly alcoholic wine from grapes picked two days late. But even before we were aware of our lower yield, we were already set to pick a bit sooner. I think we've now found the degree of ripeness we like, right around 24 to 24.5 degrees brix, which is a lot riper than what other people pick at. We normally have to add quite a bit of acid at those levels. But then, we'd have to add acid if we didn't pick them that late also. Generally I think Pinot Noir is a variety that is very pH unstable. They have these problems in Burgundy too. Even though they are not supposed to add acid and chapitalize in the same year, most places do both because they need acid even when they pick at 20 or 21 degrees brix.

It's been said that the key to Pinot Noir is pH management.

Right. I don't like the term because I don't want to manage the wine too much. I'm doing that but, on the other hand, it's not so important where the pH ends up. While I'd like it to be in a certain range, ultimately it's more important how the wine tastes. Certainly there are target pH levels, but if the wine doesn't taste good, what's the point? It's funny because our earlier vintages are really tasting good and some of them have a really high pH. In fact, the high pH wines are really easy to drink; they are really forward. If the wines are well made, you can have great wines and long lived wines with a high pH. That, of course, goes against general theories. I'm in a position where I didn't have any formal training, yet I understand the theories. So my viewpoint falls somewhere in between the two. I don't want to say if you don't have 3.5 pH or less, the wine is not going to be any good. On the other hand, I'm aware of the pH and I don't want to ignore it. It's an important factor for longevity and color. But you can get carried away with trying to make a statistically perfect wine that has nothing to offer. Then it loses all its art form and it becomes a science. I don't want winemaking to become a strict science and, luckily, I don't think it can because there are too many variables.

Generally I think California winemakers tend to control too much. I'm lucky because I've got good grapes and don't need to control much. I try to develop the potential nature has already given me. A good example of that is oak barrels. There's a lot of talk about which French forest the oak comes from and how much you toast your barrels. My theory is the coopers have been plying their trade a lot longer than we here in California have been making wine. They know a lot more about making barrels than we do. Yet California winemakers are going over there and telling them how to make their barrels. I think barrel making is an art too. I think it's great that the barrel makers are willing to work with us and I appreciate that. But it's better to have them come over here, taste our wines and then give us the barrels they think will work best with our wines. So that's an example of California winemakers' tendency to try to control too much.

So you utilize a wide variety of barrels?

We started out using some different ones but now we have mostly Francois Frere barrels. Generally we ask for center of France barrels and that's about as general as the cooper will let you get these days. Sometimes they're stamped Never or Allier because that's what they have in stock and that fills the bill. If we got it all from the same forest every time, I'd probably start to request some variability because I don't want any certain specific component in the wine. It's important to have good barrels. Just like clonal selection is important. You have to have a good clone but that's not the secret. The fact that we use mostly Francois Frere barrels is not what makes the wine great. It's just a good barrel for us and contributes what we want to the wines.

Winemaking is made up of many individual components and to talk about any component individually, divorced from the rest of the process, is almost taking that component out of context.

Right, by themselves they are insignificant, but if you put them all together, it makes a difference. For example, we have a gravity flow winery here. I'd be a fool to say our wines are better because they didn't get pumped around. I think it's a detail. But adding up all the little details, of not pumping and not interfering with the wine, ultimately help us to do what we're supposed to do and that is to preserve what we've got. So the gravity flow is just another little factor that adds up to something. It fits in well with our philosophy of minimal handling of the wine.

Do you rely on wild yeasts for your fermentations?

We've utilized native yeasts for all the wines we've made, with the exception of a small percentage that we've experimented with and later got blended in. Originally that was Josh's idea and I had no argument. As I became more aware, I wanted to find out why it was working or at least why it was a good idea. I started doing experiments to verify that we liked the native yeasts. For several years I ran various experiments with different strains of yeasts. In the case of Pinot Noir, we always found we preferred the native yeasts. But when we compared the data, the inoculated yeast strain always fermented the wines faster. I tried to use less inoculated yeast so the rates of fermentation were more comparable. Every time I inoculated, however, the wines would ferment quicker. So I'm beginning to feel that it's not so much the differences in the yeasts that we do or do not like here, it's more I'm convinced that what I like is a slow fermentation. It's maybe not that they have different chemical pathways and produce different esters than say, the Montrachet, or any other strain of yeast.

You want a slower fermentation for what reason?

Complexity. I leave everything in the tanks for a minimum of ten days. If the fermentation has stopped in eight days, we'll stop punching down and let it sit for the remaining two days, even though all activity has stopped. I just think that time is necessary for the extraction of the flavors from the skins. That ten days includes any prefermentation or maceration before it gets to the tanks, so it's not necessarily fermenting all the time. In the last several vintages, none of our tanks have finished before ten days. The average has been twelve to fourteen days. The time on the skins is really important. Whether it's actively fermenting or not, is less important. I would prefer it to be fermenting because it's safer. Occasionally we will take some active must from one tank and put it into another tank that hasn't been doing anything for a couple of days. Also, I think you're gaining something by leaving them on the skins, even after fermentation has slowed down.

You are a proponent of whole cluster fermentation?

Yes, we do one hundred percent whole cluster fermentation, with no crushing or destemming. We originally started out with fifty percent whole clusters and fifty percent crushed and destemmed fruit. We never did one hundred percent crushed and destemmed. The idea was that we always intended to go up to one hundred percent whole clusters but, in the first vintages, the yields were so low that we thought we might get too much tannin and too much extraction. So each year we increased the percentage of whole cluster fruit. In the meantime, we started purchasing grapes from other people because we were so frustrated with our own yields. We did a lot of experimenting with that fruit; if we liked what we got, the next year we would do the same thing with our estate fruit. We just wanted to verify that we were going in the right direction with the whole cluster fermentation. We found we definitely preferred the one hundred percent whole cluster method. In fact, one year we were getting grapes that were known for their herbaceousness and stemminess. When we crushed and destemmed those grapes, they reeked of stemminess but when we used whole clusters, they were more balanced and had the better structure. So it was exactly the opposite result of what you would expect. I don't know why that is and can't explain it. Sometimes, however, I think that no matter how good your destemmer is, you're getting little pieces of chopped up stems in there. Obviously, when you are using whole clusters, there are a lot more stems there that are intact and not broken up.

What's so interesting about Pinot Noir is that the winemaking techniques have to be molded to the vineyards. You can't transplant what I'm doing here to another area and get the same results. It's amazing that there's some good Pinot Noirs made with completely opposite methods. We're sure we're doing what's right and they're sure they're doing what's right.

The stem content in whole cluster fermentation is important because it adds structure and tannin, something you often find lacking in Pinot Noir. The intact fruit is important because the sugar is not all available at the beginning for the yeast to attack; that tends to slow down the fermentation. It's not a carbonic maceration in the true sense because we are punching down twice a day and that breaks the berries. We never pump over because it's not necessary and we wouldn't gain anything. Punching down the cap is the way to go; it's easier on the must and it gives better results. We now have a pneumatic tool that we use to punch down and it's quite efficient.

Whole clusters, then, regulate the rate of fermentation to some degree. I do believe there's a small percentage of fermentation that takes place within the berries themselves. That probably adds a bit of the fruitiness to the wines. The drawback to this method of fermentation is the pH problem. As I've mentioned, Pinot Noir is pH unstable and I think you make it worse by having stems in with the fruit but I'm willing to deal with the pH in order to get the benefits of whole cluster fermentation. That's one of the reasons we're using quite a bit of acid. We want to compensate for the pH rise that takes place because of the stems.

To review the fermentation: we dump the grapes into the fermenters whole, we punch down twice a day, we don't inoculate, we don't add SO_2 but do add acid as soon as we can. We'll add it before fermentation starts if we can. I'm not very concerned about what the titratable acidity is, but I try to bring the pH down to a point that I like. Even then I don't acidify so much for taste as to the pH meter. It doesn't sound as good but that's the reality of it. I just don't think that the acid you taste at that point is related to the acid that is going to be left in the end product. That's about all we do, as far as interfering at that point.

We monitor the brix and the temperature throughout fermentation. We try not to let the temperature get above 86F degrees. Often we have fermentations lower than that. Again, I'd rather have a cool and slow fermentation than a fast and hot one. I do believe you get some extraction and color with heat but I also believe you can get that with longer skin contact. So I prefer lower temperatures a little bit so it doesn't ferment so fast.

Once the cap has fallen and fermentation is finished, we drain off the fermenters by gravity flow to the level below. Because there are one hundred percent stems in the fermenter, it acts as a nice sieve and the juice runs out pretty clean. The next day we roll the press out to the tank and press the solids left into the same tank as the juice is in. In the early years, we separated free run from the press wine and kept it separate in barrel but we always added it back into the free run. Now we don't bother separating them anymore. In the early vintages, it was more important to have the option because the yields were so low. Our press is a bladder type and it's pretty gentle anyhow.

Once the wine is in barrels, we revert to our nonintervention mode. We try to leave them alone as much as possible. We don't settle the wine before putting it into barrels and it goes in pretty dirty. We do a lot of monitoring of the wine in barrels but we don't actually do much to the wine. One of the things we've found is that because we have a lot of lees in the barrels there is the potential for H_2S production. We haven't had much of a problem with it. What happens is the H_2S production starts in the lees and later gets into the wine. So we try to taste from the bottom of the barrels when the wines are pretty young. If it's starting to show up, then we'll rack it. Otherwise, we don't rack at all.

Let me qualify that. We won't rack for the first fourteen months as long as the wines are stable and sound. That's hard to judge too because Pinot Noir, when young, will not taste stable or sound. It can go through some pretty wild stages. Sometimes they might taste terrible in the barrel but they always come back. We learned the hard way about that. We didn't always refrain from racking. We used to rack pretty regularly, about every four months or so. We feel that is one reason why some of our earlier vintages are lighter. We feel that we are stripping things out of the wine. We did various racking experiments. When we racked, we tried to be as careful as possible in order to minimize the oxidation by using nitrogen pressure instead of a pump but the movement itself seems to affect the wine somehow. When you rack, you are taking some of the lees out, and the lees, we feel, are important in feeding the wine and contributing body and richness. We found we always liked the wine better when it wasn't racked. In 1983, we racked because we thought the wines were black and overly tannic. We thought racking would soften the wines a little bit. In fact, we did only one racking and it totally changed the wines; they almost fell apart.

So now we are pretty much against racking except to prevent H_2S. Sixteen months after the harvest, we nitrogen rack the wine off the lees. By that time the lees have become so compacted that you get a pretty good separation. But if we get some of the lees in there, we're not too concerned because we're not trying too hard to clean the wines up. We're starting to rack into tanks to do the fining mostly because the size of the lots have gotten larger. It's harder to fine 150 barrels than three tanks. The other point is that it's easier, on the final racking off the egg white fining, to be careful with a few containers than it is with 150 barrels. So the procedure is that the wines are racked into the tank and egg white fined there.

Through 1984 we always racked into barrels and did the fining in barrels. Now we rack into the tanks and then rack off the egg white fining into the bottling tanks. The wine gets two rackings, depending on how you define that. It's not really a racking to get rid of the lees; it's just that the wines must be stirred when they are fined and we don't want to stir all those lees up. We've spent a year and a half settling those lees!

You don't filter the Pinot Noir?

No filtering, right. We've got a filter and we use it only on the Chardonnay. We use it there for clarity of the wine more than anything else. If the consumer didn't mind a less than sparkling clear wine, and we could get away without doing that, then we would. We don't sterile filter anything.

I don't want to say we never filter because I don't believe in absolutes. I think sometimes filtering has its place. Often filtering can improve a wine if there is a defect or a microbial problem. But if you prevent whatever caused you to need to filter it in the first place, then you're better off doing that and not filtering. We have done some minimal filtering on some lots and I've found that something is always removed from the wine; it just strips the wine. Pinot Noir is so fragile that filtering is one of the most drastic things you could to do it. But again, I don't say that there hasn't been a good Pinot Noir made that has been filtered. It's just our philosophy and personal preference not to filter and so far we've been successful.

What insights did you get from your visits to Burgundy?

The thing I learned from my first trip to Burgundy was the patience involved in winemaking. They do experiments there but not the kind of experiments we do. Sometimes they don't really understand what they're doing, but through time, things have evolved and developed. They know that grapes from a particular plot of ground make better wine when vinified in a certain manner. While we want to throw a lot of technology at something and hope that solves a problem, they are patient and experiment for generations. They could benefit from our technology by being more open minded but we could benefit by acquiring some of their patience. That was the biggest philosophical thing I learned in Burgundy. You have to be patient with wine; you have to see how an experiment works for one year, but you also have to repeat it for many vintages and then see how the results look after many more years in the bottle before you can really draw a conclusion. No matter how long you're in the industry, there are always new things to learn.

Randy Dunn
DUNN VINEYARDS

*"Putting out the finest product you can is really the only way
to develop your reputation as a small winery."*

In California winemaking circles, Randy Dunn is known as the "King of Cabernet." It was a hard won title, the result of nearly twenty years of winemaking.

In the early seventies, Dunn was working on his doctorate in entomology at UC Davis, where he needed two outside fields to complete his degree. He had made some wine as part of an insecticide experiment, so it seemed natural for him to declare enology as one of his outside fields. He had also indulged in a little home winemaking while he was a student. In fact, that's how he met Charlie Wagner of Caymus Vineyards: he helped pick a second crop there and used some of the grapes to make wine at school.

When he finished his work in entomology, he decided he'd rather be making wine. In 1975, he joined the Wagner family at Caymus Vineyards as crush help. Dunn stayed on, eventually becoming the winemaker, helping Caymus establish its reputation for high quality Cabernet, as well as other varieties.

In 1978, concurrent with his winemaking duties at Caymus, he established his own winery on top of Howell Mountain, on the east side of Napa Valley. He split his time between his own winery and Caymus until 1985, when he felt financially secure enough to leave Caymus and concentrate his efforts on his own label.

Dunn produces only Cabernet but he has two different bottlings. One is a Howell Mountain appellation that utilizes grapes from his own vineyard as well as his neighbor's. The other is a Napa Valley appellation from grapes grown on the valley floor. Production is less than 4,000 cases a year and there is presently a waiting list to be put on the mailing list for his yearly Cabernet releases. The Dunn wines bring fantastic prices at wine auctions because they are so difficult to procure.

Did your experience at Caymus help form your ideas about what direction you wanted to go in establishing your own winery?

Well, I've always been the kind of guy that if something breaks, I'll fix it. That's really important in a small winery. Basically, at Caymus, it was Charlie's son, Chuck, and I who were doing everything. It didn't matter whether it was vineyard work, fixing the tractor or running the bottling line. You have to be a mechanic, an electrician, a plumber and a janitor. That's really the only way a small winery is going to survive financially. So one of the important things was just the various contacts I had in the industry; so that I knew where to get good deals on used equipment. I bought damaged stainless steel tanks and fixed them. The secret to success on a small-scale is that you can't have big interest payments; otherwise you'll dig yourself into a hole that you'll never get out of.

What was your basic approach to making wine at Caymus?

I always wanted to make the absolute best wine that we could with the grapes we had. Of course, if we didn't have good grapes, I wanted to get rid of them. Once you've got the grapes, though, you're committed and you have to make the best product you can. If I thought we could make it better by using new barrels or something else that cost money, that's what I would do. Deep down, I knew we could get money out of it when we put the wine on the market. Putting out the finest product you can is really the only way to develop your reputation as a small winery.

There are a lot of hard decisions you have to make in this business. Things like cooperage costs a lot of money. When I was first getting ready to release the 1979 Dunn Cabernet, I had to make a decision whether to bottle it or not. This was my first year, my first vintage. I tasted it and felt there was no way we could come out with this wine as our first release. So I borrowed some money, bought some more barrels and held it for another year. That was a tough decision to make; it meant we would have three vintages aging in wood.

What kinds of methods do you employ to try to achieve a high level of consistency in your wines from year to year?

It's not impossible but it's real hard to do. The only thing you can be consistent about is the fruit. For example, the Zinfandel from Amador County is totally different from the one from Lake County which is different from Napa County. One year at Caymus we had about one third of each county in a blend and I knew that each component was very different. When we dropped the Amador County grapes the next year, the wine changed; when we dropped the Lake County grapes the following year, it changed a little bit more. So it's very difficult to be consistent if the grapes aren't consistent.

Your first vintage at Dunn Vineyards was in 1979. How did you make the transition to your own winery?

It was a lot of work. I was working full-time down at Caymus and running Dunn too. Until 1985, I still worked a couple days a week at Caymus. If you don't have a lot of money, then it takes a lot of time. From our own vineyards to the designing of a label to all the government paperwork, it's just a matter of working all the time. I knew the Dunn Vineyards program would probably work by the time I released the 1982 wines. That was our fourth vintage; by this time we were selling out in a week. I could see that financially the numbers were working out in my favor too. One of the things I get a kick out of talking about with my Davis colleagues is the pay scale of winemakers. Winemakers are paid in romance, not money. Truck drivers make more money. I was able to make the transition because I had worked full-time for a living. If I had not worked for that six years and just tried to start my own winery, I'd be in a big hole, one that would take ten or fifteen years to get out of, if ever.

Did you have a strong desire to have your own winery, to be your own boss as opposed to working for somebody else?

Oh, not really. We had a lot of fun at Caymus. I think it started not to be fun when the place grew so much. And you start thinking to yourself, "My God, why am I making this wine that sells two bottles for seven dollars?" When you don't like the product that you're making, then it's time to go. It went beyond the point of necessary cash flow; it was just that they cranked the wine to keep the system happy. So my heart wasn't really in those Liberty School wines. It's really hard for me to make wine that I really don't like the taste of.

At that level, it's almost as if you are making a standardized, processed food product, like mayonnaise?

You're still making as good a wine as you can but you have the constraint of being able to pay only x number of dollars for the bulk wine. You only get a certain quality of wine if you're only willing to pay so much. It puts you in a whole different league.

At Dunn Vineyards, you are concentrating only on Cabernet. Why just one varietal?

Because every time you add a varietal to your production, you probably add twenty complications and then another twenty or thirty problems will come up in the process. That includes mickey-mouse things. Each varietal label requires separate approval. Each varietal has to be kept separate in your storage facility, which creates a lot of space problems. The list goes on and on. That was one thing that I learned at Caymus: it's a real pain in the ass if you make a lot of different varieties. If you can make one good varietal, you'll be much happier.

Why choose Cabernet?

Cabernet was definitely Caymus's strongest wine. Of all the red wines, it's the one I enjoy most. So I had a natural background in it and knew this area up here would be good for Cabernet. It was sort of unproven at the time but that was my feeling. We moved here onto the property when I bought this vineyard in 1978. We didn't have much of a crop; the vines were five years old. I think we only produced thirty gallons of wine that year on five acres. The place was a mess but we've nursed it along and we're finally getting some good fruit out of it.

What made you think this area (Howell Mountain) had the potential to produce great Cabernet?

Nothing really concrete, other than it was up in the hills. My knowledge told me that the hillside fruit was definitely better than the valley.

Why is that?

The fruit is more intense. But back to the earlier question; we picked this spot primarily because it's just a neat place to live. It wasn't that I thought this vineyard was God's gift to the wine industry. It was a nice place up here and we'll make some wine or maybe we'll sell the grapes. It wasn't a real bull-headed thing of me to do, sinking my life into this vineyard.

As far as what makes the grapes here good, that's really anybody's guess. It's definitely very different here than down in the Napa Valley. The days are ten to fifteen degrees cooler; the nights, on the other hand, are warmer. We are above the temperature inversion of the valley; in the summertime, the valley fog comes in and it'll be fifty-five degrees, whereas up here on the mountain, at six in the morning, the sun's already out and it's seventy degrees. So the theory that I learned at Davis about temperature extremes being important for color development doesn't have much validity for me right now. We don't have temperature extremes up here; possibly it's important down in the valley.

We tend to ripen earlier; because of the warm nights, the fruit doesn't cool down. Another unique thing is we can get an inch of rain during harvest and two days later we can go out and kick up dust on the surface. The soil is so light that the moisture just blows right through. It's warm in the morning, so when you get a little breeze, the moisture just dries right up.

Would you say climate is more important than soil here?

Well, the soil is different too. It's a red, volcanic soil. That can't be overlooked but that's a lot harder to talk about. It's very different than on the floor of the valley. The berries are much smaller up here than there. The fruit is therefore more intense because the surface area to volume ratio is higher. Not only is it more intense, it is differently flavored than the valley floor Cabernet. You'll hear valley floor Cabernet described as herbaceous and bell pepperish; on the negative side, you'll hear it described as vegetal. Up here on the mountain, we get kind of black pepper character. "Olivey" is a word used to describe some of the Napa Valley fruit, especially from the Stags Leap area. But we're more peppery and that pepperiness manifests itself in Zinfandel; in fact, I think it is even more evident in Zinfandel.

You make two Cabernets, one with a Howell Mountain appellation and the other with a Napa Valley appellation. What is your situation as far as estate grown grapes versus purchased grapes?

With the Howell Mountain Cabernet, about a third of the grapes come from my vineyard, one third come from a vineyard that I manage and then I buy about a third from someone else up here. So even though I control two of the vineyards, I still don't have the percentage you need to call it "estate bottled," which I felt wasn't that important anyway.

Your Napa Valley Cab is made solely from purchased grapes?

Yes, it comes from several different locations. But I'm zeroing in on a source of fruit that will represent sixty percent or more of my Napa Valley Cabernet. I really think, with this fruit making up at least sixty percent of my Napa Cabernet, that it will rival my Howell Mountain Cabernet.

Don't you feel yourself in a precarious position as a buyer of grapes if, for example, that particular vineyard changes hands or they sell their grapes to someone else?

Yes, I do. I do feel threatened in that regard. It's become so competitive that good fruit is harder and harder to find. That's why I'm making long-term commitments on the vineyard.

Tell me about your viticultural practices. What are you doing in the vineyard?

Nothing too earthshaking. One of the vineyards I manage is about twenty-seven years old and it's cane pruned. In my vineyard, I do a combination of cane and bilateral cordon. Both of them are watered a lot; we have to water a great deal up here to get any sort of crop at all. We've got drip irrigation that I usually water six or eight times out of the year. In so doing, we can get around two and a half tons per acre; if we didn't water, we'd be getting less than a ton an acre. Down in the Napa Valley, there are people that can dry farm; you can dig down into that soil and find good moisture three feet under the ground. Up here, you can't do that.

You don't subscribe to the theory that the grapes need to be stressed to get great wine?

No. I can show you some dryfarmed Zinfandel that a neighbor of mine owns up here. It's just a mess. Granted that the vines are thirty years old but they were probably a mess when they were ten years old. The vines just can't grow without water. That's pretty fundamental.

The three vineyards that make your Howell Mountain Cabernet are picked, crushed and stored separately?

Yes, I keep them separate until I'm convinced that they're all fairly equal. It all depends on the year and my racking schedule. Sometimes I'll keep them separate until a year before I bottle them. About a year before I bottle, I make the blend. I like to follow each individual lot and see how it changes. For example, at my neighbor's place, there's one area that has some red leaf in it and it has trouble getting sugar; so I usually let the grapes hang out there longer. I pick it late at lower sugar than the rest. I'm interested in seeing how that lower sugar lot comes along and develops.

So you pick selectively up here?

Yes, I might pick my little five acres on three different days and they might not all be consecutive. I'll go pick the area that I think is the ripest and see what I have in terms of sugar. Judging from that, I may wait two or three days, or even a week, before I go get the rest.

You're small enough that you can afford to do that, whereas someone else might just go in and pick an entire vineyard, even if all the grapes aren't quite ripe.

Right. I don't care how good you think you are; it's difficult to know exactly what sugar you really have. The only way to find out is to go out and pick a load. If you're a big winery and you're going into the vineyards with twenty pickers by the time they get that first load back to the winery and crushed, they might have picked another five or ten gondolas full.

What kind of numbers are you looking for at harvest time?

I'm looking for a good solid 23.5 degrees brix. I don't like 23.0 degrees; if I'm getting that, I'll quit. You sometimes have to make these weather decisions; you know, how late and how long can you hold out before you pick. But if I've got 23.5 sugar, I'll go for it.

Is part of it intuitive? You're looking at the fruit and you're looking at the numbers...

And you're looking at the vines too because there are some years that you just know the vines aren't going to give you anymore sugar. So there's no use in just leaving the fruit out there. Unless you have a case like I did in a vineyard down in Napa. I didn't think these vines were going to make anymore sugar although I wanted them to. We threw some water on them really late in the year just to keep them green because they were starting to defoliate. But the acid was too high and the pH was too low, so I just wanted to let them hang out there until these numbers were more in line. The numbers improved a bit but a hot spell started shriveling the fruit so we picked.

In Cabernet production, a lot of newcomers get scared into picking early. It's an easy thing to do. You might be looking at 22.5 degrees sugar and you think it's going to rain next week so you go out and pick. You think if it rains, it's going to ruin your whole crop. But Cabernet is really tough and it's a lot different from something like Zinfandel or Pinot Noir. If it rains on Zinfandel, you get rot real fast. But Cabernet can take it; the berries and the skins are tough. So it takes a lot of guts to let it all hang out because Mother Nature can really do you in.

Tell me a bit about your fermentation practices.

Pretty basic, really. Now that I'm getting a little bit better set up, I'm able to afford conventional stainless steel tanks as opposed to milk tanks. Now I've got 2,000 gallon typical jacketed fermenters. I usually ferment anywhere from about eighty degrees to the low nineties, so fermentation is fast. I get in and out of the tank fast because I might need to use it the following week. And most people feel you get better color extraction at high temperatures.

Do you go in for extended skin contact?

Not like a lot of people are doing. Some people are letting the wine sit with the skins up to a month after it ferments dry. The thought is that they get softer tannins out of their wine. I've tasted several trials that have been done at other wineries and I haven't been impressed. Frankly, a couple of them come across more like a Gamay Beaujolais. So I leave that kind of stuff to the big guys who've got money to throw around. I mean, if you tie up a fermentation tank for a month, you've got a serious investment. You fill that once in a year and who can afford to do that?

So a week of skin contact at the most?

Usually about a week, maybe nine days. When it goes dry, I press it into a stainless steel tank and I'll let it settle for anywhere from a day to two weeks; it depends on how much time and space I've got. Then I go into barrel, all French oak.

What's your experience in the use of new barrels versus old barrels every year?

I haven't really zeroed in on a program yet but I think when things level out it will be one third new wood every year. A lot depends on whether I continue to have three vintages in wood at one time. I've got some trials underway that indicate I could probably bottle in less than two years, so that way I would have only two vintages in wood. It would be to my advantage from the stand-point of space but to my disadvantage from the cost of barrels. If I go to only two years in wood, I'd probably end up with fifty percent in new barrels.

After the wine is in barrel, how often do you rack?

Usually I rack the wine two or three times a year. Some people rack every month, which seems a waste of time to me. Topping barrels is very important. During the winter I think the barrels can go two months without being topped but in the summertime you have to do it more often because it's warmer and dryer.

Do you attach any special importance to racking?

I think aerating is important when the wine is young. It can be important to the wine later on, if you smell them and feel they need it. Again that's a real subjective thing. I think most wines that are close to being bottled, especially if they are two or three years old, don't need a lot of air.

What about your fining and filtration procedures?

I haven't fined many red wines at all, including at Caymus. I've done some trials with egg white but basically I don't like what it does. I'm not looking to make a smooth, slick style of wine but I do believe in filtration, a little surpris-ing considering the size of our operation. A lot of small wineries are really pretty loose when it comes to filtration. They think you ruin wines by filtering them. I think filtering, when done properly, doesn't hurt the wine and it sure insures bottle consistency. There are a lot of things in wine, like yeast and bacteria, that have the capability of growing. So you can have big problems if you don't filter wine.

You want to insure its stability?

Right. If you don't put out a stable product, it's going to catch up with you.

So you don't buy the theory that filtration tends to strip the wine of its character?

What filtration does is to lighten up the color of the wine; it doesn't look quite as dark. The reason it looks really dark is that there are so many solids floating around in that unfiltered wine. If you pull those floating solids out of there, it's much clearer.

How are you able to maintain a level of consistency from year to year?

Basically, it's the fruit. If you're getting the same fruit from year to year, it's almost hard not to be consistent. If you pick the grapes at the same maturity and utilize the same practices, you're going to get similar wine.

By consistency, I also mean that you are able to produce a very high quality wine every year. People know what to expect from you and are rarely disappointed.

That's a matter of doing what you know you should do. It's not being lazy about the whole process. You have to take care of what you've got; that's the real key.

Do you do different things from year to year? I mean, do you experiment with one lot to see what the outcome will be?

No. The only thing I've been playing around with is my barrel regime. One of the problems with my facility is that I don't have extra space or time. If you were to start little experiments, you'd devote a whole nine yards to it. One of the reasons that there are very few experiments done in the industry is that it takes a lot of time and staff.

You're making 3,000 cases of Cabernet a year?

3,500; a little more of the Napa than the Howell Mountain.

All other things being equal, why couldn't you produce 20,000 cases?

Oh, I could, I could. But no one wants to believe me when I tell them I'm not going to just because it's too much trouble. I'm comfortable at this level. I don't need the marketing headaches, I don't need the staff headaches. That was one of the things that I learned at Caymus. I can make a good living doing the number of cases I'm doing right now. And there are a lot of things I enjoy doing other than working that I haven't been able to do in the last ten years.

You don't want to get trapped on the treadmill where you're constantly chasing production and keeping the marketing pipeline full?

And then the marketing aspect becomes a real worry. You feel you have to go to New York, Chicago and Miami to do tastings to promote your wine like everybody else. If you've got to beat the streets to sell your wine, it gets stale in a hurry. It's not for me.

But could you really make 20,000 cases of high quality Cabernet in the way you're doing now? And, if you couldn't, what are the limiting factors? I'm really asking about quality versus quantity.

The factor is the grapes; could you get that many tons? If you could get the grapes, you could do it. There's no question about it.

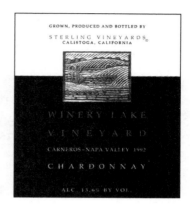

GROWN, PRODUCED AND BOTTLED BY
STERLING VINEYARDS
CALISTOGA, CALIFORNIA

WINERY LAKE
VINEYARD
CARNEROS-NAPA VALLEY 1992
CHARDONNAY

ALC. 13.6% BY VOL.

Bill Dyer
STERLING VINEYARDS

"I've never bought into the idea that because your production is large, relative to some other production, you have to abandon techniques that might be used in a small winery."

Bill Dyer and his wife, Dawnine, came to the Napa Valley in 1974 simply with the idea of working the crush that year. Nineteen years later, they're still there: Dawnine is the winemaker at Domaine Chandon and Bill is at Sterling. The move to Napa Valley proved to be fortuitous for both of them. Dawnine worked at Robert Mondavi and Inglenook before coming to Chandon. Bill worked several years at Charles Krug Winery before landing at Sterling as cellar foreman for winemaker Ric Forman. After Forman departed, he became more actively involved in the winemaking process, becoming assistant winemaker and eventually winemaker, after putting in some academic time at UC Davis.

Since 1985, when he took full control of the winemaking protocol, Dyer has been on a tireless and meticulous crusade to improve the quality of Sterling wines. His efforts have not gone unnoticed, either by consumers or the wine press. In 1989, Dan Berger, wine writer of *The Los Angeles Times*, named Dyer "Winemaker of the Year" as "a person who exemplifies what winemaking ought to be — innovative, creative and dedicated to a house style that varies only as much as Mother Nature requires." Berger goes on to say, "In the last few years, the quality of Sterling wines has slowly, silently crept up to a point where they sing notes other winemakers envy." He describes Dyer as "a person who moves forward annually, making noticeable improvements in the state of the art."

Sterling, now a subsidiary of the giant Seagrams, owns eleven vineyards comprising 1,100 acres of vines, including the famous Winery Lake Vineyard. Production is presently about a quarter of a million cases (more than Simi but less than Mondavi), concentrating on Sauvignon Blanc, Chardonnay, Merlot, Cabernet Sauvignon and Pinot Noir. Many of the smaller lots of wine with special characteristics are labeled as vineyard designated or reserve wines. Dyer is an extremely conscientious winemaker who graciously gives credit to his winemaking staff who help him maintain the high quality standards at Sterling.

You became assistant winemaker at Sterling in 1981 and then winemaker in 1985. You had some big shoes to fill, following Ric Forman, Theo Rosenbrand and Sergio Traverso. Were you secure in your knowledge and confident in your abilities?

I've never been unaware of the pressures along the way, not only from the comparison with my predecessors but also from the scrutiny brought on by the new production from the Winery Lake and Three Palms vineyards. Also the size of the production is a bigger responsibility than it was in the early eighties. I think my background allowed me to not have any fear of stepping into these shoes. For one thing, I worked closely with Ric Forman for two years. Ric, at that time, was stretched pretty far himself; he too had responsibility for all the vineyards. For work, Ric would meet with me in the morning and then would often be out in the vineyards for the rest of the day, developing the Diamond Mountain Ranch Vineyard. We had a good rapport going and my role was to fulfill his wishes in making the wine. In those two years, I got a concentrated view of how he did things. Also, I had hands-on experience, from the ground up. I can guarantee you there's not a job in the cellar I haven't done. From that standpoint, I feel really comfortable in a wine cellar. I know it from the worker's side.

What intrigues me about a larger winery is what the winemaker considers his role and main responsibilities?

There are different strategies for running a larger winery. First of all, I think I've never bought into the idea that because your production is large, relative to some other production, you have to abandon techniques that might be used in a small winery. For instance, I barrel ferment and sur lie age every bit of Chardonnay we produce here. That amounts to 2,500 barrels of Chardonnay. Yet I know other winemakers who think you can't do that when you have a winery the size of Sterling. They think you have to ferment in tanks. I don't think you have to abandon techniques because of size. It's a matter of organizing people and having people you can trust and communicate with. I was a cellar worker before I became a cellar master; I know their problems. I spend a great deal of time in the cellar. I have a cellar master here we've developed from the ground up. We have an enologist who is extremely technical and has a Ph.D. in organic chemistry. He also does the legwork of checking all those fermenting barrels of Chardonnay during harvest.

Do you consider yourself a traditionalist winemaker?

Well, certainly that's a large focus. My gut feeling is if there's a simple way to do something that has always worked, then that's the way to do it. I would rather get things done in the most simple, direct way. I don't want to handle the wine when it's not appropriate. So in that sense, I'm traditional. I've already mentioned barrel fermentation. Yet I don't absolutely reject technology. I consider it important to have stable wines in the bottle. We certainly use a lot of microbiology around here to monitor what's going on in the wines and we rely on that. I think the two things support each other. If you're familiar with what's going on in your wines, then you don't have to overuse technology in the cellar. You don't have to filter everything excessively when you know your populations are low and the wines are safe.

Is there a certain style that's evolved over the ten years that you've been here? Is there a certain way of looking at things?

I would say the style that's evolved here, with its roots going back to Ric Forman, is that the Sterling wines are meant to reveal vineyard characteristics rather than winemaking imprints. For example, I have colleagues I respect very much who might be making Chardonnay from a vineyard source in Mendocino this year and then a vineyard source in Sonoma County the next year. Just to maintain a style, they will use noticeable levels of malolactic fermentation or toasty oak. That puts an imprint of winemaking style on it. Whereas here the intention is more to have the winemaking be subtle and not call attention to itself. We're really showing the vineyard characteristics. My intention, in making Winery Lake Vineyard Chardonnay, is to capture and showcase the concentration of fruit character that gave this vineyard such a reputation. That's led me to not doing any malolactic fermentation. I don't want buttery character overlaying fruit character. Someone else might work with that fruit quite differently. So there is some winemaking style that enters into it. But it's the sense of revealing the fruit that you get instead of trying to make everything the same.

So you buy into the adage that wine is made in the vineyard?

I'm not quite willing to completely abdicate responsibility to the vineyard. I often hear a winemaker saying, "I'm just the custodian of the wine." I think some winemakers tend to downplay the profession a bit too much. I think there's more to it than that. There is the responsibility of revealing the vine-yard; certainly you cannot make good wine without paying careful attention to the whole viticultural scenario, from the site to the viticultural practices. But the winemaking is very important too. There are some techniques appropriately applied to certain vineyards and not to others.

Describe the climate and soil conditions in several of your vineyard designated sites.

The Winery Lake Vineyard is one of the few places in the Napa Valley appellation where you should grow Pinot Noir. A cool climate is certainly important for Pinot Noir. There's also a powerful story for Sterling Chardonnay there. We wanted a cool climate source of Chardonnay and Winery Lake now provides powerful, concentrated, exotic fruit aromas and a rich textured Chardonnay that enhances the estate blend and provides a showy vineyard designated wine. In the recent vintages of Pinot Noir, we've identified one hillside location as producing the best Pinot Noir. Only recently we've found there is a lot of lime in that soil from decomposed seashells back from when the bay covered the area. Previously we weren't even aware there was lime in that area. We've begun to find a lot of fossilized shells on another hill, which also has volcanic extrusions. Dr. Fiske from UC Davis told me not only is it rare to find volcanic material in Carneros but the hillside is one of the rare sites in all of North America where fossilized seashells and signs of volcanism occur together. Yet another slope at Winery Lake has shallow clay over rock and gives us an excellent Merlot that now goes into the Reserve blend.

I think soils are going to become more and more important in California winemaking. I know many people in Napa Valley who are excited about soils now. Ten years ago, everybody said the soil was all the same and that climate was all important. We're really abandoning that idea quickly.

The Three Palms Vineyard is on an alluvial fan composed of volcanic rocks that washed down a canyon in the eastern hills. Though it is well known as a Merlot vineyard, I think the Cabernet Sauvignon there is often the superior wine. Some of the proponents of dividing Napa Valley into many sub-appellations would have it believed that Cabernet Sauvignon won't do well north of St. Helena. But, Three Palms, along with a couple other vineyards like Eisele, located on rocky soils at the base of these canyons in the Calistoga area, produce very distinctive Cabernet Sauvignon because the exceptional soils are more important than the slightly warmer climate.

The Diamond Mountain Ranch Vineyard is also volcanic but less rocky. It has a light, almost chalky soil. We find again, that within that one vineyard, specific sites are quite different from each other. One area is composed of pure chalk, called tuff, and is an incredible place to grow Cabernet Franc. There are different climates within that region because Diamond Mountain Ranch is almost two separate vineyards. There's a lower region down near Diamond Creek but if you go up a dirt road, there's a higher bowl where it's a bit cooler. The Chardonnay from that higher bowl seems quite interesting. On the lower slopes, red Bordeaux varieties seem to do well. This diversity of soils throughout Napa Valley, overlaying all the climatic variations, affects the wine styles.

What are the characteristics of an ideal Cabernet in an ideal year?

Let me answer that by describing the 1985 Sterling Reserve. To me, that wine has it all. It has berrylike aromas rather than a strong herbaceous, minty character. The aroma is quite powerful; on the palate, it's quite supple rather than being a huge extracted monster. I found it enlightening to taste wines from the barrel in Bordeaux at some of the top chateaux; I realized that some of the strategies I learned as an apprentice are not the way to go. You don't need to have a huge, tannic wine to last; the structure is more important. So in blending the 1985 Reserve, I really looked for wines that gave a somewhat lean structure but a full middle and not a lot of tannin at the end. The varietal blending is also quite important. We tend to use multi-varietal blends in making Cabernet types. The 1985 Reserve, in fact, is not even labeled a Cabernet anymore. It's just labeled Sterling Reserve. It's a four variety blend with Cabernet, Petit Verdot, Cabernet Franc and Merlot.

In the Three Palms Vineyard or the Diamond Mountain Ranch Vineyard, what do you consider ripeness in Cabernet?

There are some people who say that it's ripe at a specific level and others say you can't pay attention to the numbers, that it depends on the flavors of the grapes. I'm somewhere in between these two. I think you can't ignore the sugar level. If the flavors are best when the sugars are 26 degrees brix, are you going to pick at that level? I don't think so. You have to pay attention to the alcohol level in the finished wine and that's all part of the structure too. Yet you can't pick strictly by the numbers. That's why you have to get into the vineyard, taste fruit, and pay attention. Last year the maturity wasn't very even in the clusters so we had to wait a bit longer than the numbers would have indicated.

To give you some ranges that I feel comfortable with, I like to target right around 22.5 degrees brix because that gives me an alcohol level that's in the low thirteen percent and I find that appropriate. I might be picking a bit riper as years go by though because we're starting to age it mostly in caves we have tunneled into the hill underneath the winery. The caves have a high humidity situation so you lose alcohol as you age instead of staying the same or increasing.

I find it hard to generalize about acidity and pH levels; it depends on the individual vineyard site. We're certainly watching both of them. We're watching more for the change in acid and pH. At a certain point the berries start to get a little soft and then the pH starts to go up and the acid starts to drop. That seems to be a pretty good indication of ripeness.

Generally, what are your fermentation practices with Cabernet?

In fermenting, 85F degrees would be the target for all Cabernets and Merlots. I pump over using an irrigator; some people call it a sprinkler. I vary the amount of time depending on how the fermentation goes. I don't do it for x amount of minutes based on the size of the tank. I do it based on what the must looked like yesterday and vary it, depending on what I see in terms of extraction. I also tend to pump over earlier in fermentation rather than later. I don't want gripping tannins. I tend to press at dryness. I've done a lot of experimentation with extended maceration. I haven't found it to produce long-chain, supple tannins as some people claim. I haven't closed the book entirely on that; I still experiment with it. But generally I press at dryness. I usually do the malolactic after fermentation.

What about the barrel regime? New oak versus old oak?

I think the amount of new oak you use is entirely dependent on the individual lot. More serious wines take more serious oak. For our Reserve, we are using one hundred percent new oak but utilizing barrels that previously had a white wine fermentation in them. A barrel fermentation of either Sauvignon Blanc or Chardonnay seasons the barrels. I find that works very well. Before, I found that we couldn't age Reserve in all new oak; it was just too much. Now we're doing one hundred percent new oak because of that seasoning effect. For the Diamond Mountain Ranch and Three Palms wines, I'm using roughly fifty percent new oak treated the same way. With the estate Cabernet or Merlot, there's little new oak. For those we use barrels that, on the average, are three or four years old.

For Cabernet, what's your regime of racking, fining and filtering?

I was much influenced by some of Ric Forman's techniques in this regard and he, in turn, was influenced by Bordeaux techniques. He liked to rack frequently. Yet, at one point, I learned that not every wine benefits by being racked frequently. The further up the hierarchy you go, the more the wine is going to develop and do interesting things with a little more exposure to air. For our Reserve, I rack quarterly although I don't do it on a calendar basis. I do it by tasting the wine. I might rack three times this year and four times the next year. But I think the wines that really have the aging potential and the structure to support extra handling, benefit by quarterly rackings. That's true with both the Diamond Mountain Ranch and Three Palms wines. With the estate Cabernet and Merlot, we rack less frequently.

I only use egg white fining on Cabernets and Merlots. Again, the level of fining depends on the wine. For example, I do fine the Reserve in the barrel. I think you get an exceptionally good settling in the barrel. It's not a real practical way to work, in some ways, but the Reserve is a relatively small bottling and we can afford to do it that way. I do fine the estate Cabernet and Merlot in the tank. And I only fine when I think it will enhance the wine. We do lab trials. I don't fine every vintage but most vintages get some amount of egg white fining.

Isn't there a trade off there? What's the downside of fining?

If you make a huge extracted style of wine with your fermentation techniques and then expect to finesse that wine by fining with egg whites, you can't do it. You can't touch a lot of those tannins with egg whites. So you need to have a fairly supple wine to begin with and then it's just fine-tuning with the fining.

I see all these individual techniques as part of an organic whole. One of the biggest winemaking mistakes is to focus in on some technique, not realizing that it's part of a huge context having to do, not only with the other cellaring techniques, but also maybe the region they are occurring in.

You didn't mention filtering?

In general, I filter as little as possible. In the context of that earlier umbrella philosophy, I want to do as little as possible and when I do it, it should be specific. It should be to achieve some end. I wouldn't want to overfilter for the same reason I wouldn't want to overdo anything else. I only do it as needed. On the other hand, I don't shy away from filtration when it's necessary.

I flinch when I read wine writers who take it as a given that filtration ruins a wine. Take for example some small producer in the Rhone that has made wine for generations. When the son takes over and he brings in a filter, the wine writer concludes that filtering has changed the wines and made them lousy. Maybe the son did ruin the wines by filtering but maybe he ruined them because he didn't know what he was doing. Maybe he filtered them ten times. Maybe he didn't know of certain cellar procedures that strip weird characters out of the filtering pads.

But I've always been sensitive to this argument; therefore, whenever we do a filtration, it's standard procedure here to take at least two samples from the inlet of the filter and at least two samples from the outlet. We're real specific about that. We don't take them from the beginning tank and the ending tank because that's not fair. The beginning tank wasn't moved at all and the final one had some movement. We always do that just to compare filtration. Then we do blind triangular tastings. If I look at the data from all these years, I find my preference is about fifty-fifty. Sometimes I like the one that's filtered better and sometimes I like the one that wasn't filtered better. There's not an influence of filtration that ruins the wine.

I recently set up a triangular tasting of the 1982 through 1985 Sterling Reserve for a group of winemakers and no one could tell if they were filtered. So I feel confident that when filtration is done right, it doesn't take anything away from the wine. And I feel it's important not to put wines into the bottle that are time bombs. I think some of the wines that are rated highly by certain wine writers are time bombs.

You know, brettanomyces, a spoilage yeast, can produce interesting characteristics. It can make the wines seem more complex at a certain stage in their development. But when they are in the bottle fifteen or twenty years, they won't be the same anymore. So I feel a commitment to give to the consumer a wine that will develop favorably in the bottle. I will not hesitate to filter a Cabernet to the yeast proof level of filtration, if it has brettanomyces. I never use membrane filters for the red wines because I don't feel you need to. Pad filters reliably remove spoilage yeast. Yes, there's brettanomyces in the cellar; there's brettanomyces in every cellar that exists. It's just that some people don't look for it so they don't have to deal with it. When it's in a particular wine, I get rid of it before it goes to bottle. But it usually only takes one careful filtration to do the job.

What's the theory that some low level of brettanomyces makes the wine more interesting and gives it a better flavor profile?

I believe that. It's the complexing strategy. You add a little different nuance in there and, as long as it doesn't dominate the wine, it can make it pretty interesting. So the fact that I have some in my cellar doesn't completely flip me out. I know winemakers who will never admit they have it. But it's there; it's part of the flora and fauna. The thing is, allow it in the barrels but be in control of it. Don't allow it to get out of hand. That's why we have enologists and lab technicians. But you don't want to let it get in the bottle. When sulfur levels go down and the brettanomyces has the opportunity to keep on going into the bottle, then inevitably it will always ruin the wine. When people talk about ageability of wines and always attribute it to the winemaker's skill or the region it came from, I think often the ageability factor has to do with the level of brettanomyces that were common in that particular winery. It's only in the last couple of years in Bordeaux that they've begun to realize that they've had brettanomyces. And they learned it from California winemakers. I think many wines in both Bordeaux and California lose their aging potential when bottled with brettanomyces present.

Tell me about the wine you make from the Three Palms Vineyard. One year it was forty-five percent Cabernet and fifty-five percent Merlot and the next year those percentages were reversed. It's called simply "red table wine." What's the concept behind that wine?

Three Palms fruit has been coming to the winery ever since it was established in 1969. In fact, Sloan Upton, who owns the vineyard with his brother, John, was our original vineyard manager. Over the years, the grapes were all going into our estate blend, before we began to use labels with vineyard designations. In about 1977, when Coca-Cola owned Sterling, a decision was made to release some Merlot from the long-term contract to allow Dan Duckhorn to buy some Merlot, and he went on to make the vineyard famous for that variety. And yet, the vineyard is planted primarily to Cabernet Sauvignon, which does incredibly well there. In fact, in some of the twelve vintages I've worked with the fruit, I've preferred the Cabernet Sauvignon. It shares with the Merlot a very fragrant raspberry like aroma: terroir overpowering varietal differences. So when we began vineyard designating wines recently, it seemed a natural to do Three Palms. The easy thing to have done would have been to release a Merlot. But we thought it would be interesting to just use the vineyard name on the label without varietal labeling. The concept is to leave maximum flexibility to build the blend around the most favorable combinations of varieties. In some years, Merlot will play the lead role, and in others Cabernet Sauvignon.

We are also working with the Uptons in planting Cabernet Franc, Malbec and Petit Verdot there. We hope to find the best combination of Bordeaux varieties for that site and the label we have chosen allows us to search for that combination. The wine is directed at the level of the market with the sophistication to recognize Three Palms as a great vineyard and its identity is more important on the label than varietal identity. All the Three Palms fruit, by the way, is farmed exclusively for Sterling and Duckhorn.

What's your feeling about the Meritage designation for wines made from Bordeaux style varietals? Many of these wines are presently being called red table wine and/or they have proprietary designations.

Personally, I have some sympathy for the concept. It's difficult to know what to call these wines. Sterling supported the organization when it was founded. But the name "Meritage" doesn't mean anything to me. It sounds to me like the name of another wine in that category, not what the name of the category ought to be. It's not descriptive of anything. If the intent was to demystify things for the consumer, it didn't. It just gave them another name to learn. So I'm not enthusiastic about it and I don't think we'll use it on our labels. Again, I don't like the idea that it's restricted to Bordeaux varieties. Why does it have to be all Bordeaux varieties? For instance, an exceptional Cabernet Sauvignon/Syrah blend ought to be included in a proprietary blend category.

With your Estate Chardonnays, you walk that fine line really well. They do taste really good right now and you can drink them and be perfectly happy. But several years down the line, they are going to develop wonderfully well.

I'm glad you said it and I didn't have to. It's hard for me to say that our wines are made to age long-term but they also taste good early on. People are really suspicious when they hear that. But there is something to that. If a wine is well structured, it will age well. And that doesn't mean it has to be without any interest when it's young. Long aging wines don't have to be unapproachable when they are young; they can be quite pretty and just stay young a long time. Vineyard characteristics enter into this too. If you have Carneros

Chardonnay, it's just going to be enjoyable at an early stage. But some of the mountain Chardonnays, like Diamond Mountain Ranch, when you put them in the bottle, it's kind of a leap of faith that it's worth doing.

How do you build that fresh, fruit character up front while still giving a backbone and structure that will let it age?

How not to do it is with skin contact. You can maximize flavor and aroma by bringing in some skin contact. But then the downside is the wines tend to fall apart. With skin contact, you extract more flavor and aroma but you also extract astringent phenols and get a higher pH. The wines become flabby and because of the higher pH, they go downhill quickly.

I think barrel fermentation and leaving the wine on the lees make for a more attractive wine. There's just more fruit there. Back in the early eighties when part of the wine was barrel fermented and part stainless steel fermented, they didn't go into the bottle with as much fruit. Therefore it's not as attention-getting when just released. Yet we have structured the wine in a pretty consistent way. We have always picked the grapes a bit early. There's good acidity in the wines. They're not picked at 24 degrees brix, with low acids. Generally for Estate Chardonnay, 22 to 22.5 degrees brix would be a normal target. At Winery Lake, in Carneros, it seems we need to be riper down there in order to capture the character. So we'll pick at 23 to 23.5 degrees brix for Winery Lake Chardonnay.

You seem to have a little different philosophy of making Chardonnay than some of your contemporaries. Could you explain?

Their way of looking at Chardonnay is more along the lines of "building" a wine. In that case, you start with the fruit source being important but not as definitive to the style of wine as the techniques the winemaker brings to it. So there is a style of Chardonnay that is stirred, has total malolactic fermentation and is full of toasty oak. I think the mind frame of those winemakers is that they want to make something as good as Burgundy. They feel that they can make a wine in the great Burgundian tradition in California. Well, that's not really my frame of mind. The idea is to make the best Winery Lake Chardonnay or the best Napa Valley Chardonnay. I think I can analyze myself well enough to know my orientation. Ric Forman never allowed malolactic fermentation in this winery. He still doesn't do malolactic fermentation as far as I know. He considers it detrimental to the wine. That's the context I come from. But I have begun to use some malolactic. In any given year, our Estate Chardonnay might have an eight percent to fifteen percent malolactic component. I like it to be just a hint, a flavoring. I don't want it to be noticeable though. Again, I'd like to think that I haven't decided anything for all time. For instance, on the Diamond Mountain Ranch Chardonnay, I'm playing around with more malolactic fermentation. I like the concept that you have different techniques for different vineyards. I'm much more comfortable with that instead of determining my winemaking style and then imposing that on every vineyard.

What is your barrel regime for Chardonnay?

My target is fifty percent new oak in any given year. I do that for all three Chardonnays. The other half of the oak is generally one year old barrels. I prefer buying barrels from Burgundy for Chardonnay but I don't do it exclusively because of this whole flowchart approach to barreling that I have. All of the new barrels coming here are going to have either Chardonnay or Sauvignon Blanc fermenting in them. Then some of the barrels are going to stay with the Chardonnay and some are going to go to the Reserve Cabernet and other designations. So I have some Bordeaux produced barrels that I use for Chardonnay also. I don't think the shape of the barrel matters too much. The particular forest is not as important as the tightness of the grain. We use Allier, Troncais and Nevers. The Chardonnays stay six months in the barrel; we don't want it to have excessive oak character.

I think one of the interesting things about barrel fermenting and the sur lies strategy is that you can use such large quantities of new oak without getting too much of the barrel taste. We used to wait and put the wine in the barrel for aging after it had been clarified. I found that if you used a new barrel, within eight weeks the wine would be dominated by the taste of the oak. When you barrel ferment, with all the yeast protein interacting with the barrels, you are able to go longer in the barrel with more new oak. One thing I might do in the future is go a bit longer in the barrel with the vineyard designated Chardonnays. With the Estate Chardonnay, which is a much larger volume, there are red wines waiting for those barrels after I pull the Chardonnay out. Due to the whole flow of things, it just makes sense that it comes out of barrels in springtime.

You've said fine and filter only as appropriate. Is there anything different about Chardonnay in that respect?

Just in the sense that my ideal would be to do no fining. That goes back to the philosophy of doing as little as possible to a delicate variety. You know, the wines fall very clear in barrel. The difficulty is getting them out of barrel to the tank without pulling up some of the lees with it. So if the wines are fairly cloudy in the tank, I'll let them sit there for as long as I can and see if they'll just drop on their own. I'll come back and fine them reluctantly if I need to, using isinglass which is the most gentle of the fining agents.

You know, we used to think a lot about enhancing the white wines by fining with isinglass and making them more palatable. It was certainly the regime that Ric used here for the early Chardonnays. But we're making the wines a bit differently now and I'm not sure that the fining is important for that palate refinement anymore. In the last four or five vintages, we have not been using any SO_2 in the fermenting must. First we refrained from it on reds and then we tried it on whites. There's no SO_2 being put in until after the barrel fermentation is over and then we stir it in to control malolactic mainly. With all the juice oxidation that goes on, I think that a lot of the astringent phenolic material is dropping out. I think it used to be, when you added SO_2 and protected the wines with CO_2 in all the tanks, you preserved more of that phenolic material. It probably affected the taste and maybe we needed to fine the wines. I guess I'm not a great believer in fining white wines at this point.

Because our Chardonnays have little or no malolactic fermentation, they do need to be filtered for stability. Our goal is to just do one pass through a filter with a cross-over plate, which allows a loose and tight filtration in one pass. A membrane filtration in the bottling process ensures no bacteria in the bottle. This is an area where I prefer to use the appropriate technology rather than take the approach of having to use one hundred percent malolactic fermentation just to avoid the sterile filtration. I think all this fear of stripping flavor and aroma due to the tightness of the filtration originates in the misconception that the molecules responsible for the flavors and aromas are similar in size to the bacteria and yeast the sterile filters are removing. But there is a huge difference in size between molecules and microorganisms.

Your wife, Dawnine Dyer, is the winemaker at Domaine Chandon. Do you talk shop at home?

Not very much. There was a time when we did. Wine is so much of our lives, we have to work at maintaining a little diversity. We don't really talk about work too much, on a day-to-day basis. But we do share ideas about wine. I think one of the interesting things about being married to somebody who's in the same profession is she's another palate you can bounce things off of. Even though we're not in the same realms of winemaking, she'll bring home some sparkling wine cuvees and have me taste through them. It works out well that we're not in the same area because any tendency to be competitive is diffused by that.

How do you get from philosophy into winemaking?

My flippant answer is that, after all, it's just doing fieldwork in aesthetics. I think there is some truth to that. There's probably some reason why all these philosophy majors end up in winemaking, other than the fact that you can't get a job as a metaphysician. But it's something that is aesthetic.

I think winemaking is inherently interesting because it's not like making other beverages where you take raw materials and you produce something where the whole intention is to be consistent. In winemaking it's very complex. You're taking an agricultural product and in some ways you're trying to preserve it and in some ways you're trying to transform it. There are all these choices along the way. Every vintage is different. There really are no parallels. Just the fact that you can approach it from different ends of the spectrum. Are you trying to transform it entirely or are you trying to preserve it or something in between? That's what makes it interesting.

Dawnine Dyer
DOMAINE CHANDON

"There is one thing I am continually struggling with and the dynamics of it are fascinating to me; I'm interpreting a traditional wine type for a traditional company in another country."

When Dawnine Dyer was a biology major at UC Santa Cruz, she worked summers in the wine lab at Bargetto Winery, where her husband was cellar foreman. After graduation in 1974, they came to Napa Valley to work the harvest. Less than a decade later, she had become winemaker at Domaine Chandon and her husband, Bill, had become winemaker at Sterling Vineyards.

In the interim, Dyer had spent time at Robert Mondavi Winery, Inglenook and UC Davis. It was during that period she was introduced to Edmond Maudiere, of the prestigious Champagne firm of Moët and Chandon; at the time he was in California laying the groundwork for Domaine Chandon, which was to become the first sparkling wine facility in California owned by a French company. Dyer was planning a trip to France and Maudiere arranged for her to spend several days at the Moët and Chandon cellars. On her return to California, she was asked to set up the wine lab and quality control program for Domaine Chandon, which was still under construction.

From the beginning, she had the opportunity to be completely involved with all aspects of the winery. Her professional association with Maudiere proved very rewarding in terms of tasting and blending the wine lots and establishing a sparkling wine style. By 1981, she was both winemaker and vice president of the winery. Maudiere still makes frequent visits in the role of consulting enologist. Dyer regularly returns to Moët and Chandon in Eperney to draw on Moët's considerable resources.

Although you are the winemaker at Domaine Chandon, you mentioned the sparkling wines are a team effort.

The team effort is at the heart of my philosophy of sparkling wines. The very nature of sparkling wine, the fact that it's blended, that there are many varieties that we're looking for, that there are a range of microclimates to draw our fruit from within a limited geographical area, makes the whole nature of the wine more subtle and quite complex. It tends to lend itself toward careful group decisions on wine quality. For instance, when we taste for blends, there are three of us who taste: myself, my assistant and Edmond Maudiere. The three of us are focused on different aspects of the wine; we have our own personalities and day-to-day responsibilities with the wines. Edmond has a vast range of winemaking experience from around the world. With that perspective he can sit down and look at wines that he hasn't seen for four months and have an immediate response to them.

Wines have a past and their future depends on that past. They don't just exist at a moment in time. So the nurturing process that has gone on before brings something to that as well. I think it's a wine type that does lend itself philosophically to that approach.

How do you perceive your role as winemaker at Domaine Chandon? What are your responsibilities, your priorities? What are you most focused on?

There are lots of aspects to the job I do and the focus changes. On a broad basis, I would say there is one thing I am continually struggling with and the dynamics of it are fascinating to me; I'm interpreting a traditional wine type for a traditional company in another country. It's very important to me to represent that heritage but also to have the wine be very true to itself, to reflect the grape's sources in the area and the vitality and dynamics that I see here culturally. It's a balancing act and there's some tension involved. I wouldn't say I've completely resolved that myself. I'm not displeased when someone says, "I thought this wine was from Champagne," but, at the same time, that's not really what I'm trying to do. Balancing those things is a constant fascination to me.

One thing which fascinates me about our industry is we tend to be a still wine producing country and most of the grape material that we have to work with comes from that tradition. There's a great emphasis, in my mind, that needs to be placed by sparkling wine producers to really focus on the grape material, that is, the clonal selections for both Pinot Noir and Chardonnay. We've done more work to date on Pinot Noir but I think Chardonnay perhaps is even more important. It is through our vineyard efforts, in terms of grafting programs and nursery programs, that we are able to see any appreciable amount of Pinot Meunier, which is a significant part of the grape resources in Champagne.

Another area fascinating to me is communicating information about wines to people. I think we've done a pretty good job with still wines. I find it frustrating that people who pay a lot of attention to wines in general tend to not have at their disposal ways to describe and/or remember the sparkling wines and Champagnes they taste. While I don't like to be boring about wine talk over other interesting types of conversation at meals, I think being able to describe something is a prerequisite to being able to remember it. You have to have something making that connection. So to that extent, the whole world of verbalizing flavors is very interesting to me.

Sometimes I think someone should invent a new way or new style of talking about wine. You keep seeing the same terms to describe wine.

The wineries are as guilty as anybody in being imprecise because we want to use romantic words. Writers tend to have a specific set of words they use as well. The world of descriptive analysis tends to be clinical. I think it can be good but it tends to be not very interesting to the consumer.

What did you learn from working with Moët and Chandon's Edmond Maudiere, a man who has many years of Champagne making experience? In the early years, what kind of insights did you gain from working with him?

You know I think one of the things that has been an advantage to us here has been the fact that we've had access to people who really understood the transition that was going to take place with the still wine when it became a sparkling wine with extended periods of time in the bottle with the yeast. So I would say, for the first couple of years that I worked here, I was lucky enough to be involved in the tastings right from the beginning. It was kind of on an observer level but I was there. I'd say the first few times, I was just memorizing flavors, memorizing the way people talked about them and trying to remember them myself so I could see what happened to a certain flavor when you did a certain thing. Then gradually, over a period of time, I got more comfortable with how those changes happened. And Edmond certainly brought that with him right from the very beginning: that vast experience.

Was Edmond a mentor of sorts?

Oh, without a doubt. In fact, he still serves that role. I mean, I can think of nothing better than to have access to someone with considerably more experience than me but who isn't here all the time. It gives you an opportunity to breathe and grow. I can feel a great deal of satisfaction; the work is truly mine. At the same time, I have access to that great experience.

There are so many different things going on here simultaneously at any given point in time, how do you keep everything straight in your mind?

First of all, while we are a large organization, we only make one wine type, which simplifies that to some extent. So we are a large organization; we work with 12,000 tons of fruit every year, half of which we grow ourselves. But it's all Chardonnay, Pinot Noir, Pinot Blanc or Pinot Meunier. For the most part, the fruit is grown in areas that have become very familiar to me. I think the stability of grape resources is probably one of the things really changing and helping the quality of wines in California. A good technical winemaker can watch for signs of things going wrong or well in a batch of grapes they've never seen before. But there's nothing like having worked with that same vineyard for five or six years to really start to understand how far you can push, when you need to panic and what you need to do just to prevent things from going wrong from the beginning. We have stability in that area and that helps keep our blood pressure down a bit during the critical times.

There are a lot of other people involved here from viticulturalists to assistants. One fact of life is, when you get to a point where you require a staff, you spend a little more time being briefed on things. You want to make sure you're touching bases with everybody that has a piece of that puzzle.

It's not just all winemaking; you have to be a good administrator too.

Yes. It's kind of interesting. Sparkling wine is fairly controlled, as wines go, because of the blending and the secondary fermentation. Wine really is a natural product; it wants to make itself. I often say to the people who work for me, "Once you've got the vines in the ground and the grapes on the vine, there's nothing we're going to do to stop it from happening." We're going to do it better or we're going to do it worse, but we're not going to stop the process from happening. Sometimes the best we can do is be good traffic managers and just make sure things happen in a timely way. We can stop and think about the subtleties once the grape material is all collected.

Is there a house style here? A Domaine Chandon style?

Yes, I'd say there's a house style. I think wine styles, as a topic, are rather fascinating but it can also be overdone a bit because styles evolve more than they're dictated. They reflect the things that go into them. I always find it fascinating to look at the number of European players in the sparkling wine business in California, and Domaine Chandon was among the first. But I look at the French products and the California products and I can't match them up. The styles have a lot more to do with the interpretation of the grapes than they do with anything dictated.

What we are trying to do with the fruit when we make the base wine is to look for an adequate development of grape flavors in wines but not to have them be too ripe. We try to process them in such a way that we minimize the phenolic pickup. It's a take off on the Champagne formula but it does vary a little bit here. We do have a situation where our climate is different than in Champagne. They are considerably further north than we are and have a longer growing season with less day to night variation in their temperatures. If you look at heat summations, they really don't come out all that much different. On average days from bloom to harvest, they differ by, on average over our history, nine days. We average ninety-two days from bloom to harvest; they average right around one hundred days. But there are other differences in the way heat is spread out and so there are different approaches in the way we look at maturity.

Do you rely on the sugar, acid and pH numbers in determining maturity?

We look at the numbers. But I feel it's important to be tasting the fruit too. Again, you can get to know your vineyards so you have some kind of an idea of what's going to happen, how fast the grapes are going to ripen, how fast they are going to change and what the flavors are likely to do. But one of the things of serious concern to me is making sure there are ripe flavors in the wines. If you let the fruit get too ripe, you can dominate the delicacy of the wine type. You don't leave yourself a neutral enough base to put all of the yeast autolysis on top of. But if you pick too green, you wind up with something more than neutral; it falls into a category that is a bit more coarse and common. When to harvest is a decision we have to make that really doesn't have to be made in Champagne. Their grapes simply aren't going to get much riper; in nine out of ten years, there are no decisions about when to pick there.

You, on the other hand, have to walk the tightrope. You can't pick too late but you don't want to pick too early either.

Yes. It does vary from vineyard to vineyard and also from variety to variety. But we're watching for that kind of a change in the flavor of the grape. One of the things I believe strongly about processing is you have to look at everything you do to the grape, in terms of extraction of both flavors and phenols. We talk about flavors as being positive and tannins as being negative. There's no question that the single largest source of extraction for us in this climate is temperature. If the fruit is warm, we get a lot of tannin, pigmentation and flavor out of the fruit. We're looking to minimize that kind of extraction so we look at cool fruit as being desirable. We've approached that and one other aspect of our harvest situation that's different from Champagne: the grapes are maturing fast and to bring in the kind of tonnage we're talking about in a period as short as four weeks is a challenge. We have to harvest mechanically at night. There are some tradeoffs with that that I feel are more than well balanced in favor of doing it, simply because you have cool fruit. Even though you're getting some juicing in the bins, your extraction rate is so much slower at that temperature level that you're still on the win side of that equation.

A lot of people talk about whole berry pressing, which is something we do. For whole berry processing, you have to go all the way back to the picking container and the method of conveying the fruit and take the big view of that. We spend a lot of time working on that. We're looking at some possibilities for grape cooling prior to going into the presses.

So you would pick Chardonnay at 18 or 19 degrees brix?

I think the window for Chardonnay is a little more narrow than for Pinot Noir. I'd say 18.5 to 19.5 degrees brix.

Is that fruit physiologically mature? It's not fully ripe, is it?

In California, it could go to 26 degrees brix! So the question is: what is maturity and what do you want to do with it? You can see a real physiological change at the point when the berry goes from being green to being kind of translucent. Somewhere between 17.5 to 18.5 degrees brix, you really get the first of that translucence in the skins. There is a lot of regional difference in the fruit we see. For example, we have a lot of plantings in Carneros. The Chardonnay there retains the acidity which, for our purposes, is very nice. We're looking for high acids. But it retains so much malic acid in that area that I think the maturity level on that fruit is at a higher sugar level. It's not our practice, as a general rule, to do malolactic fermentations on the wines, but in some of the areas of Carneros, you have to ask yourself if you can tolerate the alcohol going any higher. So we're looking at doing some other things to compensate for that.

With high acid Chardonnay from Carneros, you would be inclined to put the wine through malolactic, if you were a still winemaker, but you might not if you're making sparkling wine.

As a general rule, we don't. We tend to carry fairly high malates, as you might expect from picking grapes at an average of 18.5 to 19 degrees brix. If the malic acid level is too high, that is, acidity that's very aggressive, then I might use malolactic periodically to take the edge off. It's a year by year kind of decision. When we start to see the fruit in August, we can tell whether we should be doing a certain percentage of our production through malolactic. We have never gone one hundred percent malolactic and don't anticipate doing so.

Malolactic is a good tool but I had no idea that a sparkling winemaker might be using it.

It's interesting. The main characteristic of malolactic is diacetyl, that buttery kind of an aroma. Interestingly enough, that characteristic is metabolized in the secondary fermentation. So it's another thing you have to kind of see around and that's a bit difficult. You have to imagine the wine as if it didn't have that characteristic because the malolactic is metabolized by the yeasts. You lose the strong aromatics of the malolactic in the secondary fermentation but you do obviously maintain the structural changes that have taken place.

A sparkling winemaker's job is one of the toughest. You have to be able to see into a crystal ball of sorts. You have to know how a sparkling wine is going to taste upon release, after having blended a number of base wines, putting them through a secondary fermentation and then leaving them to age on the yeast.

Well, I think there is a lot of truth to that. It is complex and there are a lot of things that are going to weigh in formula. It's phenomenal just to sit down, when we're getting ready to disgorge a cuvee, and look at dosage levels. One of the things that has come to be important for me here is having a library of materials I can use in the dosage. With a dosage, we're only talking about putting eight milliliters in a bottle; it's only one percent of the volume of the bottle we're adding. It's kind of your last little chance at influencing that sparkling wine. In the dosage, you can use younger wines, or Chardonnay; you do a bit of barrel fermentation with the Chardonnay just to have that in there. I've never used one hundred percent barrel fermentation in the dosage, although, I've used little bits and pieces of it because it's amazing how much you can do with that kind of addition.

But how are you able to see into that crystal ball? How are you able to see the light at the far end of the tunnel?

I wish I could answer that. I don't really know. It has to be almost intuitive. I worked with a fellow here for a while who tasted with us. After a couple of tastings with Edmond, he commented that Edmond was really a right brained taster. I never really thought about it that way but it is kind of true. It's required that you scrutinize the little pieces on a daily basis. But there's a point at which you just have to let the gestalt of the whole thing kind of take over.

What's the margin of error here? How do you know, from all the little bits and pieces, that you're not going to have a mistake in the bottle a few years later? I guess I'm really asking about consistency.

One thing we do that helps with consistency is blending in older wines. You bring that forward with you and it helps provide some continuity from one year to the next. One recent harvest, for instance, was not a remarkable year in terms of the quality of the fruit. We had a lot of heat during the harvest period and the temperature of the grapes is one thing that concerns me. It was not ours to control that year. But I was fortunate to have additional reserves and we used a higher percentage of older, reserve wines in the blends that year. At the point of fermentation, if I saw fruit come in with balances I didn't like, I put in wines from 1986 that had good acids and low pHs, in adequate quantities to do kind of a buffering on the juice, so the fermentation could proceed along more normal lines.

With the Blanc de Noir, we had a certain amount of wines left from 1987 prior to the 1988 harvest. We were scheduled to bottle those wines in November but we held the bottling off and did an additional back blending with that to the 1988. We didn't plan to do that but it was available to us. There have been just a couple of years that the reserved wine was really critical to the quality of the wines. 1981 and 1988 were both years like that. We've had a run of really nice vintages.

You've said what you are looking for in a sparkling wine is structure and elegance plus balance and complexity. Could you elaborate?

There are a number of ways to approach the balance of a wine. Probably the most basic one is sugar/acid, tannin/acid, alcohol and how all those things are going to line up. We're looking at lower alcohols, higher acids and low phenols. For our purposes, both alcohol and acid have kind of a synergistic effect with tannins. The higher your alcohols get, the more you perceive tannins and the higher your acids, the more you perceive tannins. Thus the phenomena of some of the mid-seventies California wines that had high alcohol and high tannins. But we tend to look at what we need, which is the higher acid and the lower alcohol, and then modulate the tannins to such an extent that it works.

The other thing that we're working with is a blend of varieties. I'm talking about the one we make the most of, which is a brut blend of the four different grape varieties. The challenge there is to construct a blend out of things that are varietally distinct, yet when blended with the other components, create something that is more than just the sum of the parts.

When you're blending the base wines, what's the procedure?

We line up all the wines of a given type. There may be seventy or eighty different lots so we break them down by grape variety first. The three of us will probably go through the entire sequence, as a group, twice. We sort them out in different categories; certain lots we may designate as being typical of the harvest, certain lots are the mainstay wines and certain lots are extraordinary wines. There will always be a few lots that one or the other of us will have a problem with. So we'll take those wines that any of us have a problem with and also take the extraordinary wines and hold them out. Those might represent the two extremes. Then we'll start to work on the mid-range and play with the highlighting. We'll add back in those things that are extraordinary and/or problematic and find out, one by one, if they really are a problem in terms of the overall blend.

There will be times we'll know the Chardonnay has a particularly strong character that year and chances are we're not going to want to use as much of it. But we'll go ahead with that blending process, knowing there may be sections we want to pull out.

You do that for all four varietals? The next thing is you have to find the proper blend of the varietals together?

In fact, we tend to do that of a piece. Obviously we have vineyards that we're buying from and we hope that we're going to use most of those wines. So hopefully, we're looking roughly in the right proportions. If, for example, something crops light and we know we're out of balance, then we know that in advance and so we'll play with that. But we'll always look at trying to incorporate that in and then retreating from it. So we'll separate out those things we think are interesting to paint with because the wines of stronger flavors and more interesting characters are the ones that can really make a difference to the blend. Even though they may only constitute five percent of the wine, you can add just a little bit of that to a blend and really see a difference.

You're probably the best person to explain autolysis. What happens with that secondary fermentation in the bottle? And what happens as those yeast cells break down?

First you have the secondary fermentation itself, which is a straightforward alcoholic fermentation. What you do is put a known quantity of yeast cells in, enough cells so that they will ferment the rest of the available sugars in the bottle.

Autolysis actually starts after about eight or nine months. During the secondary fermentation you actually have a decrease of amino acids and proteins in the wine because the yeast take them into the cell body. Immediately following the fermentation, those are returned to the wine solution. Then it's not until the cells actually begin to break down that you begin to see increases in the proteins and the amino acids. The cells are pretty whole up until eight or nine months in the bottle. In fact, after three or four years, you can look at the sediment under the microscope and still find whole yeast cells; they're not completely gone.

What's happening is that the outer cell wall of the yeast cell is opening up and the constituents of that cell itself, which have been contained by the cell, spill out into the wine. So the proteins are released into the wine and then those proteins, over time, degrade into their amino acid constituents.

How does that affect the flavor of the sparkling wine?

I think that the thing you can attribute most directly to yeast autolysis is the textural characteristics of the wine. As the wine ages in contact with the yeast and as autolysis takes place, you have more and more of those rich, creamy, textural palate impressions of the wine. There's no question that there's a whole range of aromatic compounds that come from the yeast breaking down. Most of those, clinically, are sulfur compounds. They're anaerobic sulfurs that are just a bit skunky. If we were polite, we'd call them coffee or toast type characteristics, but they are in fact sulfur compounds. Striving for those qualities in the wine is a little tough, just by their nature. If they're overdone, they're too much for the wine. The straight and narrow of how you might get more or less of that kind of character, the yeast break down character, is very hard. Not to denigrate the role that yeast plays in what a sparkling wine is, but I think we may sometimes overlook the role the actual base wines themselves play and their ability to show off those characteristics. For example, one of the things

I've noticed in the Pinot Meunier that has been on the yeast for a year is it definitely has more of that bread/yeast character. The yeast in all of them is the same, but there's something in the nature of the fruit or the wine that is allowing that to show at a stage in its development when there's not a whole lot of autolysis that has happened. It is anaerobic so there may be some of those kinds of those things going on but it would be hard to call them autolytic characters.

I think Chardonnays, a problem for us historically, tend to hold that character more strongly. You see it in barrel fermented, lees-contacted Chardonnays, those are Champagne-type characteristics. We've fought so much with the strong flavor characteristics of our Chardonnays. We have a couple of mountain vineyards where the fruit character tends to be a little more subdued early on so that we can get away with a higher percentage of Chardonnay. We have small lots which tend to show more of what you think of, in Champagne terms, as autolysis characters.

The term "yeasty" as applied to the finished product of sparkling wine is a misnomer. Doesn't it manifest itself as more of a toastiness?

It's a tough one. If you look at it really straightforward, in terms of why you would use the word "yeasty," it either has to smell like yeast or you are assuming that there's a causal relationship between the smell that you're getting and the yeast. I think most, if not all, sparkling winemakers would say that, when push comes to shove, they would have a hard time saying that particular character was always just yeast.

The Domaine Chandon Reserve was first released in 1987. How do you select the lots for the Reserve?

We're lucky in that particular program. The Reserve is our brut blend that is aged longer. So it's a finished blend. It's a wine that's going to be brut or Reserve and we have a couple of extra years to make that decision. We watch it over a longer period of time. We're able to see it through the secondary fermentation and watch it for a good twelve to eighteen months before we have to decide if it fits into the Reserve program. If you would follow through the analogy with Champagne, our Reserve would be like a vintage blend of Champagne. So we're looking at something that has flavor characteristics that we think will stand up to longer aging. We don't see that every year. Those blends are complex enough, in terms of the number of components they carry, that it makes more sense to talk about the major year of that blend. For example, 1982 was a very good year for us. And the brut blends from 1982 were worthy of extra aging. At some point in the future, we would like to make something that would be a special blend that would maybe not be made every single year, like the Reserve, but would also be extra selective, in terms of the vineyard resources. From my perspective, I am seeing that now, in terms of certain vineyard lots that show consistent characteristics and quality year in and year out. We're in an interesting situation in that we are a large enough producer that we really don't want to do anything not characteristic of the style we've developed. So we're very conservative about approaching that project.

What's the single greatest Champagne you ever tasted and why?

A 1952 Moët that I tasted just a couple of years ago at a funny little restaurant in France that has an in with the cellars in Champagne. Actually I tasted a prephylloxera wine, which was not so much good but which was just fascinating to experience.

I can't think of a wine where the light bulb really went off and I said, "Oh, this is perfection. Why look any further?" It's still absolutely essential to me that there be variety in wines.

Randall Grahm
BONNY DOON VINEYARD

*"Anarchism is really the way I'd characterize
my technique."*

He's been called "eccentric," "idiosyncratic," "avant garde," "on the cutting edge" and "marching to the beat of a different drummer." The nation's most influential wine critic, Robert M. Parker, Jr., describes him as "a national treasure." In just a few short years at Bonny Doon Vineyard, Randall Grahm has generated the kind of press clippings that Hollywood would envy. But this is one case where the reputation is well deserved. Grahm's unique wines did the talking for him first; adulation from the wine press and consumers soon followed. Additionally, his caustic wit and dry sense of humor have made him the most demanded speaker on the wine symposium circuit.

After graduation from UC Santa Cruz as a philosophy major, Randall was unsure about life after college when he took a job at a wine store in his hometown of Beverly Hills. Never having set foot in a winery, he developed more than just a passing interest in wine and enrolled in winemaking courses at UC Davis. Graduating with a degree in plant science, ever confident, he only had to acquire the conventional knowledge of viticulture and winemaking. Once he understood the university propagated norms, however, he embraced the ones that fit into his winemaking philosophy and discarded the ones that did not.

The Bonny Doon label was established in 1981, followed by the completion of the winery in 1983. Possessed of a curious mind, he began to explore Rhone varietals, feeling that California's climate was well matched to little known grapes like Syrah, Grenache, Mourvedre, Marsanne, Roussanne and Viognier. As consumers acquired new tastes for these Rhone style wines, he has been thrust into the media spotlight as an unofficial spokesperson for "The Rhone Rangers," a loose confederation of winemakers whose goal is to produce the finest Rhone style wines in California.

His wide-ranging curiosity has also been instrumental in reviving interest in other arcane wine categories like eaux-de-vie and grappa as well as his "Vin de Glaciere" and fruit infusion dessert wines. Recently his interest has turned to Italian winemaking with the release of food friendly wines under his Ca' del Solo label. "It seems there are no rules in Italy anymore," he says, which certainly meshes with his style of winemaking anarchy.

You were a Pinot Noir fanatic when you were at UC Davis. Originally you thought Bonny Doon was a perfect environment for Pinot Noir. What did you learn that changed your mind?

I selected Bonny Doon (just north of Santa Cruz) because I believed it was really appropriate for Pinot Noir. Now I understand better; I have come to think that it's too warm for Pinot Noir, which really needs to be grown in a pretty marginal climate. There are other reasons for the failure. I don't think we really had the best clonal material. Maybe I just didn't give it enough time. It might have turned out better if I had given the vines more time. The problem was I was buying better Pinot Noir grapes out of Oregon; unless I could produce grapes as good as I could buy, there was no point in doing it. So that's why I abandoned Pinot Noir, at least at Bonny Doon.

You were a Pinot Noir fanatic? And a total Burgundian fanatic also? What led to your love affair with Rhone wines?

At the time, I still was a wine consumer above all. I hooked up with Kermit Lynch (wine importer) and he got me interested in Rhone wines. Eventually, I traveled over there and I was tremendously impressed with the people and the wines. I was also struck with the climatic similarity between the Rhone and much of coastal California. So I began experimenting on a small scale. In 1982, I had made a little Grenache. In 1983, I made some Syrah. In 1984, I made Syrah and Grenache, which ultimately went into the Le Cigare Volant bottling. It wasn't so long ago actually. But I was fortunate my intuition was fulfilled. Sometimes my intuitions are totally wrong. In this case, it was right. I was really lucky to have such instant validation of my hypothesis. I could have just as easily tried Grenache and it could have come out with no color and no flavor, and that would have been the end of it. But it turned out that this was just a great Grenache vineyard. Subsequently I've bought grapes from other Grenache vineyards that produced totally insipid wines.

What do you perceive as similar between the Rhone and coastal California?

When you talk about the Rhone, you really have to distinguish between the northern and the southern Rhone. The northern Rhone has a fairly unique, distinctive microclimate. Growing Syrah grapes requires clearly fastidious or rigorous growing conditions. The most important thing is that it be relatively cool and that the grapes receive a tremendous amount of light. Over and over, you find the best northern Rhone vineyards on slopes that get a full day's sunshine. The soil must be very poor. Pretty much I find that if you grow Syrah in a soil that's not too rich and under fairly cool conditions, you'll end up with a wine that's got good character.

In the southern Rhone, you get quite a bit of sunshine. Again, you need low soil fertility. It's warm but it's not so blisteringly warm that the wines have no character. I think a lot of our coastal California climate falls under these conditions. You might want to call it high Region II or low Region III. I think that it's really a perfect spot for southern Rhone grapes.

I should also add, the chief similarity is a lot of sunshine and no summer rain. The grapes ripen to full maturity without rot or other problems, so they are clean, flavorful and fruity. Whereas grapes grown in more of a continental climate may not fully ripen and may have problems with rot. They're not as clean or as expressive.

What about your own vineyard at Bonny Doon near Santa Cruz? Don't you get a lot of rainfall?

A lot of winter rain, but I don't think that really has much bearing on the quality of the grapes. Indirectly, the soils are fairly leached out; they're not fertile soils. They're sandy and light. Bonny Doon is temperate; maybe a low Region II, above the fog line, but with a good deal of marine influence. We get bright days with a lot of great sunshine and fairly temperate weather. I believe our climate is perfectly suited for northern Rhone varieties. I'm not sure if we have enough heat for southern Rhone varieties, although I have some new theories and want to try growing some southern Rhone grapes.

What was your approach viticulturally, as far as clonal variety, spacing and trellising?

These are very complex and somewhat painful issues for me. We started from scratch. I tried to get the best clonal material I could find. Basically, I looked for vineyards in California producing wines I liked. I looked at the grapes and tried to find those with the most character. A lot of it was intuitive and maybe a little bit premature. I wish I had about ten years maturity or experience before I started this process. I would have saved many, many dollars.

Which leads to the question: "If you knew what you know now, what would you have done differently?"

Virtually everything. It's been fits and starts. Many of the things that I was groping for intuitively, were steps in the right direction but I had an imperfect understanding of the whole process. Take close spacing, for example. I started the vineyard with six by eight foot spacing, which is fairly close. Then I went to France and got a dose of close spacing religion and ended up interplanting the vineyard. So I am now three foot by eight foot, which I think basically is all to the good.

The problem has been getting a trellising system that will deal with the amount of canopy, the amount of growth that you get in this kind of dense spacing. It's been frustrating because we end up with such a dense canopy that the plants end up shading one another and don't give fruitful buds. Without fruitful buds, there's no crop. The vines grow ever more vegetatively and we get caught in a vicious cycle. Then I started thinking about how I could spread the canopy out. I then went to a split canopy. I had a divided canopy whereby I had two columns of foliage. The problem was they weren't spread out far enough; they were a foot apart and it still wasn't far enough. I spread them two feet apart and it wasn't far enough; they were still growing together. Now, gradually I'm moving in the right direction. The problem is that these things are tedious and expensive to retrofit. Currently, I'm looking at changing over to what they call a Scott Henry two tier canopy or a modification of that. If I do that, the canopy will be spread out to the point where the canes are exposed. I think that will work well but I'm not there yet. If I could have started out at that point, I would have been miles ahead.

What kind of yield were you looking for originally?

It was just pie in the sky. Again like a Burgundian true believer, I felt that limiting the yield was important. At this point, I feel, however, that I know nothing about viticulture, in a sense, that I have to relearn everything. The conditions that exist in Europe do not in California. On the face of it, it does not appear that restricting the yield to a fixed amount gives the same results as in Europe. I think you need to take elements of what we know in California and what we believe in France and somehow make a synthesis. There's no road map. There's no one who can say, "This is what you have to do."

It's hard to get the big picture. Viticulturally, you may think you want a particular trellising system but there are so many other components making up the winemaking regime that if you just change one component, you've changed the whole equation.

To give an example, the big question you have to look at is how to manage the vigor of the vines. In France, you can grow vines a meter by a meter and a half because the soil is so lean. They have poor soil, a limited amount of sunlight and nematodes and viruses that we don't have. We do the same thing here, planting our vines not even that close together and we end up with so much vigor that we literally cannot manage the vines. So, as I plant additional vineyards, I'm looking at devigorating rootstocks or what I can do physiologically to get the vines to function as they do in Europe in a great vintage. How can I simulate those conditions?

And really, we don't know. Because if we do the same things here, the results are not necessarily the same?

Exactly. When I was at UC Davis and thinking about Pinot Noir, it was sort of a joke that every week I would have a new revelation. One week limestone soil was the answer; the next week it was surface area to volume ratio; the next week it was close spacing.

I'm kind of going back to certain theoretical models in my thinking now. I'm trying to create growing conditions that will produce the most intense fruit, given my understanding of how grapes function physiologically. I keep going back to cool, temperate climates, long growing days and well exposed vines that get a full day of sun and a tremendous amount of light. If there were one key, that would be it.

Will the next big leap in quality come from the vineyard?

We've got the vinification down, I think. We understand that well. The next improvement must come from growing better grapes. I think our winemaking is really sound. Again, in Europe, in a great vintage, most everyone makes really good wine. It's not because someone came through that village in the spring and gave everyone enology lessons. Something happened out in the vineyard such that the grapes arrived in real good shape.

Do you consider yourself to be a traditionalist winemaker?

I don't know; I don't consider myself to be anything. I like to look at what has gone before. I like to study old winemaking techniques. But basically I see myself as an empiricist and do what works. I want to try as many different things as I can. If it works, I'm going to use it. I really see myself as being experimental. I use whatever way is most expeditious, if it gives me the result I want, whether it's an old technique or a new technique. It turns out often that it's a very old technique.

Why do you think that is?

Because things were valued differently. I believe there was more value placed on quality previously than now. People do things now for a number of reasons but I don't think quality is always foremost in their minds. Winemaking is done with many motives. Quality is one of them; cost is another. So are producing the wine quickly, turning the tanks over quickly and having the consumers accept it.

Great winemaking can be pretty expensive. Certainly the conditions that existed one hundred years ago in European vineyards will never exist again. They had unlimited cheap labor; that's never going to happen again. Maybe we will be clever and resourceful enough to mechanize to the point where we can simulate some of those conditions. Maybe we will have machines to do things that once required hundreds of people. But whatever we do, it's probably going to be different.

Wine is made in the vineyard?

I agree with that completely.

Are you just the caretaker of the wine? How do you view your role?

I don't know; you can't be objective about your own contribution. I believe that my strength as a winemaker is my good palate. I'm not a really great technician but I'm smart enough or experienced enough to know if I've done something good, even if I've done it that way by accident. I'm clever enough to realize that it is good and I will try to figure out how to do it again. Another strength is that I have a background in viticulture; I think a lot about the viticultural contribution to the wine. If I ever make really great wines, I think it will be my viticultural interest that will enable me to do that.

Where are you getting your Syrah grapes?

Right now I'm buying them from the Bien Nacido vineyards in Santa Barbara County and I'm growing some myself. I'm not getting any more Syrah from Paso Robles.

What do you find are the differences in the Syrah from the different areas?

The Bien Nacido Syrah is aggressive, very flavorful and aromatic. Our own vineyard Syrah may not have the varietal intensity but it seems to have slightly more concentration and depth. Hopefully, I can improve on the aromatics and they can improve on the depth.

What are you looking for as ripeness in Syrah, as far as the numbers? Do you play the numbers game?

Yes and no. I'm trying to play the numbers game less and less. I'm trying to get to the point where I'm really looking at flavor more than anything else.

And how do you determine that? Just to your own taste?

Really by taste. I'd like to look at certain phenological measurements. You could look at the level of anthocyanins in the grape and that's often a good indicator of ripeness. The problem is that it involves a lot of analysis and often these determinations have to be made posthaste. So you don't have the luxury. You can pretend that these things are very scientific and very analytical but often it depends on when I can get a truck down there for picking, or, "It looks like it's going to be 104F degrees tomorrow so we better pick now." It's often a logistical thing.

I look at pH. But again, every vineyard is different. I also look at the number of days from flowering; that often is about as useful as anything else.

Obviously, you keep every lot from every vineyard separate?

It is separate, although, on occasion, logistics will compel us to consolidate or improvise. One year, for example, the Syrah came in very ripe. Also there was a lot less than I thought so we were only able to fill the tank half way. We had some Grenache coming in about a week later. I've always wanted to coferment Grenache and Syrah, so I ended up crushing the Grenache on top of the Syrah. The Grenache was a little lower in sugar than I would have liked, so it really sort of worked itself out just fine. That was one of the components of Le Cigare Volant.

Explain what Le Cigare Volant is all about.

Le Cigare Volant is my loose rendition of a Chateauneuf-du-Pape. Who knows what it will evolve into but that's what it started out as. It's a blend that's primarily Grenache based; I use Syrah, Mourvedre and when I can find it, Cinsault. Ultimately I'd like to have all thirteen Chateauneuf-du-Pape varieties but I know I'm dreaming.

Explain what Old Telegram is all about.

Old Telegram is one hundred percent Mourvedre. I make it when I can make it distinct from Le Cigare Volant; when I have lots of Mourvedre that is special enough or distinctive enough to really bring out the Mourvedre character. I made it in 1986 and again in 1988. If my understanding of how to bring out this Mourvedre character improves enough, I can perhaps make it every year.

How do you handle the Mourvedre grape?

Mourvedre is an interesting grape. I like whole cluster fermentation for Mourvedre. I think that's really the way to go. The stems make a big contribution to the wine, adding a nice spiciness. Again, these are Mourvedre grapes from a fairly warm climate in Oakley. If I were growing Mourvedre in a cool climate, I might consider destemming them.

You've been on a recent rampage to plant the white Rhone grapes: Marsanne, Roussanne and Viognier. Why are you interested in those grapes in California?

I think they're exquisite. All things considered, I think they will produce the most interesting white wines in California. I think I can say that with some certainty, although there will be people who will disagree with me. These grapes do well in our warmer climate. The problem in California is that, when you grow grapes in a warm climate, often they will just not retain much in the way of nuance or perfume. With these varieties, when you grow them in a slightly warmer climate, they still have the spiciness and the fragrance. I think that's what we need in California. We need wines with some degree of elegance. On a real preliminary basis, at Bonny Doon, these grapes have it.

Are you presently bottling Marsanne or Roussanne?

We've done a blend of Marsanne and Roussanne called Le Sophiste. We have fifty cases in a good year. I feel like the boy who cried "Marsanne" or the boy who cried "Viognier." I keep threatening to release all these wines but we just can't seem to get our vineyards into production. One of these days it will come. I have problems with gophers. The first year they wiped out a quarter of our vines. I have problems with yellow jackets attacking the fruit. But I'm slowly working these things out; it's just taking a while.

You have said that our preoccupation with Chardonnay and Cabernet may just be a passing fad; "varietal imperialism," you called it. That, in twenty years, we may have taken to all these other varietals that you're talking about.

I said that somewhat gratuitously but I actually believe it. I really do. I don't think Cabernet or Chardonnay will be extinct but I feel that varieties like Marsanne, Roussanne and Viognier will have a much more prominent role. They'll be the dominant white grape varieties in the future.

The problem, of course, is that we're trying to grow premium grape varieties in California but we just haven't looked in the right places. Sauvignon Blanc is not the answer for California. Even the other grape varieties we've experimented with, like Pinot Blanc, are not warm climate grapes. They are cool climate grapes and should probably be grown in Oregon. If we're serious in California about producing high quality grapes, the first places I'd look is Rhone, Provence and Italy. Those are the grapes we should be experimenting with here. There's a Provencal variety called Rolle, a truly interesting grape. When I was at UC Davis recently, I was excited because they seemed to have some plants of the Rolle variety. It turns out that they did have it, they indexed it and the plants died; now there are none. Unfortunately, UC Davis has no money to acquire these varieties and index them. We're really not making a lot of progress in that respect.

There are also Italian grapes like Nebbiolo and Sangiovese.

Sangiovese, I think, is the red variety in California's future. Perhaps as much so as Syrah. I think the most interesting wines being made right now are Sangioveses in Tuscany. They're incredible, simply incredible.

Generally, what are your vinification practices?

I do a couple of different things. I do some whole clusters; it's actually not a true carbonic maceration. I begin it whole cluster and then midway through the fermentation I take the tops off of the variable fermentation tanks and really stomp the grapes very well. Then the fermentation is finished with the top off. Part of it will get conventional California techniques, punching down and pumping over. I like the variable capacity tanks because we can get in on the top of the tank and manipulate the grape cap easily. I can also seal up the tanks for a long cuvaison. I leave the wine in the tanks for three or four weeks, which is a long cuvaison for California.

You're talking about the Grenache, Syrah and Mourvedre. How long does fermentation take?

Usually ten to fourteen days; I'll leave it in an additional week after it's gone dry. By putting the top on and lowering the lid to just over the level of the cap, I can protect the wine from oxidation or acetification and just leave it.

What does that do for the wine?

I think it really improves the extract and gives the wine a lot more depth.

What about the Marsanne and Roussanne? Are they all barrel fermented?

Such as it is, yes. Two barrels worth!

I mean, traditional French methods: barrel fermented and aged on the lees?

Well, I'm not so sure if there's any such thing as a traditional technique.

As opposed to a California technique, with fermentation in stainless steel?

If you go over to the Rhone, you see fermenters that look like something out of "The Nutty Professor." Most of it is done in stainless steel; very little is done in barrels. These people don't have a lot of money to spend on their winemaking. You'll see epoxy-lined tanks and not that much temperature control. Stainless steel is a pretty radical development in most places. It's real primitive there. I'm not sure frankly whether barrel fermentation is the answer for Marsanne. This is a really radical thing for me to say, being a Burgundian at heart, but I'm not sure Burgundian winemaking is necessarily the way to go. Perhaps cool, temperature controlled fermentation is the way to go. I really haven't made up my mind yet on the appropriate technique for California. Having never had enough wine to work with, I have to ferment it in the barrel because it's the only thing that's small enough.

Aren't there a lot of French models for the wines you're talking about? Is that model the starting point for you?

It was the starting point. As I said before, I think the most interesting wines are being made in Italy, where there seems to be no more rules. Anarchism is really the way I'd characterize my technique. When you start thinking about blending Rhone varieties with Burgundian varieties with Italian varieties, who knows where it will end? I don't want to limit myself. For a while, when I first started this Rhone binge, I thought I'd just be a Rhone kind of guy and just do Rhone varieties. But then why limit yourself?

You have your hands in so many things at Bonny Doon. You do fruit infusion wines, which are fermented fruit (raspberry, blackberry or strawberry) with neutral grape spirits. What is the process for producing them?

We take incredibly ripe fruit and let it ferment slightly and then infuse them with high proof spirits in which the fruit macerates. We purchase the high proof spirits because we're not set up to distill that efficiently or economically. The fruit macerates for six weeks, then we press it and bottle it. It's really not the main thrust of our business; we just do it for fun. Originally, for economic reasons, I thought it would be an efficient use of the facility in the off time, when a lot of crushing and winemaking activity isn't going on. As it turns out, I decided I only like Washington state berries. The strawberries have to be very fresh and it turns out they come in two weeks before harvest. So it's a big mess; it ends up conflicting with harvest and becoming a big pain in the neck, but we do it anyway.

You also do eaux-de-vie?

We're doing a number of fruit eaux-de-vie: apples, cherries, pears and apricots. We're doing a grappa too. The grappa is made by fermenting and distilling the skins and the juice together. I think that stuff is great. We're also doing marc from the skins of the grapes that go into the Le Cigare Volant. So obviously that would be called Marc de Cigare.

We also do the ice wines; actually I shouldn't say that. They are "Vins de Glaciere," which translates as "wines of the icebox." These are wines that are made by harvesting grapes at fairly normal ripeness and maturity. Again, we're harvesting for flavor. When we get the maximum flavor intensity, then that's when we'll pick. We then freeze the grapes. We bring them up to the winery and press them while they are frozen. Actually they've just begun to thaw. What this does is concentrate the sugar in the juice considerably. The juice is settled and the wine is fermented. It's a fairly normal fermentation; we use a couple of different yeast strains. It ferments until it stops; we don't stop it. I've found the starting numbers that give us the ending numbers we want with those wines. So the fermentation takes care of itself. It's pretty straightforward. We ferment very cool and simply filter and bottle it. We do it in the off season when we're not doing a lot of other things so we can really give it our full attention. It's very labor intensive but it's the only thing we're doing at that time so it's not a real hardship at all.

Do great grapes equal great wine? If you have great grapes, how can you go wrong?

Generally you can't. If you avoid screwing up a good thing, the wine's going to come out just fine. When you go to Burgundy and talk with people who are all making wines differently and all are turning out well, you come away with the idea that there's no answer. If there is an answer, it's the fact that they really have some wonderful grapes in their vineyards. There are many roads to make wine that will come out just fine. But the whole key is starting out with the right grapes.

The only thing that I really believe with regard to winemaking techniques is that I don't believe filtration benefits red wines. I think that generally the less you do to the wine, the better it turns out.

What about racking and fining for the red wines?

If I have a tannic red wine, like Cabernet or Syrah, I obviously rack those wines more often and expose them to oxygen a lot more. I believe that more delicate wines, like Grenache, do not benefit from racking. I generally like to leave the wines alone, partially because we're really busy and we don't have the time to mess around with it. Generally we don't rack the wines very much. We do fining trials every year and find that we don't like the results as much as we like the wine just left by itself. We never filter red wines; I really feel that strips the wine. We like low levels of sulfur dioxide but I'm aware that this can be a dicey business. I keep an eye out for brettanomyces.

I like to put white wines through malolactic fermentation, if possible, to avoid the necessity of sterile filtering. If a wine doesn't completely go through malolactic, then I sterile filter. I do it when I have to, but somewhat reluctantly.

Some winemakers say that if you don't filter red wines, you may have an unstable product on store shelves?

If the winemaking is sound, the product will be stable. If the wine is fermented to dryness, if it has finished malolactic fermentation, if you don't have any microbiological problems, then there shouldn't be a problem.

You have great press clippings! Among other things, you're described as, "eccentric, idiosyncratic, avant garde, on the cutting edge, marching to the beat of a different drummer and a national treasure." How do you react to these kind of comments?

Sometimes it just sort of shocks me. Just last night, at a tasting, I was shocked at the intensity of interest and the admiration, if you will. I feel somehow unworthy of it. I think I have to be careful that it doesn't go to my head. Part of the problem is, from a strictly business standpoint, once the propaganda machine is in place, you sort of have to keep it going. I've kind of created this monster where people want to hear me and talk to me. I understand it's part of the business and I don't mind doing all the promotional things. At a certain point, it really does begin to take away from your time. The problem is you really can't turn back the clock. It's difficult to tell people they can't see me because I'm too busy. Then they perceive you as arrogant.

The ironic thing, of course, is that I never really tried very hard to do any of this stuff. But I have so many projects, I just wish there were more hours in the day. I feel myself being pulled in so many different directions that I think I want to just sort of step back and consider where I'm going. It sometimes seems like a runaway train.

David Graves

and

Richard Ward

SAINTSBURY

*"I would argue that the level of achievement in Pinot Noir has shown
the greatest improvement of any variety of the decade."*

If partners David Graves and Richard Ward ever decide to give up winemaking, they might make a go of it as a comedy act along the lines of Abbott and Costello. They have worked side by side for so long they seem like brothers, finishing each other's sentences without missing a beat. Graves is the garrulous one and quick to joke, while Ward, with his wry sense of humor, is the perfect straight man. It's no joke, however, that within a decade's time, they have established a reputation for producing complex Chardonnay and Pinot Noir from Carneros grapes.

Graves and Ward met at UC Davis where they were both studying winemaking, although neither finished his degree work because the siren song of the vineyards and the real world of winemaking beckoned. They did learn, however, just enough to be dangerous and more than enough to know that winemaking would be their chosen career. Graves got hands-on experience at Chappellet, Joseph Phelps and Domaine Chandon, while Ward paid his dues at Stag's Leap Wine Cellars, Pine Ridge and Santa Ynez Winery. In 1981, they finally put together a plan for a joint venture that they had always talked about: crushing in leased facilities and producing 3,000 cases of wine. They named their enterprise "Saintsbury," after George Saintsbury, a literary scholar, whose slim volume, *Notes on a Cellar-Book*, has become a cult classic on wine appreciation since its publication in 1920. By 1983, they had formed a limited partnership, raised a substantial amount of money and built a rustic, wooden barn winery in Carneros.

Today, due to the demand for their wines, they have expanded the winery to a production capacity of 36,000 cases, continuing to focus on Pinot Noir and Chardonnay. They were one of the first wineries to utilize Carneros grapes and feature the appellation prominently on their label. "Saintsbury," they say, "is very much a work in progress." A vertical tasting of their wines confirms that a great deal of progress has already been made and it may now be only a matter of refining those small, but all important details. Each harvest, they examine their assumptions and attempt to find ways they can make a positive contribution in improving their wines.

What was your winemaking approach in the beginning and how has it evolved over time?

Graves: There was some confidence about the direction we wanted to go. I think both of us feel that one trait we share is confidence in our abilities. It may be misplaced occasionally but I don't think there was a lot of agonizing, at the beginning, about what to do. We felt we had a plan, in terms of a winemaking style. Neither of us cared for the then current high alcohol and high oak style of Chardonnay. What followed that style, the foodwine style, was, in some ways, equally bad. There was a willingness to accept certain styles that were a little bit out of the mainstream. They have become more assimilated into the mainstream since. But we did not agonize over making barrel fermented, malolactic Chardonnay. This is not an evolutionary thing for us. This is what we did from the outset.

Let me walk you through how we started to make Chardonnay and what's changed about that since we began. We only make Chardonnay and Pinot Noir; that's why our T-shirt says, "Beaune in the U.S.A." That's pretty much our focus and has been since we started. We always had a cool climate sourcing of fruit. Western Sonoma County, where Iron Horse Winery is, and Carneros were the sources of Chardonnay for the first two years. In 1983, we became essentially a Carneros winery. We cut loose the western Sonoma fruit, not because we didn't like it but because we wanted to be focused in terms of an appellation. I think that area still has a lot of interest in doing a different version of the same kind of wines we make. Obviously they are not going to taste like Carneros wines but they'll be of very high quality.

We didn't care for skin contact of the Chardonnay as a style. We had decided to abandon sulfites and let the juice be relatively oxidized. Obviously we looked after the wine carefully. But the juice was allowed to brown. We were committed to fermenting from juice into wine in barrel; in other words, when we barrel ferment, it's juice that goes into the barrel at 23.0 brix with the yeast cells. We're not able to put a lot of juice into the barrels because the juice has a very riotous early period of fermentation. Finally, we add malolactic bacteria. We started the malolactic fermentation in the first vintage. Every vintage of our wine has gone through malolactic fermentation, basically to completion.

This remains the basic outline of what we do. I think a lot more wine is made that way now than when we started. Now you can call that inside luck, or the market moving toward that style. As soon as we could afford them, we were using all Burgundy coopered barrels. We have shied away from a heavy toast on the barrels. I think our wines have gradually gotten a little more oak character as we evolved and understood our vineyards better. We use about thirty percent new barrels every year. To break in a Pinot Noir barrel, we ferment Chardonnay in it. You can imagine the logistics. If you're filling the barrels with forty-eight gallons of juice and you want to end up with all the white barrels full, you're not going to have enough barrels to barrel ferment the wine. The other consideration is that we don't necessarily want new oak character, from a brand new barrel that's never had wine in it, as a character of the Pinot Noir. We tend to go for a light to medium toast on all our barrels. We use Vosges and Nevers more than Allier in Chardonnay; Allier and Nevers in Pinot Noir. We are now retiring barrels after their fourth vintage. But if you go in the cellar, there are a lot more old barrels there now than there will be next year because, as we've grown, we've wanted to have a ballast of old barrels to counteract the growth and volume that came from new barrels. If we used only new barrels, we'd end up with wines that are oakier than the house style.

What you're saying is that your original concepts from the first vintage are sound. You're continuing on and refining them?

Graves: We're more aware of the positive benefits of lees contact now. We're not stirrers at this point. But we make little attempt to clean up the wine. Everything gets pumped out of barrel so that the whole lot can finish malolactic. We sulfite the entire lot; then we resuspend the lees in the tank and put that lot back into barrels. We don't top; we don't move the wine. We've abandoned racking the lots of Chardonnay unless they become stinky. Basically they're left undisturbed from the time they are sulfited until they are racked up to be bottled. That's also true of the Pinot Noir. As the average vine age has risen, we have realized that there's enough richness in ninety percent of the Chardonnay to stand on its own. Then there's another ten percent, the richest of all, that can turn into what we call the reserve bottling, which is the logical end point of our winemaking style with Chardonnay from Carneros. In other words, in January we taste the lots blind and then select the richest three or so to become candidates for the reserve wine.

Ward: Traditionally, our regular Chardonnay has not been that impressive when young. A lot of people think it's a delicious wine. But the wine writers out there who are plugging the world's greatest Chardonnays to buy have not often included ours. But when they come back and taste it six or eight years later, it's suddenly a lot more impressive compared to the other wines they've been plugging early on. The reserve gives us a chance to say that we're making wines that have plenty of richness but also delicacy, like the great white Burgundies. We've never had that opportunity in California. When you have richness, it's often because you end up with high alcohol and totally sacrifice delicacy.

In fermenting the Chardonnay, do you inoculate or go with wild yeasts?

Graves: We throw Ed, the wine cat, in the fermenter, let him swim around in the juice a bit, then haul him out. He's been in the vineyards and has gotten wild yeast on his coat!

Ward: The answer to that is: both. We don't do anything to inhibit wild yeast; at the same time, we inoculate with pure culture. We've tended toward inoculating with smaller and smaller amounts of pure culture.

Do you inoculate in order to feel more secure about the fermentation?

Graves: Given that we have a low sulfite environment, we're sure that the yeast is there but we do want our wines to go dry and not have too many aldehydic or other off characters. It's the same when we inoculate with malolactic bacteria. The increment of quality from wild fermentation is probably small compared to the risks of degrading the final product as a result of fermentation difficulties.

What's your cellar regime for filtering and fining the Chardonnay?

Ward: In general, we try to do as little as possible. Each year we end up probably coming closer to that ideal of doing only what is necessary and nothing in addition. The wines are put to bed dirty in barrel. There is no intervention from the time they finish malolactic until the time we rack them up to get them ready for bottling. For Chardonnay, we tend to fine. In Burgundy, traditionally, white wines have always been fined. We're not talking about fining with bentonite here because that's more of a stability factor rather than what we consider fining, i.e., to make a wine more fine. In Burgundy, it's traditionally done, while in California, it's not; although there's been a reverse in trend, in the last few years. So we would look at casein for fining Chardonnay with small amounts of PVPP to look at the total fraction of molecular weight phenolics in the wine. We're talking about one-eighth or one-sixth of a pound per thousand. Each year is slightly different. Our idea of no SO_2, oxidation of phenolics in the juice, natural fining during barrel fermentation and rapid pressing leads to a generally low overall phenolic level in white wines. So we're really talking about minor adjustments right before bottling. Maybe we'll use tiny amounts of isinglass for clarity.

In terms of filtration, we'd be looking at a diatomaceous earth filtration with a follow-up of sterile pads. In the past, we've tried not to sterile filter the Chardonnay but our malolactic cultures are so active that they do not die and settle out; we end up with lots of malolactic bacteria in a filtered wine unless we filter through sterile pads.

Graves: The wines are stable. 1982 was the last year the wines didn't finish malolactic completely. They're very much through malolactic but the perpetrators are still floating around. Even with an extended period of not being disturbed and with a careful racking, the bacteria are still abundant in the tank.

Ward: If you sample a barrel that's been sitting there for six months untouched and put it under the microscope, there are a few yeast cells but lots of malolactic bacteria. They're not going to be removed unless you're sterile filtering.

Why put the Chardonnay through malolactic fermentation? What are the benefits and the side effects of doing it?

Ward: One aspect of Carneros is that, in cooler years like 1985, 1986 and 1987, we have higher malic acid content in Chardonnay than practically any other Chardonnay growing region in the world. It's higher than Burgundy, higher than Oregon and higher than the Central Coast. As a result, if we don't put it through malolactic, the titratable acidity is quite high and you get that green apple, harsh, treble end Chardonnay. You get so much of your titratable acidity as malic acid that, in a year like 1986, you would have to end up deacidulating, not from the aspect of the numbers you're getting but from the aspect of taste balance.

Graves: There are also some flavor characters that change in a positive way when you add some of this complexity. We haven't done a nonmalolactic Chardonnay ever here. Our colleagues, who have more time to indulge in these things, have done these and have reached the same conclusion we have over three years, as they've gone from ten percent malolactic to one hundred percent malolactic with fruit from basically the same vineyards, using the same production techniques that we use. We often observe, when we pour wine for people, that sometimes they're surprised the wine has gone through malolactic because it doesn't have the overblown malolactic character with a butterscotchy taste.

Why is that?

Graves: Well, I think our bugs (bacteria) don't necessarily lend themselves to that. They're efficient and relatively tolerant of being in wine, so they finish the job fairly early. They're growing in the presence of yeast because we inoculate during the primary fermentation. The yeast seems to take up some of the malolactic bug by-products, especially diacetyl, and therefore reduces that butterscotchy aroma. Because the musts are naturally suited to this, we don't end up with flat, oily characters. I think that oiliness is what has led people to believe that malolactic is not appropriate in Chardonnay. It's the caricature of malolactic that they hold up as the reason they don't like malolactic. I don't think most people would hold our wine up and say this is the reason they don't like malolactic.

There is apparent fruit character in the wine as well. In other words, you don't just add French oak, barrel toast, lees character and malolactic aromas. Those things are there but they are balanced against a strong fruit component. Dick mentioned earlier the aging of the Chardonnays. I think they do develop in a way that's interesting with time. If you were interested in bottle aging Chardonnay, I think ours have performed better than I thought they would early on. Our first vintages, in many ways, entered a graceful middle age and have been there for quite a while.

Are you looking for fruit or complexity in your Chardonnay? Or are you looking for a balance of both?

Ward: We're looking for a balance. That's what it's all about. We don't want too much malolactic character and we don't want too much bright fruit. We want the wine well integrated, because if well integrated when young, it's likely to be well integrated when it's old. It will age gracefully.

Some winemakers don't care about the fruit and are more concerned with the wine's complexity and the ability to age well.

Ward: If you look at both Pinot Noir and Chardonnay, our philosophy would be that we want that wine, when it's bottled a year after it was fermented, to seem young, fresh and maybe not complex because a wine that's only a year old shouldn't be complex if those complexities come from rapid aging. With Pinot Noir, winemakers have been sucked into thinking, "Gee, this wine seems Burgundian." Yet they don't ask themselves, "Does this wine seem like a nine-month-old Pinot Noir?" or "Does it seem like a three- or four-year-old Pinot Noir that's only nine months old?" They get really excited about how developed the wine is at that stage and we're saying that's the first sign of problems. So we want some complexity there from barrel aging, malolactic and careful winemaking but the wine should seem young, it should seem fresh, it should have fruit. I think that's one of the hallmarks of our Pinot Noir. It shows lots of fruit and yet it hasn't gotten the highest marks from certain wine writers because it's not that Burgundian, that complex and developed when it's released. We want to see those qualities occur with age because that's the only way the wine is going to be graceful. If you have those qualities in the beginning, there are potential problems.

Graves: That brings us into a natural examination of how our Pinot Noir style has changed over time. I think we did a lot of things right with our first vintage; it was a combination of luck and skill. We were sensitive to the idea that there was a delicious, lighter red wine (Garnet) working in those fermenters that wasn't going to turn into a delicious, bigger Pinot Noir. If we treated it right, it was going to reward us and the wine drinker with a wine that had lots of flavor but in a lighter vein than most of the Pinot Noirs that were around in

1981. There was a tendency early to mind the pH. We looked at some wines recently that had a pH of 4.1. That's kind of a no-no here at Saintsbury. But we've always liked warm fermentations and we've handled the wine very little in the cellar. Those things are unchanged.

We have more small vineyards of Pinot Noir than we have of Chardonnay. I think the diversity of the Pinot Noir is larger by its nature. That's certainly more in keeping with its reputation. All of the Pinot Noir comes from within a mile and a half of the winery. Yet, if you line them up, they are really different. Even vineyards that are relatively close to each other physically are not necessarily close to each other stylistically. That's why we have chosen not to make a vineyard designated bottling. The diversity we get from the vineyards, vintage to vintage, is fairly constant but the kind of character each vineyard presents may change quite a bit. One vineyard may be included in the Garnet bottling one year, then be in a more richly extracted style with more stuffing the next year. We have some older vineyards and a cadre of younger vineyards that, as they've matured, have changed.

It's a matter of being sensitive to what each vineyard wants to be within the framework of how we make Pinot Noir. Which is to say, we use a Demoisy because we're not looking for an entire crushed berry. We're not using stems. I think the way we might be evolving is perhaps using the crusher that allows more whole berries to survive in the Demoisy. It's a relatively gentle machine but there are gentler ones available. It's logistically difficult for us to use a whole cluster regime, given that we use relatively large closedtop fermenters instead of relatively small opentop fermenters. What we gain by using larger closedtop fermenters is the ability to macerate on the skins after dryness without being compelled to press because we find a strong, volatile character coming off the fermenting cap and we need to press right away. Instead we're able to button those fermenters up, control the head spaces and keep the wine on the skins a lot longer than we would be able to with open tops.

How long do you leave the Pinot Noir on the skins?

Ward: Twelve to fifteen days.
Graves: The wines would actually be dry in five to six days.

Pinot Noir has a fairly fast fermentation?

Graves: I think it makes better wine when it ferments warmer. So we're setting the jackets at 83F degrees to 85F degrees and the cap is warmer than that. We've taken to using an irrigator to do the pumpovers so we have a relatively gentle but thorough wetting of the cap. Early on, we wet it about three times a day. That gradually slows down as fermentation slows down until finally we're not pumping it over in the last couple of days before it's pressed.

Do you think you would get more extract or more character if you slowed fermentation down?

Graves: The latest thing in Burgundy is not to slow fermentation down but to not ferment for four or five days. In other words, have the wine do a sort of cold soak on skin; the juice soaks with the skins and then you start fermentation.

Ward: Another thing people are trying is not allowing the tank to cool back down after the log phase of fermentation is over. Once you have that temperature rise to the 85F degrees to 90F degree range, you keep it there as long as possible.

At Saintsbury, we have made a lot of important changes. We no longer pump our pomace to the press. We rake it out of the fermenter, put it in a box and dump it back into the press. We use the irrigator as a pumpover device, the kind Dave talked about, which breaks up the skins a lot less. So everything moves toward less solids generation, more careful handling and less oxidation. By scraping the pomace out and dumping it into the press, we don't have to pump. We are taking the free run that is drained out of the tank and going directly to barrel with it because there are relatively less solids. You don't have to settle it to put it in barrel. So now the wine doesn't get racked at all out of barrel. It goes directly to barrel from the tank. It finishes malolactic in barrel. We make any small acid adjustments and add our SO_2 in place, in barrel. The only time it will get racked is when we're getting ready to bottle.

You don't rack the Pinot Noir. What's your approach to fining and filtering?

Ward: In general, we don't fine red wines because we don't have to. And this gets back to the question of what to do about stems. We find that we get good intensity, character, color and tannin balance without stems. In the richest of years, it's possible that stems might add a little characteristic of complexity in flavors and aromas as well as the tannin balance. But, in the lighter years, you run into the potential of ending up with bitter wines. It's difficult to tell ahead of time which are going to be the richer and which are going to be the lighter years. So that's the basis for our decision not to use stems. Plus handling in the cellar is easier without the stems.

Graves: In addition to causing some potential tannin imbalance problems, the uncritical use of stems can lead to some of the vegetal, dill pickle characters in Pinot Noir that, to my way of thinking, are not acceptable or certainly not the house style here at Saintsbury. You know, we've touched on the Burgundian ideal here in this conversation. I think if you set five very different Burgundies in front of five different people and asked them to pick which one was the most Burgundian, you would probably get five different answers. Given the diversity of wine styles and the making of Pinot Noir in Burgundy, that's always seemed like a funny way to analyze what this wine tastes like. We certainly see that in tasting the 1985 vintage, you'd think that because it was a very good year in terms of ripeness, the house style would tend to move to the background and the vintage would come forward. But they are still all over the map. So I think uncritical acceptance of what they do in Burgundy has led a lot of winemakers down a primrose path, only to fall down a slippery slope into a chasm.

Do you do a light filtration?

Ward: We do a diatomaceous earth filtration and then a pad filtration. We're not so worried about removing all the malolactic bacteria. There's a moderate amount of malolactic bacteria in the Pinot Noirs.

In the past, why haven't we consistently been able to make great Pinot Noir in California?

Graves: I think that's a moving target. I would argue that the level of achievement in Pinot Noir has shown the greatest improvement of any variety of the decade. It's sort of a "When did you stop beating your wife?" question in some ways. I mean, we've now stopped trying to get good Pinot Noir to come out of every area where you can grow Cabernet Sauvignon, as was the case twenty years ago. We've figured out that Carneros and western Sonoma County are good places for growing Pinot Noir. We've stopped trying to do it in a lot of places where it didn't work and have concentrated on refining the match between vineyard and winemaking technique in these areas where there is good potential on a year-in and year-out basis to make good Pinot Noir. So I would say that the bad old days are officially over for Pinot Noir as of the 1982 vintage.

Ward: We've seen a steady and constant improvement in our wines. Every year we are more and more pleased with the results we get. That's because we're smarter each year, we get grapes from more vineyards and we have more diversity; we actually can handle things in a better way as we make more wine. We've seen our neighbors produce better and better wine every year. So there's a great increase in quality overall among the producers who care and think. We're not at the peak yet; we're going to continue to see that trend move upward. We're only now putting a lot of effort into clones, trellising and canopy management. We haven't even seen the result of those efforts in the wines yet. So that's the next step in making better wines.

Then the next big leap in quality is going to come from the vineyards?

Ward: Yes. All the people interested in looking to the future in Napa and Sonoma agree with that too. That's why you see so much money and effort being spent on redoing vineyards and planting new ones in truly modern ways. There's a realization by those people that that's the only place where we are going to be able to make great strides in wine quality. Sure, you may be able to improve five percent in the cellar, but if you're talking about an improvement of fifty to one hundred percent, it's going to come from winemaking in the vineyard.

What is it that you like about Carneros fruit?

Graves: It comes from nearby the winery!
Ward: It's only an hour from San Francisco. We have a lot of friends here!

I know you have the cool climate. What about the soil?

Ward: The soil conditions are heavy, acidic, clay loams. Although heavier soils have traditionally produced good Pinot Noir, they are a little lower in pH than we would like for optimum vine growth and grape quality. But that can be addressed over the years. We believe in the overall blend of microclimate and soil. I think Carneros Pinot Noir tends to have raspberry, black cherry, and strawberry characteristics in the fruit with overtones of cloves and spice. The other nice thing about Carneros is it has a longish history, as far as Pinot Noir in California is concerned, of making good wines on a consistent basis. That's very attractive from both a winemaking and a business point of view. Being close to a large metropolitan area is another benefit. The fact that we're in Napa Valley is important, although we look up on Carneros as a viticultural area of its own that makes a lot of sense from an appellation point of view. In the greater marketplace out there, we're in Napa Valley and that has some benefit.

Richard, you were quoted as saying, "We don't employ Burgundian techniques." Could you explain that?

Ward: We don't blindly follow traditional Burgundian characteristic techniques because that's what they do in Burgundy. They make great wines in Burgundy. We're in California.
Graves: We're trying to develop good Carneros techniques!
Ward: And produce the best Pinot Noir we can. Now if that eventually leads us down the same path as the great winemakers in Burgundy, that's fine. But we're not going to say, a priori, "This is the way to do it." We're going to hopefully find out the way to do it, given our circumstances here.
Graves: It's very much a work-in-progress approach. We think about technique each year and we can examine our assumptions pretty widely. We probably wouldn't, for example, do all fermentation with wild yeast next year. I

don't think that would be the kind of thing we would say is useful. But again, we might think about the crusher/pump combination to see if we could have more whole fruit survival. We've already talked about a number of changes we've made. All this is a matter of examining assumptions and seeing where you can really make a positive difference, as opposed to just doing the same sorts of things because you view the match of vineyard and winemaking technique as essentially a done deal.

Ward: The flip side of that is we made certain large decisions back in 1981 about how to make wine. I don't think our years of experience since then have led us to change those decisions much. They've pointed us in new directions to better refine how we do it. We tried to address the big picture in the early going, without trying to impose fine-tuning on it by deciding that's the way it should be done, until we learn what that fine-tuning should be, instead of doing what someone else is doing.

Graves: We're very much a Carneros winery. We're one of the first to use only Carneros as an appellation. If you're going to be a Carneros winery, you're going to make Chardonnay and Pinot Noir. We saw that we had a lot of room to make a statement with Pinot Noir, whereas with Cabernet, we were going to try to squeeze in a new little wrinkle that might have caused us to be completely lost in the shuffle. Focusing on Pinot Noir has served Saintsbury very well and I think we've made some very good Pinot Noirs. And there's a lot of room to make some fabulous Pinot Noirs. I don't think either of us feels so complacent that we say, "That 1990 Pinot Noir was really good; I guess we'll just do things that way from now on."

Ward: I would add that because we can't go out in that vineyard and say, if we do this, this and the rest of it, we will get the kind of grapes we want year after year and we will know enough about it. It's very exciting, from the scientific side of both our characters, that we don't know enough about it and yet we're learning a lot each year. Getting to that point where we can control it probably will not happen in our lifetime. We've got the art, the craft, the science, the fun, the camaraderie and the enjoyment of life that extends past going to work.

Scott Harvey
SANTINO WINERY

"My goal here is to be the guy that made Amador County work. . . . I'm an Amador County winemaker; I don't plan on going anywhere else."

Scott Harvey has an unusual background for a California winemaker. Born in Germany, his family returned to El Dorado County in the Sierra Foothills when he was five. However, in high school, he returned to Germany on the AFS student exchange program and lived with a family in the Rhineland Pfalz. Back in California, he finished high school and began working at Montevina Winery, but once again Germany beckoned. He hopped a freight to Texas, hitchhiked to Tampa, got on a freighter to Rotterdam and hitchhiked back to Germany. He showed up on his AFS family's doorstep and announced he wanted to become a winemaker. He enrolled in a traditional school and, with intense effort, he finished the two year degree winemaking program in one year.

Confident in his abilities, he returned to the Sierra Foothills and put his knowledge to use at several wineries. In 1979, he helped found Santino Winery and has been winemaker there ever since. An eloquent spokesperson and full-time booster of Amador County wines, he aims to make the appellation a household word among wine drinkers.

While White Zinfandel is a mainstay at Santino, Harvey's pride in the county's climatic and viticultural differences are reflected in his big, gutsy Zinfandels and Barberas. His German winemaking background serves him well in making limited quantities of dessert wines such as a Trockenbeerenauslesen style late harvest Riesling and a unique Zinfandel "frost" wine. His planting of Rhone style grapes in the region are starting to bear fruit and the future is promising for these varietals in Amador.

What kind of perspective did the German winemaking background give you?

A German winemaking background, first of all, teaches you cleanliness, with which the Germans are good. You understand the importance of good records to keep track of everything in the cellar. They will make twenty or thirty different wines in small lots in the cellar. Germany is full of small, family-operated wineries and the school is geared to teaching you how to run that type of winery. You learn cash flow and cost analysis. The school itself was a winery so when a cork salesman wanted to sell his corks, he had to get up before the whole class and present his price and quality to the class. The school is really geared to hands-on, small winery management, which was perfect training for a winery like Santino.

As far as making tannic wines like we do in Amador County, the Germans have no idea about those kinds of wines. But at Santino we make a White Zinfandel that's very dramatic. The wines produced here tend to have more acidity, on the average, than wines from wineries in the same area. I'm not afraid of acidity as much as other California winemakers because of the nature of my background. And the Trockenbeerenauslesen and the ice wines we make here all come from the German training.

You generally had free run at Santino since the beginning; what are your goals here?

My goal here is to be the guy that made Amador County work. Hopefully, a future generation will look back and say, "Scott Harvey at Santino Winery was the guy that developed the wine type that works for us; the guy that developed the best wine for this soil." I'm an Amador County winemaker; I don't plan on going anywhere else. I'm going to make this appellation work. Santino Winery is a great vehicle for doing that because it's a well financed, state of the art facility. This winery lends itself to me doing what I want.

Personally, I feel that tannin is a regional problem in Amador County and tannin management is very important in Amador County Zinfandel. If you fine Amador County Zinfandel with tannin binding agents, which would be egg whites or gelatin, you end up destroying too much fruit, even more so than the tannins. So the resulting wine tastes even more tannic than it did before you fined it. You have to learn how to manage the wine early, which is partial carbonic maceration, submerged cap fermentation and aging in the bottle.

Santino bottle ages all of its Zinfandel two years before it releases them. It wouldn't be possible to do that in a winery that was bank financed because they would need that cash flow turn around. Santino has already paid that expense. I have two vintages of Zinfandels just patiently aging in the bottle. A lot of wineries say they sell no wine before it's time and then the banker comes in and tells them, "It's time." That's unfortunate. When you're marketing a product, you have to figure out what you have that your competition doesn't and play on it. Santino has wines that have been bottle aged and my competition doesn't. I'm in the best situation, as an Amador County winemaker, to be the trendsetter, to be the person that develops things that can work.

Do you own any vineyards?

The winery sits on a forty acre parcel and it has no vineyards, except for experimental plots. I personally own a vineyard which is across the road from the winery. It's bottled at Santino as an estate bottled wine, even though it's not owned by Santino, because it's a contiguous piece of property and the winemaking is controlled from the grape growing all the way through to the end. The vineyard is called Grandpere, because it's the oldest producing Zinfandel vineyard in the state. I sell those grapes to Santino, as well as to other wineries in the area. Again, my whole philosophy is to make every winery work in this area, not just Santino. All the knowledge and all the experience that is gained here is open to all the other wineries in the area.

You don't own any vineyards, so you're contracting out with local growers for your grapes?

Nearly all of our grapes come from Amador County and it comes from the same growers and the same vineyards every year. I've got long-term relationships with my growers and I feel they are very important.

How do you control the quality of the fruit you're getting?

First, I pay my growers on time and I pay the going price or higher. So they want to sell to Santino. Secondly, I develop a friendly, personal relationship with my growers. That's important. Thirdly, communication is the key. We talk about vineyard practices. I don't tell them what to do but I show them what I'm doing in my vineyard. I explain to them the kind of wines I want to make. If there is a problem with the grapes, I tell them. Then we'll talk about what they can do next year so I can get what I want.

I live in this county and I want these people to be my friends and neighbors for years to come. Developing a good relationship with your growers is very important in a community like this.

What kind of soil do you have here?

The soil in the Shenandoah Valley area are what is called Sierra series soils. There are pockets of Sierra series soils throughout the Foothill region. It's a sandy loam type soil that drains fairly well and is fairly deep. But most of the Foothill soils are very shallow with granite right underneath them. There is a lot of cattle grazing in those areas. But here you can tell by the size of the oak and walnut trees that the soils are fairly deep. This area lends itself to dry land farming. Irrigating up here doesn't do much good. Irrigating might increase yield by a ton per acre, but then quality just goes to hell.

The characteristics that come from our grapes are due more to climatic conditions rather than soil conditions. What happens in these dry farmed vineyards is the Zinfandel vines, just before the grapes get ripe at about 21 or 22 degrees brix, start shutting down and start sucking moisture back out of the grapes themselves. So the perfect Zinfandel bunch is a lot of nice full berries and a certain amount of shriveled berries. It's not raisining, the berries are just dehydrated. So to pick Zinfandel requires years of experience; you have to walk through the vineyards and eat the grapes. You can't just run a sample because a sample is usually off from what's really there. You have to tell by the percent of shriveling and the taste of the grapes. The bottom line is that you can't pick the grapes until the flavor is there. And the best flavor comes from the grapes that have hung the longest, usually after a rain, where the sugar has stopped and then started back up again. You get more of that jam characteristic from the Zinfandel after the first rain.

So what kind of numbers, as far as sugar, pH and acidity, are you looking for in Zinfandel?

There aren't any.

So a lot of it is pretty intuitive?

In 1980, we had a new winemaker in the county; he was from UC Davis. We were in the middle of the harvest and he told me that his grapes were coming in just perfect. He said they were 23 degrees brix, .8 acid and 3.2 pH. I told him that those sounded like good numbers but what did the grapes taste like? He didn't know what I was talking about. My philosophy is it's better to pick the grapes when the flavor is there and then deal with the must when you get it in the tank. If the sugar is too high, then blend it down, either with water or with a wine that has a lower sugar content. It is illegal to add water now in California; the State has decided. You make wine in the fermenter before you ferment it. Fermentation is a great marrier; it's what marries the components. If you blend wines after fermentation it takes much longer for them to marry together. So it's better if you can make the wine in the fermenter.

Elaborate on that a bit.

If you're going to make an adjustment, you make it before fermentation. You don't make the wine, ferment it up to sixteen percent alcohol and then decide you need to do something. When the wine has fermented it's become a unit. Let me tell you about my White Zinfandel. I put Sauvignon Blanc in it, but I put it in before I ferment the wine, not after. Then when I make the White Zinfandel, I stop the fermentation by dropping the temperature and adding sulfur. I do that rather than letting it ferment dry and adding a foreign dosage element later. You don't get a complete wine then. You get a wine that takes years to marry.

It's a more organic way to incorporate that?

Right. In the fermentation, you're dealing with tannin and alcohol management, which are regional problems in Amador County. So you deal with these problems in the fermentation process rather than trying to deal with it later by using egg whites or gelatin fining agents. We have submerged cap fermenters; they are stainless steel tanks with grids that we bolt in during harvest. We pump in, underneath the cap, about eighty percent to ninety percent of the grapes crushed and they get locked underneath this grid. Then ten percent to twenty percent of the grapes, whole berries now, are thrown on top of the cap. So some grapes are immersed in juice and some are not. The amount of whole berries you throw on top depends on the percent of shrivel, the strength of the skins and how much deterioration there is; the more deterioration, the more tannin extraction you have. Then you inoculate your tank and the fermentation takes off with carbonic maceration and submerged cap fermentation going on in the same tank. When you pumpover, you're pumping over into whole berries on top, rather than into crushed grapes. You have no maceration of the cap whatsoever. Again, your sugar level is important; you have to decide if you need to add anything to the must. Because you don't want a really high alcohol level at the end of fermentation; the alcohol pulls a tremendous amount of tannin out of the skins.

Fermentation temperature is very important. If you want to run a warm fermentation, a characteristic we like, then do it early when the alcohol content is low. Then cool the fermentation down toward the end when the alcohol is higher. Generally, as a winemaker, all you're doing is creating paths that this thing, that God is making, can go down. You create a condition so the wine has to go down this path rather than that path.

Do you believe the old adage that wine is made in the vineyards?

Oh yes. I was reading an article about some famous winemaker who bought a vineyard in Montrachet. He said, "You have to talk to every vine." And I think he's right. You've got to go out there and get involved in the vineyards. I have a crew do some of my pruning but I do as much of it as I can. You've got to go hoe them and sucker them. You just can't be an absentee landowner. You have to be involved in crop size, crop yields and integrated pest management. It really makes a difference. I see it in the wine I make from the Grandpere Vineyard, as opposed to the wine I make from the growers I buy grapes from. I'm not saying that these growers aren't good but their primary factor isn't quality, it's return of dollars per acre. You have to convince them that what you want is going to return them the most money per acre over the long haul.

I think a winery that owns its own vineyards has a real advantage, as far as the best quality they can obtain from that vineyard. The disadvantage of that is they don't have the possibility of picking and choosing from the best vineyard sites in the county. I go to Fiddletown and work with Chester Eschen and we get the best grapes the area has to offer. I get all the D'agastini Vineyard grapes; it's the highest elevation vineyard in the county and has great fruit. So I can pick and choose. As long as I take care of my growers and they want to become part of the Santino team, then it all works. This last year, when Zinfandel was really scarce, Santino ended up with 200 tons more than it usually does. I made a lot of White Zinfandel out of it and sold it on the bulk market. This winery produces about twice as much White Zinfandel as it sells in bottles. I do that for a lot of reasons. I buy a lot of grapes from wine growers and it keeps them happy if I take their entire crop. I then have the ability to keep the best tanks for the Santino label and sell the rest of it in bulk. This also generates a good amount of cash flow right after harvest and allows me to pay the growers right away. So it has worked out very well for us.

Is the fascination with White Zinfandel a fad or is it here to stay?

If people think it's going to be a passing fad, then it will be. The wine industry tends to kill its own golden eggs. I think there is a long-term place for White Zinfandel, if we treat it with respect.

I like to drink the White Zinfandel that I make. I'm very serious about it. I take a lot of time and energy in making it. Actually, we make two White Zinfandels here. One is a bone dry, barrel fermented, Tavel style rosé (200 cases). The rest of it, which is 12,000 cases, has about 2.5 percent residual sugar. I stop the fermentation when the acid masks the sugar and the sugar masks the acidity. Then you get that sweet and sour counterbalancing effect, which is the trick to making German style wines. The wine is .9 acid and 2.4 percent residual sugar this year. The fermentation is stopped by dropping the temperature to about 29C degrees and it's kept at that temperature until it's bottled. So the CO_2, developed by the yeast in fermentation, is locked into the wine and held there. We describe it as California's festive White Zinfandel and that's exactly what I want it to be. I think White Zinfandel should either be a picnic wine for people who like softer, lighter wines or else a bone dry rose. Winemakers who are making White Zinfandel at .8 percent or 1.2 percent residual sugar are trying to hit both those markets but not hitting either one. So we have a tremendous clientele for White Zinfandel because we are one of the sweeter ones and we have a distinctive goal and style in mind. The American consumer is also a cold beverage consumer; it's also the right color for the American consumer. They like the pink color. Lastly, Zinfandel is America's own grape variety. It has a lot of things going for it so it should be around for some time.

What is your case production and how is it divided up?

We produce about 30,000 cases of wine; the rest of it is either bulk sales or custom crushed. A little over half of our production is White Zinfandel; the rest are red wines. We also do very small lots of special wines like the Trockenbeerenauslesen Riesling or a White Zinfandel ice wine. We do make an Orange Muscat and a Port. Then we make a wine that I think is unique and has a real future once the consumer accepts it. It's a Muscat Canelli Amabile. I don't think Amador County has a white variety yet that really works well, as a dry wine. But the Muscat we make is made in an Italian style that's called Muscato d'Asti. It's 7.1 percent alcohol, 10-12 percent residual sugar, high acidity and very spritzy. It's an idea that came from Darrell Corti in Sacramento. It's a hard wine to sell because most people aren't familiar with it. But people who sample it in the tasting room end up buying it.

What about the climate here in Amador County?

The elevation of the Shenandoah Valley is anywhere from 1200-1700 feet, as it climbs to the east. Santino Winery is at 1400 feet. Usually the vineyards at the higher points of the valley tend to have more flavor characteristics. The vineyards at the lower end tend to have a little less acidity and a little less of that bright, cherry fruit but a lot more of the jam, earthy, pruney characteristics. During the day, the heat rises up out of the Sacramento Valley and comes across us here. The daytime temperatures can warm up to 110F degrees but generally they are 85F degrees to 95F degrees. We do get a week or so of 100F+ degrees temperatures. At night, the wind direction changes and the cold air starts fleecing down off the snow caps in the mountains to the east. There's a ridge along the other side of Plymouth and I think cold air is hitting that ridge and rolling back into this valley and filling it up. The night temperatures always drop below 60F degrees. That's what is needed to grow good red wine grapes: the fluctuation between the night and day temperatures.

Tell me how you made the 1986 Trockenbeerenauslesen Riesling. These were totally botrytis affected grapes that were picked in Sonoma County in late October at 45 degrees brix?

1986 was a vintage with a fair amount of rain during the harvest. So there was the potential for botrytis to develop. These Sonoma County grapes were destined to go to a large winery over there. But that particular winery didn't want to deal with botrytised grapes in that small a quantity. So I got a phone call from the grower and I told him to bring a bucket of fruit by so I could see what he had. They were perfect and I bought the whole crop.

With a Trockenbeerenauslesen, you can't run it through the equipment; the stuff is too dry, we can't pump it. We have two old crushers here that belong to old-timers in the area. They are not destemmers, just old crushers with a little motor on them. You set the crusher up across a couple of four by fours right on top of a bin. Then you just crush everything right down into the bin. At that point, it looks just like mincemeat pie. You let it soak for a day or two or until the volatile acidity becomes too high for comfort. You lift the bins up to the press and shovel them in; there's no way you can pump that grape material in. Then you press the hell out of it and keep pressing it all night long. When the stuff comes out of the conveyor at the end of the auger, the wind just blows it away. The skins are so delicate anyway that they get pressed down to literally nothing.

You end up with a product at 45 degrees brix. That's Trockenbeerenauslesen specifications rather than Beerenauslesen specifications, and there's a big difference. A Beerenauslesen will ferment to the point where the only limiting factor that kills the yeast is alcohol. Which means that it will go to seventeen or eighteen percent alcohol. A Trockenbeerenauslesen has such high sugars that the limiting factor that will kill the yeast is a combination of alcohol, acid and residual sugar. In a situation like that, your parameters flip over. You don't ferment cold anymore to preserve the fruit; you have to ferment warm to develop enough CO_2 to blanket the wine so that the wine doesn't acetify on you. Otherwise it will turn to vinegar faster than it turns to alcohol. You have to make it in full containers; you cannot make it in a partially full container. If you do that, there's always oxygen that sneaks back to the surface of that wine and acetifies it. You warm the wine up to 65F degrees to 70F degrees and you keep it there until it just won't go anymore. The first Trockenbeerenauslesen that we made fermented for thirteen months!

After that, the processing is fairly simple. You want to run it through protein stability and bentonite it. Sometimes tannin is a problem because of the stems you had in there. I found the best tannin fining agent for a Trockenbeerenauslesen is usually Jell-O brand gelatin from the grocery store. Usually the best flavor of gelatin is whichever one the wine lacks, say cherry or whatever! One packet of gelatin works pretty well for a 1,000 gallon tank, if you need it. The 1986 Riesling wasn't fined at all, except for bentonite.

Do you or can you filter this type of wine?

First, you lees filter it through a lees press, which is a diatomaceous earth filter. Then you pad filter it. When you bottle it, you filter it through sterile pads into the bottling machine. It's very hard to get this stuff to go through a membrane filter. Hopefully the wine is fairly stable then.

The botrytis grapes are just a fortuitous occurrence; you can't plan for that. It's something that just falls into your lap and you have to seize the opportunity.

Right. We didn't have any of this type or grape material for a couple years afterwards. I was trying to think of something to make that would fall into that same dessert wine category. I called around, even as far as Washington state, looking for botrytised fruit, with no luck. We went out on November 28th to pick a batch of White Zinfandel that I was just going to run through the press and sell off in bulk. The night before, it had dipped below freezing. The temperature gauge that morning at my house read 19F degrees. When I went to pick the grapes, they were frozen so I immediately thought of making an ice wine. While we were picking, the grapes started to thaw too quickly so we took them down to and put them in cold storage in Sacramento. We kept them there until we had the time to make the whole batch of ice wine at one time. This was the first Zinfandel ice wine ever made in the United States. The wine is 26 percent residual sugar, 1.6 acid, 2.1 pH and 8.1 percent alcohol. It's a really interesting wine.

There's enough acid there so that the wine is balanced?

I added the acid. I brought it up to 1.6 acid before fermentation. The fermentation procedure was that I took the grapes out of cold storage, brought them here, lifted the bins up to the press and shoveled them right in. I pressed them for about sixteen hours and just pressed the hell out of them. The juice comes out real fast but sixteen hours later you run the pressure up to two atmospheres and leave it there for half an hour and you end up with maybe a half cup of juice. When I dumped the press out at the end, I had nothing but little ice balls. I ended up with 45 degrees sugar but the first stuff that came out was closer to 55-60 degrees brix. As I kept pressing though, that went down. The rest of fermentation was the same as for the Riesling. As far as the wine quality, it really doesn't make any difference whether it's naturally or commercially frozen. Cryogenics is being used extensively now in Sauternes so that even a nonvintage year is a vintage year. If they don't have botrytis every year, they just freeze the grapes. In Germany, however, it is illegal to produce an ice wine from commercially frozen grapes.

Let's talk about red Zinfandel; do you make different styles of Zinfandel?

No, they are all made the same but they turn out differently because of the vineyards. We make three Zinfandels here: the Amador Zinfandel from the D'agastini Vineyard, the Fiddletown Zinfandel from the Eschen Vineyard and the Grandpere from my vineyard. They are all fermented in the same style, with the submerged cap and carbonic maceration on the top. They are all aged in French oak; some are aged in newer oak than others. I don't use any brand new cooperage; I don't believe in it. What I really like to do is buy two to four year old French oak barrels from wineries that are producing Pinot Noir.

What is it that you don't like about new French oak barrels?

New oak and Zinfandel don't blend well together. New oak does blend well with Pinot Noir and Cabernet. But Zinfandel does need some oak. So if I'm going to leave the wine in barrels for two years, it's best not to have new cooperage. The younger wines go into the newer barrels and the second year they go into older cooperage. The Zinfandel is pressed directly from the press to the cooperage because I want the lees in the barrels. Then they are left on the lees to settle out because I want that autolysized character. I want the lees to start breaking down before it goes to hydrogen sulfide. Again, it comes right back to tannin management. A wine that's left on the lees tends to have softer tannins. The wines are left on their gross lees until about January or February and then we rack them for the first time. They won't get racked again until we're through the first warm part of the summer; I let the cellar warm up until they go through malolactic. At that point, they are racked and blended. Then they are put back into barrel and left there until they are bottled, which is the following year. So basically, the wine is put into barrels dirty, racked in six months, racked again just before the next harvest and then not racked again until they are ready to be bottled. They are coarse filtered only; no polish filtration or fining agents are utilized.

You're a strong believer in bottle aging the wine before releasing it to the consumer?

Right, Zinfandel is bottle aged for two years and Barbera is bottled aged for one year. Bottle bouquet in Amador County Zinfandel is just phenomenal. They probably drink best when they are five to ten years old.

In my view the most important part is the blending. And the fewer times you move the wine, the less you lose. I know a lot of wineries that really believe in rigorous racking. Also, I get my first fermentation going with natural yeast and then I cross inoculate. I add a little bit of sulfur at the crusher to retard bacteria. Actually, if the grapes look pretty good, I don't add any because I really don't think you need it. Then I get them in the tank and take the bottom valve off another fermenter where there's a bunch of lees and I just pump it right in for about thirty seconds or so. Then I've got my inoculation, a high population of good bacteria. With yeasts, about ninety-eight percent of all the yeasts that are floating around out there only survive up to about six percent alcohol. They're the ones that produce the aldehydes and the off alcohols that you really don't want. The other two percent of yeasts that are floating around are the yeasts that you want; those are the good guys. So if you get a fermentation going, and you run it up above six percent alcohol, you've eliminated all the bad guys and you have a huge population of the other two percent. You take those good guys and you put a whole bunch of them into the next tank and the fermentation proceeds. So the ninety-eight percent category of yeasts doesn't have a chance. I've always had a better experience with wild yeast than I've had with a commercial yeast like Montrachet.

Do you think the consumer is still somewhat confused about what Zinfandel should taste like? In the seventies, Zinfandel was made in a late harvest style, a Beaujolais style and everything in between.

I think it should be that way. I think that there should be everything in between. Why, if you make Zinfandel, should you curl up and die? Why should you stop experimenting and growing? Just because the wine writers are confused on Zinfandel styles it doesn't mean we have to put up with it.

In the future, I think you're going to see Zinfandel dropped from the label in Amador County and you're going to see us making a wine called "Amador." Just like the Chianti region makes Chianti. That's my goal: to develop the best wine from the soil. Zinfandel is going to play a very big role in it. But Barbera is going to be part of it and Rhone varieties are going to be part of it. That's where we're headed. I want the consumer to buy "Amador." I want the consumer to say, "I'm cooking leg of lamb or prime rib tonight and I want a wine that has the characteristics that Amador has." No matter which wines you taste here, the Amador characteristics come through on every one of them.

Dan Lee
MORGAN WINERY

*"Our reputation has been built on the fact that we can take grapes
from different vineyards and perhaps do the best job
that anyone could do with those grapes."*

In the early seventies, Monterey County got a bad reputation for producing unpleasant, vegetative wines. Dan Lee, who became winemaker at Jekel Winery in 1978, was instrumental in helping establish Monterey County as a first-rate appellation. He produced a series of excellent wines at Jekel, particularly Cabernet Sauvignon, that solidified Jekel's renown as well as his own.

Originally a pre-med UC Davis undergraduate, he gravitated to the enology department because it combined science and agriculture with a bit of individual creativity. After four years at Jekel, he was confident enough, with family backing, to start his own operation in 1982. Morgan is a medium-sized winery that focuses on the "big four" varietals: Cabernet Sauvignon, Chardonnay, Pinot Noir and Sauvignon Blanc. All the wines are true to their type, in a style that accents the fruit. At the same time, they are never ponderous or heavy-handed; the wines display a suppleness and finesse that sometimes gets lost in comparative tastings.

What is even more impressive is that Lee can make wine of this quality, since he contracts with various grape growers throughout the northern part of the state for most of his fruit. In addition to the vagaries of the vintage, Lee also has to worry about procuring new grape sources when a particular vineyard is no longer available to him. The appellations range from the Alexander Valley in Sonoma County to a small hillside plot in Carmel Valley.

Lee's approach to winemaking is deceptively simple: obtain the best possible grapes, then pay strict attention to the use of appropriate winemaking techniques that will enhance rather than mask the quality of the fruit.

What do you like about the Cabernet grapes from Carmel Valley? What's special about them?

There is an entirely different climate and weather pattern in Carmel Valley; they get much more rainfall there. The soils are different too; they have a different consistency than the Salinas Valley. It's a small valley and the grapes are grown quite a ways up in the hills and away from the ocean. Carmel Valley is almost a miniature version of Salinas Valley. It runs almost in the same direction away from the ocean but it's about ten times smaller.

In the Salinas Valley close to the ocean, it's cool; further away from the ocean, it warms up progressively so that the Gonzales area is about the first area you can grow grapes and ripen them. It's still a cool area so you must plant the right varieties for cool climate wines there. When you get down to King City, it's quite warm and below King City is hotter. In the Carmel Valley, those temperature changes take place over a smaller area. By the time you get up to Carmel Valley Village, it's almost like being in King City as far as warmth goes. The area where the Cabernet comes from is ten miles further, where hills block the winds and fog from the ocean. The valley, where we get our Cabernet grapes, is a sunny, warm valley but it's up the hills and gets some ocean influence. In the summer, the days are warm, in the 80F degrees to 95F degrees range. But once the sun goes down, the nighttime temperature drops drastically. So you have a combination of warm days and cool nights. It gets warm enough so that it cooks out the excess varietal character in Cabernet. That, coupled with the cool nights, tends to bring out a lot of good color, tannin and flavor in Cabernet. With that type of fruit you can make big Cabernets with nice fruit characteristics that have more of a Napa, or even Mayacamas mountain range, Cabernet style. It has cedary, cigar box and cassis-like character with no herbaceousness at all. We think that's mostly because of the warmer climate there. You get sun for a longer period of time and you have less wind because of the hills.

You don't own any vineyards? You are working entirely with purchased grapes?

Although we have an acre and a half down the hill here that we've planted for nursery stock, all our grapes are purchased. We have long-term contracts with most of our growers.

Do you work closely with your growers as far as the viticultural practices? Does that help insure the quality of your fruit?

I try to, as much as possible. One of the premises when we were looking at vineyards was the grower's viticultural training and expertise. That's part of the selection process when deciding on a vineyard. Most of the time the vineyards are already well managed before we go in. So we find that we don't have to advise the growers much. Most of them know their vineyards better than we do as purchasers of grapes. After harvest time, we take a look at the wines to see if there's something we don't like that is vineyard related. For example, the Pinot Noir might have less color than we'd like. So we might suggest the grower do some leaf pulling the next year to give the grapes a little more exposure. Most of the growers are very cooperative because they want to please us. We have good working relationships with them. For the most part, we don't tell them what to do.

Since I left school, my whole focus has been on the winery end of things; I don't own any vineyards. The marketing and business aspects take up a lot of time too. So I've gotten away from the vineyards a bit. I know good fruit and I know good wine. I know enough about what's going on in viticulture to guide the vineyards as much as possible.

1982 and 1983 were difficult years because we had rains during harvest. I remember going out to one of our Chardonnay vineyards in 1983 after a moderate rain. It had cleared up and the breezes were blowing. This particular vineyard had a large canopy hanging down on the ground a bit. The vineyard rows were already dry but when I lifted up the canopy, I found the ground underneath the canopy was still wet. It was 75F degrees with high humidity and it was like a sauna underneath the canopy. Sure enough, within a day or so, we started seeing botrytis show up on the grapes. In a matter of a few days, the whole vineyard was starting to go that way. So we picked immediately. But the next year I went back to the grower and talked about the excess canopy in his vineyard. He went in and hedged it all to give much more air circulation in the vineyards. With obvious things like that, we politely ask the grower to help us out. And if it's feasible, they'll do it because we are both trying to achieve the same result: the highest quality fruit possible.

Going back to Cabernet, fifteen years ago the Cabernets from Monterey County were quite vegetal and herbaceous. You've obviously solved that problem in your wines. What is your theory on the excessive herbaceousness of Monterey Cabernet?

It was a combination of two things. Vineyards were planted to Cabernet in the wrong area and the winemaking was not very good.

But lousy Cabernet from a few wineries stigmatized all the Monterey County Cabernets.

They sure did. It had a lot to do with the mismatch of climate and variety. Cabernet was planted in areas that were too cool. There were viticultural problems with the vineyard owners too. Here in Monterey a lot of the vineyards were set up as partnerships or investment companies. At that point in time, they wanted negative cash flows for a few years and positive cash flows thereafter. The vineyards provided negative cash flows because of the costs of purchasing, planting and developing them. You didn't get any fruit from the vineyards for four years. Once you started getting good fruit, the idea was to provide some positive cash flows and investment returns.

In that type of situation, you didn't have the individual farmer/owner like you do in Napa or Sonoma, where the same family may have farmed that property for fifty years. In Monterey there was more of a business focus on return on investment. What they did was look at what grape was commanding the highest price in the market. There was a shortage of Cabernet then. It was going for $800 a ton, while everything else was going for $400 to $500 a ton. Since that grape was giving the highest return, they planted everything to Cabernet, without regard to climate or soil. It was purely a monetary decision. You had investors from Wall Street making grape growing decisions instead of wine growers.

I sense that you see yourself as a traditionalist?

Our goal is to produce the best wine we can in each of the four varieties we work with. We'd like to be recognized as one of the top five producers in each variety. We utilize modern technology in the areas of equipment and wine analysis but we combine it with very old world, traditional winemaking techniques. We wear different hats depending on the variety. For example, our Chardonnay is one hundred percent barrel fermented. We put our cooler vineyards through malolactic fermentation; in a normal year, forty percent to seventy percent of the Chardonnay goes through malolactic. We age on the lees and we do a little stirring of the lees.

We use only the higher toast level, Burgundian oak barrels. We use a lot of new oak every year, approximately forty percent . We have used fifty percent new oak but you could only leave the wine in the barrels for six or seven months at that level. Now we're going with a little less new oak and leaving the wine in barrels for nine or ten months. We like the new oak every year because there's just something special about a brand new barrel's impact on the aroma and flavor of Chardonnay. We don't, however, want to overdo it or let it become a predominant factor in the wine.

We're looking for cooler vineyards. We have two or three vineyards we utilize in the Gonzales area, which is the coolest part of the Monterey growing area. We're on the borderline of just ripening every year because it's so cool. In those vineyards we usually have to wait for acid levels to drop, more than anything else. Sometimes we pick at a little bit higher sugar level than we want because the acidity is still too high. We've used a vineyard a little further down the valley and it usually comes in at average acidity and it's a good balance for the higher acidity fruit.

If doing sixty percent malolactic is good, why not go one hundred percent malolactic?

At some point in time, we might go to one hundred percent malolactic. But what I sometimes see in one hundred percent malolactic California Chardonnays is the malolactic character becoming the predominant character in the wine at the expense of the fruit. That's what I'm trying to avoid. Our first year was about twenty-five percent malolactic and we've been increasing that percentage since then. We're still not quite comfortable with putting our warmer vineyards through malolactic. That has a tendency to become more malolactic in character than we really want.

Right now we like what's happening with the wine at the malolactic levels we've established. With the cooler area fruit, we had batches that are non-malolactic that some people think have gone through malolactic because of its rich character. We're finding, if we get the malolactic finished with a good pH level and a good acidity level, the fruit character shows very well also. So we make our decision every year depending on what the pH and acid is on the fruit when it comes in. If the acids are below 1.0 or so, depending on the malic levels, we might acidulate a little bit if we want that batch to go through malolactic. We've done very little acidulation in Chardonnay. In fact, we're usually fighting too high an acid level so we're increasing our malolactic percentage for acidity reasons. We're finding if it's done early on with good acidity levels, the fruit doesn't suffer and the wine doesn't have too much malolactic character.

It's interesting you say that because, in tasting your Chardonnay, I couldn't tell if it had gone through malolactic or not.

I enjoy hearing you say that. When I taste a nice white Burgundy, I can tell if some of them have gone through malolactic, but for the most part they don't have a pronounced malolactic character. So I like producing a wine that keeps you guessing. If that's the case, I'm happy because I feel that the wine is balanced. Our 1987 Chardonnay has a nice amount of buttery character from the malolactic. We could have done a little more on that because it's only about forty-five percent malolactic. In retrospect, we think we could have gone up sixty percent to sixty-five percent and brought that character out a little more. But that character will develop in the bottle with age. So I think in a year's time it will be tasting even better.

What about your fining and filtering regime?

Every year it's a little different. For the most part, we do little fining other than the normal bentonite fining for protein stability. We're not campy enough where we want to put out a product that throws sediment. We want the wines to be relatively stable so we do protein fining. Occasionally we might use a little gelatin to fine, if the wine seems rough.

We do a bentonite addition at fermentation. The Chardonnay traditionally takes about three to four pounds of bentonite total. So what we usually do is add about one and a half to two pounds at fermentation and then we get some protein stability during fermentation. But we want to leave it slightly protein unstable so we can use bentonite at the end too. What we've found is, once we pull the wine out of the barrels, it's cloudy with the yeast, especially the portion that goes through malolactic. But then we like to use a pound or two of bentonite to really clarify the wine before we filter. By doing that, we've found the filtration process goes a lot smoother. You end up with a clearer wine to start your filtration on. You can also filter quite a few more gallons through the same set of pads than you would otherwise. We have a filter with a cross-over plate so that in one pass, we can do both a rough and a fine filtration. One of the things we try to do here is not pump the wine around very much so we do minimal handling in the cellar. At any one particular time, not all the Chardonnay is in barrels. We usually have ten percent to fifteen percent in tanks. Then we will exchange a batch of Chardonnay that's been in barrels the longest with the batch that's in the tanks.

Is that an economic consideration or an aesthetic one?

A little bit of both. With all of the new oak we bring in, it's a hedge against getting the wine too oaky. It's economic in the sense that you don't have to buy barrels for all your wine. If you have some wine in a neutral container, you have something to blend back to in case you got a bit more oak than you would have liked.

With the Sauvignon Blanc, we want that fruit to show through a little more. With the Chardonnay, it's really a blend of fruit. But Chardonnay fruit is more neutral; it doesn't have a distinctive fruit quality all its own. So it's more a combination of the fruit and those complexing factors. But we want the fruit character to be more of a focus in the Sauvignon Blanc than the Chardonnay. So we usually do about forty percent to forty-five percent barrel fermentation for Sauvignon Blanc and the balance is fermented in stainless steel. We age it on the yeast for the most part but not quite as much as the Chardonnay. If we do a racking we may not suck as much yeast over in the racking as we do with the Chardonnay. The Sauvignon Blanc does not go through malolactic. We use only Bordeaux barrels for it. We get the harder woods, Nevers and Allier for the most part. We use Bordeaux barrels for Sauvignon Blanc and Cabernet and Burgundy barrels for Chardonnay and Pinot Noir.

About half the Sauvignon Blanc is in barrels for six months or so while the balance is in the tank. Then we do one exchange every year. The barrels are sixty percent to seventy percent new every year. So all the Sauvignon Blanc will spend some time in barrels. We decided on that regime because we wanted the fruit character to be the primary focus. We want a touch of oak but we don't want it to be too strong. We employ the same fining and filtering regime as we do with the Chardonnay. The Sauvignon Blanc is from Alexander Valley where it's warm. The fruit usually comes in at about .8 or .9 grams per liter acid and in some years we had to add just a little acid to it. We try to do any acid adjustments before fermentation because we find that it marries and blends nicely to the point where you can't tell if it was added or natural. You can do a little acid adjustment after fermentation but when you reach a certain point you start tasting the tangy characteristics of the acid.

The Sauvignon Blanc is a simple wine to drink, a little more straightforward because of the absence of malolactic. It's clean with a little bit of oak. We are starting to make our Sauvignon Blanc with more barrel fermentation. It's tending to be more of what I consider a Chardonnay style Sauvignon Blanc, where there is some wood poking through it. We're trying to give it a little richer mouth feel and not be so steely, tart and austere. We're consciously gearing it toward more of a richer style.

My impression of that wine is that there is some grassiness and some herbaceousness. So many Sauvignon Blancs have been neutered. But yours displays some varietal character.

We want varietal character but not too much. And the varietal character we're looking for is more of a light, clean grassiness with some floral, melon and fig notes. That's as opposed to a weedy herbaceousness or grassiness that has a heavy characteristic of mown hay bordering on bell peppers. That's a style of grassiness that I think is an aggressive style of varietal character. We're looking for enough character to let you know that it's Sauvignon Blanc but not much more. We want to give a richer mouth feel, a rounder mouth feel. We want it to always be a recognizable varietal but hedging toward the Chardonnay in terms of tactile fruit. That's the style I enjoy but I also like the strong steely, austere style. But that style is not as well accepted in the marketplace. Most of the American public doesn't drink much Sauvignon Blanc and I think it's because the aggressive, grassy components that you sometimes find in Sauvignon Blanc have turned people off.

Do you think you have a handle on Pinot Noir?

We are experimenting more with Pinot Noir than any other varietal. We don't have a set game plan on it. The first year we used sixty percent Monterey County fruit and forty percent Carneros fruit. We liked that wine quite a bit. But I was thinking about going toward a little bit more of a firmer structure and a bit more berry fruit. The second year we went overboard in using eighty percent Carneros fruit and twenty percent Monterey fruit. It was a firmer wine and more berryish and cherryish. But it was a simpler wine and more one-dimensional. It was not quite as interesting a wine. We've moved to a blend that's in between those two, with sixty-five percent Carneros fruit and thirty-five percent Monterey. But that's not set in stone either and I don't think it ever will be. More than any other variety, Pinot Noir is still a real education not only for ourselves but for most producers. I have an idea of where I'm going with it but it's more of a set taste that I'm shooting for. With most of the wines I make, I have an ideal wine in my taste bud memory that I'm aiming for. So we're always doing things that go in that direction. With Pinot Noir I think it will be a longer road to achieve that ideal than any other variety. It's a long-term education. In the meantime, we're going to produce the very best Pinot Noir we can.

Pinot Noir has two less color pigments than any other red wine. If we have our choice, we'd rather have a darker Pinot but it's not absolutely necessary. Flavors are the most important consideration. We're shooting for as much color extraction as we can get but we're not going to go overboard extracting the wine just to get an ounce more color out of it.

The Pinot Noir goes through a rather warm fermentation. We often hit 90F degrees in the fermenter. The Pinot Noir ferments quite rapidly. It takes a couple of days to really get perking. We throw a lesser amount of yeast in it so that it will start slower. Then, once it starts going, it goes quickly and ferments dry in four or five days. It sometimes drops from 20 degrees brix to 5 degrees brix almost overnight. Then it will finish up a little slower. We leave it for extended maceration on the skins. Often the entire fermentation process will be done in eight or nine days but we leave it for an extra five or six days on the skins. We give it a fairly gentle pressing with a bladder press. We don't do any separation. Everything gets blended back together because it's a pretty gentle pressing. Once it's fermented, we treat it much like we treat Chardonnay. We put it in Burgundy barrels on the yeast. We don't do a lot of rackings. We pretty much do it anaerobically. We roll about half the barrels and leave them like that and the other half we top on a biweekly basis to let a little bit of air in.

We pretty much just let it sit and treat it much like a Chardonnay. We do a light egg white fining just to take off the rough edges. We do a coarse pad filtration on it before bottling.

What is your winemaking approach to Cabernet?

Cabernet, more than any other wine, basically makes itself. It really depends on the characteristics of the fruit from the vineyard. We'd like to pick right around 22.5 to 23 degrees brix. We find that beyond 23 degrees brix we start to get a raisiny character. The vines we're getting our fruit from are mostly on the young side so that's why we're shooting for 23 degrees brix. As those vines mature, we'll probably be looking more for 22.5 degrees brix. The grapes have moderate acidity, coming in at about .8 acid. The pH is usually in the 3.3 to 3.5 range. When you look at Cabernet grapes, you see this kind of blue-purple, velvet covering on the fruit. It almost looks like blueberries. It has a dark blue dusty look to it. When you see that in Cabernet, you know you've got something good. And all this Cabernet in Carmel Valley is like that; it's just beautiful stuff.

We do a moderately warm fermentation, say 85F degrees or so. Then we do an extended maceration time. The fermentation finishes in about ten days and we leave it on the skins for five days more. We press it off and again, we don't separate any press fractions. Then we put it in Bordeaux barrels. Cabernet is funny because it's pretty god-awful in the early going. It doesn't start tasting like Cabernet for six or eight months. But as it sits in the barrels it starts gaining character and loses its young, big, fat fermentation characters. The first vintage was a high percentage of new oak so we left that in barrels for about fourteen months. The second vintage will be in barrels for eighteen or nineteen months.

We're experimenting with using some American oak. The first vintage was about ten percent American oak, the second vintage a bit less. The main thing in Cabernet is playing with that blend of French oak versus American oak barrels. I prefer the French oak barrels overall. You get tannins and a nice character from it. But there's a nice little blast of vanilla you get out of American oak barrels.

How often do you rack the Cabernet?

We rack it about three times a year. The first year we top the barrels and the second year we roll most of the barrels without topping them at all. We rack three or four times the first year and maybe twice in the second. Again, we haven't quite figured out our ideal racking regime. We're still working on it but we probably rack more than most people.

Cabernet is really the easiest wine for us to make. We pretty much let it develop on its own. The hardest decisions for us are how much oak we want and what our fining levels will be. We're shooting for a Cabernet that is drinkable when released but also with good aging potential. We'd like the wine to be a little softer and more approachable on release. Down the line, we might do a reserve bottling that would be meant for longer-term aging.

Cabernet, when it's aging in the winery, you can almost forget about. You may not taste it from the barrel for a month and find it doesn't change all that quickly.

It seems like it's fairly easy to make wine. The hard part, for the winemaker, is finding a way to take the wine to a more flavorful, more complex level. After a winemaker gets to a certain point, it seems to be a matter of fine-tuning the details.

Yes, for the most part, that's true. The way I view it, we've almost developed a recipe for several wines we've done. The Chardonnay has been successful and we think we have a pretty good recipe. Of course, the so-called recipe changes slightly from year to year, as we learn about and try different things. But you can really change the overall quality in the vineyard. We are always on the lookout for new vineyards doing a good job. Every year we're trying new vineyards. For example, for our 1987 Chardonnay, we brought in ten percent to fifteen percent of our grapes from the MacGregor Vineyard in Edna Valley. It's a cool area and we like that fruit. Our reputation has been built on the fact that we can take grapes from different vineyards and perhaps do the best job anyone could do with those grapes. We don't chauvinistically favor one wine growing region over another. Our Sauvignon Blanc is from Alexander Valley but the small percentage of Semillon we blend into it is from

Carmel Valley. A lot of our Pinot Noir is coming from Carneros. If we get hooked up with the right vineyards, we might do a Napa or Sonoma Cabernet. We're really out to make the best wines we can and we're not so naive as to think our region produces all the best wines in the state. We think this region does well with certain varieties but there might be better areas for certain grapes. We want to make good wines and it doesn't matter if the grapes come from Napa, Sonoma or Monterey.

How much do you rely on the empirical, scientific data in the lab versus your own taste and experience?

In making wine, I'm really much more like an old Italian winemaker. The direction we go here is mostly based on how the wines taste, how they turn out on the palate. We take a look at all the numbers but most of our decisions are made on what we taste and what we like. We then will back up that judgment by looking at the numbers but it's almost secondary to our palates. I still think your palate is the most important thing in winemaking. That seems to be more of the art, if you start doing things more by your palate than by the numbers. I'd say ninety percent of my decisions are based on taste.

You use your science for the details. You test for stability because that's something you can't taste. You need the science but I view that as the minor details of winemaking. Producing good flavors and good balance is the hardest part and I think you use almost nonscientific means to try to achieve those things.

In school you're taught to make technically sound wines without defects. But they may be fairly sterile wines. I've only learned how to make flavorful and distinctive wines since I've gotten out of school. But they are still technically sound wines. California has a reputation in the world winemaking community for making technically sound wines using modern technology and modern equipment. What interests me, however, is that we are going back and using traditional, old world techniques as far as production. I'm talking about barrel fermentation, aging on the yeast and things like that. And then we're using our technology to achieve a means of producing better wines, for example, by finding a way to move the wine around more gently in the winery.

But we're using a lot of old world techniques and we're finding that some of those techniques are technically very sound. The whole process has kind of gone full circle and we're finding there were sound reasons that these old techniques were utilized.

QUPÉ

19 91

SYRAH
Santa Barbara County
Bien Nacido Reserve

PRODUCED AND BOTTLED BY ROBERT N. LINDQUIST
SANTA MARIA, CALIFORNIA   ALC. 12.5% BY VOL.

Bob Lindquist
QUPÉ WINE CELLARS

"When I first started learning about and collecting Rhone wines, the main reason was that they tasted so good and offered all these unique flavor components. And by unique, I mean different than Bordeaux or Burgundy."

Bob Lindquist never started out to be a trendsetter in California winemaking; he trusted his own instincts and made the kind of wines he liked to drink. During the five years he was at Zaca Mesa Winery, he saw cool climate, high acid grapes coming into the winery and felt this fruit would be ideal for making a traditional, barrel fermented, malolactic Chardonnay, a style not much in favor in the late seventies. He had a special fondness for the wines of the Rhone region and also had access to Syrah grapes, which were then primarily used for blending. In 1982, while working at Zaca Mesa, he began making wines under his Qupé Wine Cellars label, based on his confidence in interpreting Chardonnay and Syrah grapes in a traditional manner.

The history of Rhone style wines in California is a fairly short one. Although Phelps, McDowell and Estrella River had done some work with Syrah grapes, for them it was more of a sideline. It was Lindquist, along with Randall Grahm of Bonny Doon, who helped bring Syrah to the forefront. The first Syrah from Qupé made Lindquist's reputation and proved that delicious wines of this type could be made in the benevolent climate of California's Central Coast.

Lindquist continued his exploration of Rhone varietals, bottling single vineyard designated Syrahs from grapes planted in the cooler Santa Ynez Valley. He also grafted over several acres of vines to Marsanne and Viognier, both traditional white wines of the Rhone. Following his own taste and championing Rhone style wines has proved serendipitous for him, as wine consumers now embrace these wines as an alternative to Cabernet and Chardonnay. Current production is around 8,000 cases. Lindquist is also involved with Jim Clendenen of Au Bon Climat in producing several thousand cases of red and white Bordeaux style varietals from Central Coast fruit under the Vita Nova label.

You are really a big proponent of the Rhone varietals. Why are you so partial to these wines?

In the late seventies, when I first started learning about and collecting Rhone wines, the main reason was that they tasted so good and offered all these unique flavor components. And by unique, I mean different than Bordeaux or Burgundy. At that time, Rhone wines were bargains, partially because they were overlooked in the marketplace. You could buy a really good Cotes du Rhone, which was the lowest level of this wine, for $2.99! You could buy the highest level, like Hermitage or Cote Rotie, for $10. That's why they intrigued me so much and why I drank more of them than I did Bordeaux or Burgundy. Also, I was influenced by the way we eat at home. We tend to grill a lot, using strong, spicy flavors, which seem better matching with the kind of wilder flavors of

Rhone wines. They are a bit less subtle than the wines of Bordeaux and Burgundy, and less complicated.

When I released my first Syrah, the 1982 vintage, I priced it based not on what other California Syrahs were selling for but on what other comparable Rhone wines were selling for at that time. I was drinking some really good Rhone wines, from St. Joseph and Cornas, for $7 or $8 and I thought that's where my Syrah belonged. A lot of my retail accounts wanted me to sell it for more because it was such a bold style of California Syrah. But I priced it at $7.50 because you could buy similar wines from France for that price. In the last couple of years, thanks in big part to wine writer Robert Parker, prices of Rhone wines have really climbed. A lot of that is due to the amount of press Rhone wines are now getting plus the fact that there aren't many or much of them. The best Rhones are produced in small quantities and there is a demand for them now.

How did you get your own label off the ground initially?

What I did was lease space from Zaca Mesa to make wine. I bought some barrels, bought some grapes and made wine there. I paid Zaca Mesa a fee for using their equipment, which I actually traded in services for the first vintage. That's how Qupé was started in 1982. Besides Chardonnay from cool climate vineyards in Santa Barbara County, I also wanted to make Syrah. Nobody was making Syrah in this area but I have a real love for Rhone wines. I contacted Estrella River Winery in Paso Robles which had a large vineyard of Syrah grapes, some of which Estrella was willing to sell me. That's where I got my Syrah grapes. They were having marketing problems. Syrah was a new variety and they weren't lighting the world on fire with it.

You are one of a handful of California winemakers who are experimenting with other Rhone varietals. You are working with small amounts of Marsanne, Mourvedre and Viognier. Why?

Because they are unique. It's something that's hardly been done in California until very recently. That's a big part of it. It's also because I love those wines. I'm not overwhelmed by white Rhones; I drink them on occasion but they are not wines I really aspire to make. But nobody is making Marsanne in California and I thought that I should make another white wine besides Chardonnay. This will make me a little more diverse and I'll enjoy the experience. So I've decided to make Marsanne as a second white wine.

Do Marsanne grapes and other Rhone varietals grow well in California soil and climate?

I think so, although it's a little too soon to tell. My experience so far has been with Marsanne from vines I grafted over and it turned out very nice. I got good sugar, acid and pH levels. The vines looked healthy, the grapes looked fine and there was a good crop level.

What about the two other Rhone varietals, the Mourvedre and the Viognier? What are you doing with those?

Well, I didn't plant any of those grapevines. Instead I grafted over an existing vineyard to those varietals. It's much less expensive than planting a new vineyard. Also, the roots of the vines are already established so one year after you graft the vines, you have grapes. You miss only one vintage and the following year you have a crop.

The reason for grafting over to Mourvedre is that I really enjoy wines from France that are made from Mourvedre. I also recognize its potential as a grape to blend with Syrah. Mourvedre has a lot of the same characteristics as Syrah; it doesn't have the fruit or the spice but it has the rich backbone and the tannin. What I think I need are Grenache grapes, to flesh out the Mourvedre and Syrah. I see Syrah as something here on the left and Mourvedre as something here on the right. Grenache would be in the middle and could bring the wine together. All this comes from just what I taste in the wines so far.

What about the Viognier?

The Viognier is the grape of a small appellation in the northern Rhone called Condrieu. It makes an aromatic, delicate, white wine. In France, it's hard to grow and doesn't yield well. It's apparently a very temperamental grape variety. Because of that, a lot of California winemakers, who may have been interested, have shied away from it. But it seems this grape grows just fine here. In France, probably the combination of where it's grown and the climate it's grown in maybe wouldn't affect it here. A lot of that probably has to do with the high quality of the wine in France. If you took Viognier and grew it in the San Joaquin Valley, you probably couldn't distinguish it from French Colombard. My thinking is to take a variety like Viognier and grow it in a cool climate where it will be stressed to a certain point. But because we're growing it in California, where we have a lot of sunshine and good growing conditions, maybe we'll get a decent crop from it every year and hopefully make something of quality. There aren't that many Viognier vines in the United States right now and the amount of bud wood each vine produces that can then be sold to growers to plant Viognier grapes is very limited.

Why aren't there more winemakers doing this kind of experimentation in California?

Actually there are but they're all fledgling operations so you don't hear a lot about them. A couple years back, I went to a gathering of California winemakers who make Rhone varieties. At that dinner, we all brought barrel samples to taste beforehand and we all sat down to a multicourse dinner with wines. I tasted five different California Viogniers, two different California Marsannes, a California Roussanne, several different California Mourvedres and about a dozen different California Syrahs. It was very impressive, fascinating to me because, although I'd heard about these things going on in California, it was the first time we'd gotten together to talk about our interests. I realized I wasn't alone in pursuing these varietals.

Do you consider yourself a traditionalist winemaker?

Yes, very much so. Traditional in the sense of going back to the way wines used to be made. I certainly like to use all the modern technology that is appropriate. But the basic style and production techniques of how the wines are made are traditional. For instance, with Chardonnay, the wine is completely barrel fermented. That's not like some wineries that start the fermentation in stainless steel tanks and then, once the wine is halfway through and the wine is cold, they put it in barrels to finish fermentation. That's just partial barrel fermentation. Barrel fermentation is putting juice that is mucky and full of solids right into the barrel. You start fermentation in the barrel and finish it in the barrel.

Another traditional technique is to leave the wine in the barrel on the lees, which are the solids that settle out, during its aging period. Then, put the wine through its secondary malolactic fermentation, which is an important part of the winemaking process in the style of Chardonnay that I make.

Let's back up a little on your methods for making Chardonnay. You get most of the grapes from the Sierra Madre Vineyard in Santa Barbara County. Is that a cool, Region I, according to the UC Davis classification?

Very much so. It's one of the coldest vineyards in Santa Barbara County, and Santa Barbara County is one of the coldest areas for grape growing in the state. It's a popular misconception that central to southern California is a very hot region. If you look at a map of California, all of the mountain ranges run north to south except for those in Santa Barbara County, where they run east to west. What that does is open up the coastal valleys of this area directly to influences from the ocean. We get cooling breezes every afternoon. We get a lot of fog and cold air moving in at night. It's not uncommon to have a summer day in which temperatures get up to 90F degrees and then go down to 40F degrees at night. That's an important part of grape growing here. It's not how hot it gets but the average temperature of the day that affects the way the grape grows. The Sierra Madre Vineyard falls right in the middle of Region I.

What do you like about the Chardonnay grapes that you get from the Sierra Madre Vineyard?

One thing I like is the fact that they're really stressed. They grow on sand essentially. It's funny that I happened to take one of my partners up to the Sierra Madre Vineyard one day during harvest. He looked at the grapes and said, "You mean, we're making wine from these grapes? They look terrible." They look terrible but they make great wine. They get sunburned, they get a little mold on them and they're scraggly little clusters with not many grapes on them. I guess he was expecting them to look like a bunch of Thompson Seed-less grapes you buy at the grocery store. He expected beautiful grapes like the kind you see in Gallo commercials. They're not like that at all. Part of their character comes from being in this stressed situation. A lot of wind blows through there and consequently the vines look tattered. They don't get much nourishment because they're growing in sand.

What about the sugar levels of the Chardonnay?

Because it's cooler here, the grapes stay on the vine longer and the growing season is longer. Consequently the grapes get ripe and have more character and flavor, at a lower sugar level, than if they were grown in a warmer area. In 1983, 1984 and 1985, all the Chardonnay grapes were perfectly ripe at 21.5 brix. So that's when I picked. The grapes were ready and the acid and pH were in perfect balance. The flavor was there. Some other winemakers in the area, who don't make the same style of Chardonnay that I do, thought those grapes weren't ripe and left them on the vine longer. They got more sugar from the grapes but I don't think they were as well balanced by the time they picked them. With the grapes picked at 21.5 brix, you still get twelve percent alcohol, which is plenty for Chardonnay.

In 1986, we had an extremely cooler than normal vintage. At 21.5 brix that year, the grapes weren't ready; they were still green. The acid was way too high so I waited. I finally brought the grapes in at 22.8 brix. It took a long time for them to go from 21.5 to 22.8 brix because it was so cool. Consequently the 1986 Chardonnay is a little heavier and richer than the previous vintages.

Do you have to add acid to the fruit from this region?

I do. But I haven't had to add acid to any of the Sierra Madre Vineyard Chardonnay. I've made other wines with grapes from this area that I've added acid to. Certainly the Syrah, which comes from a much warmer area in Paso Robles, gets a lot of acid added to it.

The reason for that is that nature hasn't really done its job in that area, at least for you to do what you want to do with the grapes. How do you determine how much acid to add? Is it scientifically determined?

Well, it is. But it's not anything that's precise. I like to start with acids around 10 to 12 grams per liter, also stated as 1.0 to 1.2. This is all determined in the lab. So if the grapes come in at 0.8, for instance, then I'll generally add 3 grams of acid to take it up to 1.1. That's a real common number for the Paso Robles Syrah to come in at, right around 0.8. When I bump it up to 1.1, it's in balance.

Now if you didn't add acid to this Syrah, what would happen?

The wine would be too soft and flabby. It would taste flat and just not have the flavor. But also, if the wine is low in acid, it's usually higher in pH. Once you get a little higher pH and lower acidity, bacteria can have a field day in the wine. Lower pH and higher acidity keep the wine fresher and more stable, protecting it from bacteria, spoilage and oxidation.

So in your Chardonnay you're generally looking for low sugar levels, high acidity and a good pH. And a good pH to you is?

For Chardonnay, a pH of 3.0 or 3.3, with 3.1 to 3.2 being ideal.

We've discussed sugar levels, acidity and pH. These are the three important numbers you're looking at. How do those numbers translate when the consumer opens that bottle at the table? What does it all really mean, as an end result, to the person who is drinking it?

If the wine has good acidity, low pH and lower alcohol, it means that the wine will taste good. The wine will be in balance and harmony in the mouth. Acidity gives it the liveliness and freshness. Low alcohol makes it easier to drink. High alcohol in Chardonnay can make the wine a bit hot and harsh to taste. It will be heavier; when you're drinking it with food, it can overwhelm the food. So that's what I'm shooting for: a wine that has a lot of flavor because of the style in which it was made and is also nicely balanced to drink with a meal.

Why is malolactic fermentation of the Chardonnay important to you? Is it because of the nature of the fruit you're getting?

That's a determining factor. But also I want fruit that can be put through malolactic because I like what malolactic fermentation does to the flavor of the wine.

And what does it do, in your experience?

It softens the acidity, which you might think is a contradiction because I want high acid. But I only want high acid to a point. If it's too high in acid and then it's too tart and will be less enjoyable to drink. It might be like sucking on a lemon. But if you start with high acid, also have a low pH, by the time the wine finishes malolactic, the acid is toned down and the pH is still low. Malic acid, which is one of the principal flavor acids in grapes, is very tart and one-dimensional. It's the principal flavor acid in apples, for example. When you bite into a crisp, green apple, it can be very pleasing but the tartness can be a bit annoying. Lactic acid is a more complex acid; it's softer and has more of a lush flavor. So the benefit of malolactic fermentation, that is, the malic acid being changed into lactic acid, is that you get a rounder feeling in the mouth from that wine.

Then there are other side benefits that don't necessarily come from the malolactic fermentation itself but are a result of it. One is that you get a bit more oxidation of the wine early on because, when I put the wine through malolactic, I don't add any sulfur to the wine until after the malolactic process is finished. So the wine gets more oxidation, more air, during that period. That's something you have to control very carefully. A lot of California Chardonnays that have been put through malolactic haven't been carefully tended and, as a result, they tend to get brown and overly buttery and soft. That's something you want to avoid.

Any other side benefits from malolactic?

When you're putting a wine through malolactic, you want to leave it on the lees, which is part of a style of winemaking. The lees have a lot of nourishment that feed the malolactic bacteria. What you're getting is more of an infusion of the flavor from the lees because you have this activity going on in the barrel. You're also creating new lees, because the malolactic bacteria grow; when they're finished, they die and settle to the bottom of the barrel. They create a new flavor component of lees in the barrel; this addition of lees adds another dimension of flavor.

Do you subscribe to the idea that malolactic fermentation adds complexity to the wine?

Absolutely. My feeling is if you don't make Chardonnay from grapes grown in a cool climate, if you don't barrel ferment it and if you don't put it through malolactic fermentation, you're missing the boat. You are not making real Chardonnay. There are a lot of nice wines made from Chardonnay using other techniques but they are not traditional and not what Chardonnay is all about.

In barrel fermentation, you're putting the must right in the barrel. How do you control the temperature of your fermentation, or is the barrel a self-regulating unit?

That's it. After the grapes are crushed and pressed, I don't put the juice into the barrels right at that moment because logistically it's not possible to pump it from the press to the barrels. So I collect all the juice in a stainless steel tank and chill it. A lot of the time, the grapes come in cool and don't need much chilling. But if it's a warm day when the grapes are crushed, then the juice is warm and bacteria and wild yeast can start moving in on it. So I chill the juice down to about 50F degrees and the next day I put the wine into barrels. When the juice goes into barrels, it's fairly cold. I put it in with all the solids. I don't settle the juice at all; I just draw it right off the bottom valve of the tank. When it goes into barrels, I add starter, which is wine that's already fermenting, with the type of yeast I want to use with that wine. It usually takes a day or two to start fermenting. It starts slowly and, once it builds up, it goes pretty quickly.

But the fact that it is in a sixty gallon barrel regulates the temperature. Assuming you have a cool cellar, the barrel itself will stay pretty cool.

One reason for keeping Chardonnay cool and fermenting it cool is to preserve the fruit character in the wine. Here I'm talking about wineries that ferment in stainless steel with temperature-controlled jackets. I don't make fruity Chardonnay; I don't care about the fruit. If you get a little bit of fruit character, that's okay. But the style of Chardonnay that I make accentuates the lees, the wood and the body as opposed to the fruit.

We are back to the question of balance again. There are a lot of wines that win blind tastings because they have a lot of impact, or a lot of oak. But if you sat down at the dinner table with these wines, after one glass you might not want anymore because their heaviness overpowers the food. I like to think the style of Chardonnay I make is a wine that you can keep drinking throughout your meal and keep enjoying without tiring of it.

Tell me about your cellar procedures for Chardonnay, with respect to racking, fining and filtering.

I age the wine on the lees and since I bottle it in May or June, I rack the wine for the first time in the early part of May. The wine has been sitting on the lees since September. I rack it off the lees, fine it with bentonite and skim milk. The skim milk helps lighten the color of the wine and gives it a little nicer finish. This is a traditional fining agent used in France. Because of the style of Chardonnay I make, the wine hasn't had any SO_2 in the beginning, so it tends to get a little darker in color than a wine that has a lot of SO_2 or a wine that has been kept in stainless steel. My style of Chardonnay will get golden. Skim milk doesn't do anything for the stability of the wine, it just helps the appearance by lightening it up a bit. Bentonite is a clay that binds unstable proteins in wine and settles them out. Sometimes I rack wine and then filter it; other times I filter while I'm racking it. Then I bottle it. I usually don't filter when I bottle.

You're a proponent of handling the wine as little as possible?

Yes, except where filtration is concerned. Because if a Chardonnay has gone totally dry and gone through malolactic, theoretically you don't need to filter it at all. But I do anyway because I want the wine to be clear. I don't want sediment in my Chardonnay, not that it would hurt the quality, but the public doesn't expect to find sediment in a white wine.

The Marsanne is a new variety in California. In fact, your 1987 Marsanne is the first commercially released California Marsanne. What has been your fermentation method and cellar regime with it thus far?

The Marsanne is entirely barrel fermented in older barrels, as opposed to the Chardonnay which has a percentage of fermentation in new barrels. The idea with the Marsanne is to prevent the oak from becoming an influencing factor in aroma and flavor. Obviously the method by which it's made is a factor but the actual oak character doesn't come into play. With the Marsanne, I settle the juice, ideally for around twenty-four hours, to get most of the solids out so that they don't become a big factor in the flavor of the wine. As soon as malolactic fermentation is over, the wine is racked off the lees into old barrels. I like lees flavors in Chardonnay but I don't think it's appropriate for Marsanne. I'm trying to preserve more of the fruitiness and make the Marsanne cleaner and crisper.

Tell me about your production methods for Syrah, a grape you've been working with since 1982.

With the Syrah I usually ferment with thirty percent to fifty percent whole clusters in small open top fermenters. Then the grapes are stomped on to break the skins and to pack them into the fermenter. They're not stomped on enough to break up most of the berries, just some of them. The balance of the fermenter is filled with crushed and destemmed fruit. That's a change from what I did originally. From 1982 through 1986, I used one hundred percent whole clusters. But in 1985 and 1986, I had trouble getting as much color and extract as I would have liked. Also with one hundred percent stems in the fermenter, you have more pH problems. In 1987, I switched to a combination of whole clusters and crushed fruit. I like the results a lot more.

What did you achieve by switching to this combination?

There is a lot more juice so the cap is easier to punch down. Because there are fewer stems, the potential of a pH problem is reduced. Another benefit is that I can put more fruit into a fermenter and get maximum use of it. The biggest advantage is having a juicier must to work with; it's more pliable and easier to punch down so it's easier to extract tannin from. By having whole clusters at the bottom of the fermenter, there is still plenty of carbonic character.

So there's still some carbonic maceration going on?

Right. In fact, when I press and empty out the fermenters, at least half of the whole clusters still have whole berries and have fermented carbonically. If you break open those berries to take a look, you'll find that they are sizzling away inside. That helps add to the aroma and provides a more fruity, spicy component.

After fermentation, I press and then collect all the wine in a tank temporarily. Then I put it into barrels. The idea is to put it into the barrels with almost all the solids that come out of the press. I allow it to go through malolactic fermentation with a lot of solid content in there. After malolactic, I SO_2 the wine right in the barrels. I don't rack it at that point; I leave it undisturbed through the winter and spring. At the end of spring, when the cellar is fairly warm, I rack it. The only other racking it gets is when it comes out of the barrels for bottling. The vineyard designated Syrahs may get racked one more time before they are bottled. It all depends on how the wines are showing in the barrels. The reason for racking is that the wine starts to get a little reduced; it stinks a bit and seems that it could use some aeration. I don't like to rack Syrah too much because I like to handle the wine as little as possible.

What is your fining and filtering regime for the Syrah?

It's fined with egg whites. The amount of egg whites depends on the year, the amount of tannin and the way the wine feels in the finish. Usually it's five or six egg whites per barrel. Depending on how well the wine falls clear from the fining, it will go through a rough filtration and a polish filtration before bottling.

You always filter your Syrahs. What do you feel the controversy is about filtering versus not filtering?

Filtration helps clarify the wine, it makes it easier to sell commercially and makes it easier for a restaurant to deal with. Because I only put it through a polish filtration, there's still going to be a little sediment that falls out over time in the bottle. I have trouble getting the wine clear enough by racking alone. I'm not satisfied with the overall clarity. The other problem is that if you have a lot of solids or sediment, the wine is more susceptible to bacterial spoilage. The presence of bacteria might be higher and there's also more nutrients for the bacteria to feed on. So I like to get the wine fairly clear before it's bottled.

What is it about the cooler climate Los Olivos and Bien Nacido fruit that you like better?

Because of the cooler climate and longer growing season, the varietal character tends to be more pronounced. It's the same thing that happens with Cabernet Sauvignon. If you grow Cabernet in a Region I, you get a strong herbaceous, bell pepper character from it. Since Syrah is not a very herbaceous variety, you get a stronger raspberry and pepper character. The other advantage of a cooler climate is having lower pH and higher acidity at the time of ripeness.

So a cooler climate is more appropriate for Syrah?

I think so, especially if you're going to make a varietal Syrah. If you're going to blend it with other varieties, then there are more options. There are a lot of wineries that are now blending Syrah, Mourvedre and Grenache. In that circumstance, it might be better to grow Syrah in a slightly warmer climate because the Mourvedre, which likes a warmer climate, will have the acidity to balance the softer acid in the Syrah.

What type of barrels are you using for Syrah?

I use all Francois Frere barrels. For the Syrah I use older barrels which were previously used for Chardonnay. For the Los Olivos and Bien Nacido Syrah, I'm using a small percentage of new oak, just to give those wines a bit more complexity.

You and Jim Clendenen are making wine under the Vita Nova label. Part of the reason for Vita Nova's existence is to see what you and Jim could do with Cabernet fruit from this area?

Exactly. Cabernet from this area isn't that highly regarded. We thought that it would be a real challenge. We also felt that Cabernet could be a very important variety in this area, if we could zero in on the right vineyards and maintain certain production methods.

What are the traditional production methods you are utilizing for Cabernet?

We crush and destem completely and then put the fruit in small opentop fermenters. We do a pretty standard opentop fermentation. But at the end of the primary fermentation, we seal up the tanks and let the wine soak with the skins for an additional ten to fifteen days. The extended maceration softens the tannins in the wine and creates more complex, richer flavors. It's something that you have to be careful with because you don't want the wine to get too volatile. The wine is exposed to more oxygen and it's not protected from the CO_2 of fermentation anymore. You have to make sure your tank is sealed up very tight and that any head space is protected with carbon dioxide. We use quite a bit of new oak because the Cabernet varieties can stand up to oak character. The other important thing we do is quarterly rackings with air.

What insights did you get from visiting the French wine regions?

One of the things I found most important is to maintain good cellar practices. All the wineries I visited were small. The winemakers work all different aspects of the operation and have total control over what they are doing.

Tasting the Syrahs in the different areas of the Rhone was interesting to me. I tasted Syrah from the southern Rhone before it got blended with Grenache and Mourvedre and I noted how similar it was to Syrah from the Paso Robles area. As I moved up the Rhone, into a cooler climate, I noticed how the flavors and characteristics were more like the Bien Nacido and Los Olivos Syrahs that I make. It reaffirmed my feeling that a cooler climate is preferable in making Syrah.

I also found that, for certain wines, oak isn't all that important. Marsanne would be an example. As long as you have good fruit to work with, you don't need oak barrels to make the wine into something distinctive. The same is true for Sauvignon Blanc. I visited quite a few wineries in the eastern Loire area, in Pouilly Fume and Sancerre. Quite a few of them don't use oak barrels because they have high quality fruit from unique soils and vines that were stressed. Their wines are distinctive without the oak. Wineries that did use oak barrels also made distinctive wines but in a different vein. I tasted a number of Marsannes that were made with different techniques but they were all very good wines.

In France, it's pretty much a given that to make fine wines you have to have fine grapes to start with. That was affirmed over and over again.

SIMI

Chardonnay

MENDOCINO COUNTY 34%
SONOMA COUNTY 59%
NAPA COUNTY 7%

1991

Zelma Long
SIMI WINERY

"I don't think there are any absolutes. I've tasted good wines made many, many different ways. The people who make the best wines know the raw materials they are working with, they know what they want and they adapt their techniques to accomplish it."

Zelma Long never intended to become a winemaker. At Oregon State, she was a home economics major who hated home economics but had thoughts of a career as a nutritionist. So she took chemistry and microbiology courses required for her nutrition minor and then switched to a general science major. Ironically, this was an excellent background for pursuing a graduate degree in enology. She enrolled in UC Davis but interrupted her studies when Mike Grgich, then at Robert Mondavi Winery, asked her to work the crush in 1970. She stayed on and, when Grgich left Mondavi the following year, she became head enologist and helped balance the great expansion in volume with appropriate quality controls over the next eight years.

In 1979, she was hired as winemaker at Simi Winery, a somewhat moribund Sonoma County winery that had changed ownership a few times and had seen better days. She immediately rolled up her sleeves and went to work, overseeing an extensive renovation and modernization of the winemaking facility. She looked to the vineyards and procured better grape sources for the style of wines she wanted to make. Furthermore, she has never given up experimenting, either in the vineyard or the cellar, to improve the quality of the wines.

Always one to keep an open mind, Long has never believed in a winemaking "formula." Her recent focus has been on improving the quality of both the Chardonnay and Cabernet. As the ongoing research in the vineyards evolve, so will the winemaking response to it. After over twenty years in the business, her open-mindedness has kept her on the leading edge of research and technology. She is perhaps the best example of how a person's natural curiosity and tenacity can have a dramatic impact on the quality of the wines. Four years ago her continuing commitment to excellence was acknowledged and Long was named president of Simi Winery.

Give me some sense of what those early years at Robert Mondavi Winery were like. What was exciting about it?

1970 was the beginning of the new era in winemaking. It was an exciting time to be at Mondavi as it nearly doubled in size three years in a row. In 1973, we crushed 7,400 tons of grapes versus 1,700 tons in 1970. There was an enormous increase in the volume of work and the physical capacity of the winery.

During that period, the Mondavis had a penchant for experimenting. We tried half a dozen types of wine presses; we bought centrifuges to use. We brought Cabernet grapes down from Washington State; we bought grapes from all over California. In the early seventies, the Mondavis hired a German winemaker as a consultant and I learned about German winemaking techniques. In 1973, I traveled to Europe for the first time, then again in 1976 with Andre Tchelistcheff and again in 1978 with Robert Mondavi.

In those ten years, we developed a full-fledged experimental program with a full-time experimental enologist. We experimented with different fermentation temperatures and barrels. We tested all the new techniques that we, as an industry, are confident about now. In those ten years we explored the basics of the winemaking we do now. That was a very special time for me.

How do you feel that background served you when you came to Simi Winery in 1979?

At UC Davis, I was fortunate in the two years I was studying and commuting back and forth. There were small numbers of students then, so I knew all my professors well. That, to me, established a close link to Davis that I've never lost. I continue to look at the Viticulture and Enology Department as a tremendously valuable resource for winemaking. People ask me, "Did you learn to make wine at Davis?" You don't learn to make wine at Davis but you learn the context in which you're working. You learn the process and you understand the chemistry, microbiology and viticulture.

I think Mondavi gave me the opportunity to have a tremendously broad base of experience with people, equipment, winemaking procedures and grapes. It allowed me to go through California and around the world to see what was going on. It was probably unparalleled in the context of producing quantities of high quality wine. When I think of that combination of breadth of experience and high quality winemaking, I doubt there was an equal.

When you came to Simi in 1979, what was the state-of-the-art equipment at the winery?

There wasn't any. I went from a winery that was very state-of-the-art to a winery that was not. Simi represented much more the traditional winemaking techniques. There were open, wooden fermenters, which hardly existed anywhere else. Simi had a workable but old-fashioned press. The winery had relatively little fermentation capacity compared to the amount of grapes that were coming into the winery.

Did you come to the job with your eyes open to all that?

Yes, I viewed it as a wonderful opportunity. The people that owned Simi, the Schieffelin Company, had owned it for about three years. During that time, they had decided that there was great value in the wine industry and they were ready to make a large capital commitment to the winery. They were looking for someone to change the direction of the winery. They wanted someone to physically modernize it. Those opportunities are rare and whenever you find one, you have to ask, "Will these people sustain their dream?" Many people come into the wine industry with a dream of having a winery a certain way but they can't do it. But in fact, Schieffelin did sustain their dream.

Michael Dixon, who was Simi's president, gave me a free hand to buy the grapes and we moved fairly quickly into buying land for vineyards. I had control in hiring and training people, designing the cellar, remodeling the old winery and getting all the equipment needed. I set wine style and winemaking procedures. In wineries, the title of winemaker can mean many things. In some wineries, the actual control the winemaker has over what affects the wine is more limited than others. Here, I was presented with an opportunity to impact all the different areas that would affect the wines and I had the financial backing to make it happen. As it turned out, it was a tremendous opportunity.

What kind of changes did you make when you came to Simi?

First of all, I was given a plan of the amounts and kinds of wines Simi wanted to produce. They had already made the commitment to build a new cellar but they hadn't gone into detail. I took crush tonnage projections and laid out an anticipated grape delivery schedule. We figured out the size of the fermenting room.

Then I went back to basics. When you design a house, the architect says, "How do you want to live in this house?" With a winery, you have to ask, "What kind of wine do I want to make with this winery?" I knew I wanted to make the winery work well for the people working in it. At harvest, everyone is overloaded with work and if you make your winery inefficient and difficult to work with, all the energy goes into overcoming the difficulties and you can't apply the energy where it should be applied, which is thinking about the wines and the winemaking. I wanted the winery operation to be smooth; I didn't want excess movement in the handling of the wine. So I developed a set of concepts of how we wanted to make Chardonnay and Cabernet and proceeded to design the system to accomplish that.

The first step is asking, "What kind of wine do you want to make? What style? What quality?" The winery is the tool to do that so you work out the necessary details. They had American oak; I wanted to switch to French. There were redwood tanks being used; I wanted to remove them to get away from using redwood and to free up room for barrel storage. I wanted to change the systems for stacking the barrels to make them more flexible and accessible.

We made many physical changes in the old winery. We changed our red fermentation system. We increased the number of tanks for each ton of grapes we brought in. We were trying to assure that, even in a very short harvest season, with many grapes coming in at the same time, we would have the cooperage to receive the grapes when they were ripe and ready. So we designed a winery that had a large cooperage volume relative to the number of tons we were going to crush; we minimized our risk. Careful winery design is crucial to fine winemaking.

I had to look at the vineyards. A substantial number of grapes were under contract. The Chardonnay under contract I liked very much so we kept that contract and extended it. We had Cabernet under contract in 1980-81 and I decided that I wanted to look at others. We dropped that contact and began to develop new Cabernet sources. We started making Sauvignon Blanc in 1982 and built its winemaking procedures from scratch. We started by defining what we wanted to accomplish with Sauvignon Blanc, developing a style and then developing grape sources and the winemaking techniques together. I spent the first four years at Simi learning about Sonoma and Mendocino County grapes and developing grape sources for all the varieties we make.

We also reduced the number of varieties. Simi was making about eight varieties when I arrived. I wasn't keen about making all those varieties. It's important to think about who you want to be and focus your efforts. The decision to focus on a fewer number of varieties was considered a good decision both from a winemaking and marketing point of view. We dropped Gewurztraminer, Zinfandel, Pinot Noir and Gamay Beaujolais.

In 1982, we started to develop vineyards. We now have 175 acres in Alexander Valley; 120 are Bordeaux varieties: Cabernet Sauvignon, Cabernet Franc, Merlot and Petite Verdot.

As soon as I came to Simi and started to have responsibility for buying grapes and deciding when they were to be harvested, I realized that the system in wide use during the seventies, of paying growers on the basis of sugar levels, was not a good system. Because the quality of grapes doesn't relate to how much sugar is in them, but to their flavor and balance "ripeness," we set out to develop better systems for assessing ripeness. We began to use grape color, texture, vine condition, juice aroma and grape flavor as better clues to ripeness.

I had many viticulture friends and we all had a growing need to look at what we could do in the vineyards to affect wine quality. We wanted to go beyond the standard way viticulture experiments were evaluated at UC Davis, that is in terms of effect on brix, acid and brix/acid ratio. We wanted to look at other quality clues in the wine chemistry like phenolics and color; we wanted to think about balance and interactions between components in addition to just the components themselves. So we set up a Simi vineyard to do experimental work. We planted a twenty acre close spacing trial of Cabernet and a clonal block, more properly called a selection block, of different red Bordeaux varieties and different selections within each variety. We developed different trellis systems (TK2T, U, Lyre, vertical shoot position) and planted different root stocks (AXR, SO4, 110R).

We've looked at the whole winery from top to bottom. That started because of Schieffelin. I don't think they knew all the details but they had a commitment to change the winery's direction and the money to do it. When Moët purchased Schieffelin in 1981, they not only continued but reinforced our direction.

Simi now calls itself "wine growers." But in 1977, Simi only owned three acres of Riesling. Now you own 175 acres. Do you feel you have more control over the winemaking process, being in more of an estate grown situation?

Yes. You have an opportunity to look at all aspects of wine growing closely. You make decisions in the vineyard and live with them. I must admit I have a soft spot in my heart for both growing and buying grapes.

Let me talk about buying grapes first. For a winery to be successful in buying grapes, you look for growers who are committed to quality. It's wonderful, and not surprising, that there are people growing grapes who are very proud of what they do. It goes beyond economics. They want to sell their grapes to a winery who can and will make fine wine out of them. If you're a winery that wants to make fine wine, that's something in your favor when you seek to buy grapes. We look for the growers who have the technical expertise to do the job; it's not enough just to want to do it. I've had experiences in purchasing grapes from small, part-time growers who have another profession and take care of their vineyards on weekends. They struggle because they are not professional grape growers. When the time comes for harvest, they may have difficulty getting a harvest crew. No matter how much they want to produce good grapes, they may not be able to harvest them when they should be harvested. It's not just the desire; the professional ability to do the job is crucial. Then the terroir, the interaction of the grape variety, the soil and the climate has to be right.

The first year we buy grapes from a vineyard, we don't know the personality of the grapes. Are they going to be ripe at a higher brix or lower brix? Are they going to have small berries or large berries? We aren't going to be as skillful at adapting our winemaking to the characteristics of the grape until we understand it. For example, we have a vineyard that has small Chardonnay grapes. We know that if we do skin contact with the vineyard, because it already has so much skin to juice ratio, it can produce a heavy, coarse wine. So when that vineyard comes in, we put priority on crushing the grapes direct to press. It makes wonderful wine that way.

After about three years, we can be relatively confident of that vineyard's behavior. After five years, we've seen the vineyard in diverse weather conditions; by that time, you truly know the grapes. I put a high premium on little things; knowing the variations of the soil within the vineyard will help you do a better job sampling the vineyard accurately. The vineyard sample will more closely parallel the grapes as they actually come into the winery.

It would be difficult or impossible to ask a grower to do all the experiments we do in our own vineyards. For example, our close spacing vineyard was three times as expensive to install as a normal vineyard. We didn't know, and won't know for several years, what the close spacing will accomplish in quality and yield. We hope it will give us dramatically increased quality. The TK2T (Te Kawata Two Tier) trellis system that we tried with Cabernet was a completely new system developed by Richard Smart, a New Zealand viticulturalist. It has never been tried in California before and it appeared to be a little crazy but it's made wonderful wine for us. It's much easier to take those risks upon yourself than to ask someone else to do it.

Let me explain what I think is most wonderful about having our own vineyards: the ability to make better wine in the vineyard. There's a map on the wall with all our different vineyard blocks, thirty-six different blocks that are different by virtue of variety, clone, rootstock, soil or trellising system. Something makes each different from the other. They are like wines; each has to be considered an individual. Within the same blocks, most of which are no larger than three acres, there are soil differences, so we have to subdivide how we manage the block. Each block comes into the winery and is kept separate. In December, our winemakers, vineyard manager, viticulturalist and myself will sit down and taste each lot. Of course, it won't be the first time we've tasted them, but it will be a formal tasting and discussion. We'll taste and talk about our impressions of each block's personality. An example of our comments will be, "This block has excellent concentration; this block is a little herbal; this block has soft tannins." When we find characteristics in a block that we want to improve, we explore why the block is that way and how it can be modified. For example, what can we do to increase the concentration of flavor? Specific viticultural techniques can enhance Cabernet flavor. That's what's exciting about viticulture today. More is understood about the vine physiology, grape growing and viticultural effects on grape composition.

Based on our tasting and discussion, we go back into the vineyard and change the way we're managing a block. Let me give you an example. We have a rocky vineyard that is half Cabernet Sauvignon and half Cabernet Franc. The Cabernet Franc grows very differently from the Cabernet Sauvignon. The Cabernet Sauvignon has strong growth while the Cabernet Franc has weaker vegetative growth and tends to crop heavily. We went into the Cabernet Franc and pulled off the crop and cut back on the pruning so that the vegetative growth would be stronger. We found we had to water the Cabernet Franc more often. The first harvest of Cabernet Franc had high sugar but didn't seem to be ripe; it was green and astringent. We thought perhaps the grapes were stressed for water and weren't continuing the ripening process. The next year we watered the Cabernet Franc more frequently and made a much better wine; it was fruitier with softer tannins. We had made an impact.

Diane Kenworthy, our viticulturist, hired a botanist to study the Cabernet Franc at harvest. All the vine leaves have tiny openings, called stomates. When they're open, they take in CO_2 and photosynthesize; they also respire water like the pores of your skin when you perspire. She found that in the heat of the day the Cabernet Sauvignon would close its stomates and protect its water supply. The Cabernet Franc, however, would still be photosynthesizing and respiring water. It was respiring more water growing in the same conditions as Cabernet Sauvignon and therefore needed more water from irrigation. What we learned from observation, we verified scientifically; we responded with changes in vineyard management and made a better wine the next year.

The first part of what I call the grape/winemaking circle is keeping all vineyard blocks separate during vinification, tasting them and evaluating their strengths and weaknesses. The second part is the viticultural response to the wine. What do you want to change and how do you do it? Vineyard management practices have to respond to and improve the wine. The third part is back again at harvest. You taste the grapes in each block and ask yourself, "What are the characteristics of these grapes? Are the grapes big? Are the tannins soft or rough? How are we going to make this Cabernet? Are we going to do longer skin contact? More pumping over?" We must understand each block of grapes in this vintage and tailor our winemaking to it. Then back to step one again: "What kind of wines did we make and what are we going to do next year in each block to make the wines better?" The next harvest you ask, "How should our winemaking respond to the characteristics of this block this year?" That type of circular building of the winemaking/grape growing cycle is difficult unless you're living with your vineyard. Each block is different and you must manage the nuances of the pruning, the canopy and the watering.

With that kind of approach, the winemaking response will be different every year.

Yes, that's something that we have to learn in our industry. I had a conversation with Paul Pontallier, the manager of Chateau Margaux. They have a cellar book that tells about all their different vineyard blocks and how you vinify each block under different conditions. That cellar book was written in the seventeenth century! So they have an enormous depth of experience with their vineyards. He also told me that, in 1986, they chapitalized some of their wines, not because they needed alcohol but because they perceived that the grapes that year were higher in tannins than normal. They felt that the alcohol in the wine must balance the tannins. What this shows is great attention to the characteristics of the grapes in that vintage and the appropriate winemaking response to those grapes.

I feel that our industry has moved from the acquisition of basic, good winemaking techniques in the seventies to the application of basic, good vineyard management practices for wine growing in the eighties and to much more finesse, both in the grape growing and the winemaking.

I know you have been partially barrel fermenting your Chardonnay and putting it through malolactic fermentation. What kind of response is that to what is happening in the vineyards and the style of wine you want to make?

Barrel fermentation, for me, falls into the category of style. I see barrel fermentation as a tool to achieve a certain style of wine. I look at wines that are fermented in stainless steel as a little leaner, tighter, fruitier and simpler in style than Chardonnay fermented in barrels. Barrel fermented wines tend to be less fruity, a little softer and more complex in flavor. Also, I look at barrel fermentation as a way to successfully integrate new wood into the barrel aging process. If you take a finished wine and put it into a new barrel, you tend to get a wine that is woody, simple and somewhat phenolic or dry. If you had fermented that wine in a new barrel, the wine would not be woody. The wine has the sense of the wood flavors but they're well integrated. You don't get a phenolic impression. Winemakers commonly believe the reason for this is that the yeast, generated during fermentation, has a fining effect on the phenolic compounds that are extracted from the wood. Barrel fermentation is a style consideration.

In barrel fermentation the winemaking response to the vineyard would be the use of older versus new French oak. It's been our experience, with both Chardonnay and Cabernet, that grapes have intrinsic structure and flavor concentration profiles that make them appropriate or inappropriate for use with new oak. If you ferment a Chardonnay in a new oak barrel and then six months later it tastes woody, that's the wine's way of telling you that the structure wasn't right for the new oak.

For example, we have taken Cabernet from three different vineyards of the same vintage, harvested at the same relative degree of ripeness, put them into barrels made by the same cooper and fourteen months later, one tastes woody and the other two don't. The French acknowledge it as well—they say that a great vintage, with great structure and flavor concentration and high quantities of good quality tannins, can be kept in a new barrel "forever." That is an exaggeration, but the wine just doesn't get woody. The winemaking response to the grapes relative to barrels is whether to use new oak or not and more subtle decisions as to kind of oak, barrel preparation, etc. It all depends on the structure of the wine, which depends on the vineyard. And you learn that by working with the vineyard. There are vineyards that ninety percent of the time have the structure to carry new oak. In 1986, we pulled our wine out of barrels sooner; the 1986 Chardonnay didn't seem to have the structure to carry the wood like the 1985 vintage did. The vintage has an impact on structure and concentration and the vineyard does too. To have the best wine, you want to respond perfectly.

Another advantage associated with barrel fermentation is leaving the wine on the yeast lees. Originally, I considered that an advantage because we weren't moving the wine; I think of Chardonnay as a wine you need to protect. You put it in barrel as juice; you ferment it, you top it up and you let it sit and age on its lees for six months. This is much less movement than a wine fermented in a tank and subsequently moved into a barrel. An additional virtue is the effect the lees may have on the wine. At Mondavi, we put Fume Blanc into barrels right at the end of fermentation when it was loaded with yeast. From our experiments, we found that the wine that went into barrels loaded with yeast, as opposed to the wine that went in later when it was clear, had a fuller, rounder flavor. Currently at the Enological Institute in Bordeaux, they are studying polysaccharides, carbohydrate related compounds. They have shown that increases in time on the yeast lees change the polysaccharide content and may account for the textural change. So there's good scientific support for yeast contact.

Many winemakers in Europe originally felt that the yeast protected the wine; as long as you leave the wine on the lees, you had more of a reductive condition and didn't have to adjust SO_2. We've experimented with SO_2 reduction in barrel fermented lots that are left on the yeast lees. We found that SO_2 reduction is a possibility and, in fact, an advantage to mouth feel in many cases. We're not confident we can reduce SO_2 if we have a finished wine in the barrel but not on the lees. There are more and more good reasons coming to light to support barrel fermentation. It's simple, and there's a lot to be said for simplicity in winemaking.

You have been cutting back on the skin contact time of the grapes. Five years ago, it might have been twelve hours contact, now it's been considerably diminished. What was that a response to? What did you find out there?

In 1981, I bought a must chiller based on an instinctive feeling that it would be better to cool those hot grapes right away when they came in from the vineyards. It wasn't based on experience or any technical data. But we did set up an experiment that year to evaluate the effect of must chilling and fortunately the results supported the decision. We did a twenty-four hour skin contact with the grapes at four different temperatures. I learned something very important about skin contact that I hadn't seen before: temperature is more important than time. I knew, from my work at Mondavi, the compositional effects of skin contact: increased phenolics, increased pH and decreased acidity. But we had never thought about temperature as important to control; instead we were always concerned about the time on the skins. At Simi during the 1981 experiment, at each temperature we took samples every few hours and looked at the wine phenolic content. The rate of increase in phenolics was much more related to temperature than time. Grapes that were cold had a lower level of phenolics after twenty-four hours skin contact than grapes that were very warm after three hours of skin contact. It was dramatic. Temperature makes a big difference and time makes a difference but less so.

Skin contact has an impact on style. We tasted those four wines over a period of four years. In the first tasting, about three months after harvest, the cold skin contact, the less extracted, low phenolic wine, was closed up and not nearly as pretty as the others. The warm, twenty-four hour skin contact was more like those late seventies wines that were big, rich and "up front." But that wine died in about six months. In that same period, the cold skin contact lot had begun to develop. After a year and a half, it was the most beautiful wine. Stylistically, we wanted to move away from heaviness and coarseness; we wanted flavor, but we wanted delicacy. So we switched to chilling our grapes, which had an immediate impact. Then we switched to reducing skin contact time. Skin contact time was adjusted vineyard by vineyard. The vineyard that had a high flavor profile or high phenolic profile, like the small grape Chardonnay, would get no skin contact.

You seem to be among a handful of winemakers who are always experimenting, always doing something new, whether it's in the vineyard or the cellar. You always keep an open mind.

You can't get settled into a "this is the way to make wine" mentality. The way wine was made, say twelve years ago, might have worked for those grapes and those expectations at that time. But tastes change; my tastes have changed and the public's tastes have changed. I think we have a much more sophisticated audience than we did ten years ago. So what works at one time may not necessarily be appropriate later.

Winemaking is a system and it's a system of interaction. When you make changes in the system from using new barrels to older barrels, more barrel fermentation to less barrel fermentation, more skin contact to less skin contact, the change affects the whole system and you may have to change other things in response. I've always had a problem with people who say that a certain technique is the best or only one. I don't think there are any absolutes. I've tasted good wines made many, many different ways. The people who make the best wines know the raw material they are working with, they know what they want and they adapt their techniques to accomplish it. They don't have a formula.

We're very proud of both our Chardonnay and reserve Chardonnay. We've been successful in making a distinctive style and we're recognized for the quality of both those wines. You could almost say we could rest on our laurels. But that's not possible. What are we going to be doing ten years from now with Chardonnay to still be on top? I'm confident it's not exactly what we're doing today. There are always possibilities for improvement.

It won't be anything radical but the small details and little pieces of information give you a greater understanding of the whole picture.

For Simi and the North Coast in general, there will be a radical difference between 1980 and 1990 in the vineyards. There were radical differences between the 1970s and the 1980s in winemaking. After major changes occur in the vineyards so that we're getting more flavor concentration, softer tannins and different acid balance, the industry will have to go back and restructure the winemaking because we won't be working with the same raw materials anymore. As we perfect our ability to grow better grapes, our winemaking will change in response.

In a large winery, such as Simi, how do you perceive your role and what do you see as your priorities?

First of all, I don't think of Simi as large. I've always thought about winemaking as threading all its various aspects together into a whole system. When I came to Simi, I wanted to design the cellar, buy the equipment, build a staff and develop winemaking procedures because I knew all those things counted for the wine. That's the way I still feel. I have an outstanding group of people working for me. All are experienced in what they do. I see myself as standing back and asking, "Where do we need to be going? What do we need to explore or focus on?" I came to Simi with a depth of winemaking skills and once we'd gotten the basic system established in the winery and vineyards, I asked myself, "Where do I need to invest my technical efforts for the greatest result?" The answer was in the vineyards. What I saw in the early eighties was that the greatest result would come if I invested my time in the vineyards, learning about viticulture and how to integrate that into the winemaking.

Because Simi is small and we don't have a large number of people, we can't concentrate on everything at once. For my first five years, much of our experimental work and energy was concentrated on Chardonnay development. Then, in conjunction with our vineyard development, we started on a major Cabernet program. After our Cabernet vineyards were planted and started to come into production, I went to Bordeaux to explore what they see as critical to making great Cabernet. I came back with a good concept of the answers to that question. I began to physically change the winery, modifying our winemaking and working with our vineyards to achieve our Cabernet goals.

What kind of discipline is winemaking? How would you categorize it?

I like to think of wine growing as an art. Maybe the art is the integration of the craft, the science and the agriculture. That's why it's so interesting; it has so many facets. People today are a bit shy about science and technology but it is a great gift to winemakers. I mentioned the experiment with polysaccharides: it's wonderful to have wine science provide you with an understanding of what you are observing. Another good science example is the research being done on the effect of light on the leaves and fruit in growing Cabernet. The research shows that different kinds and amounts of light affect color, flavor, acid balance and phenolic composition. But science doesn't even scratch the surface of all the questions we can develop about winemaking. Much is still experimental and intuitive. And much can be said about the quality of people's palates. I think the better taster I am, the better winemaker I am.

Tim Mondavi
ROBERT MONDAVI WINERY

"I see myself not so much as a winemaker but rather as a wine grower."

Tim Mondavi entered the wine business in the traditional European way: he was born into it. His grandparents were originally involved in the California bulk wine business and, in 1943, they purchased Charles Krug Winery in Napa Valley. His father, Robert, and his uncle, Peter, operated the winery for several decades until a well-publicized family rift prompted his father to establish Robert Mondavi Winery in 1966. The founding of the winery ushered in the modern era of winemaking in California: it was the first major winery built since Prohibition. Robert Mondavi broke from the past and revamped sleepy winemaking traditions, experimenting and creating the most high technology winery money could buy. With the day-to-day operation of the winery in the hands of his children, Robert is now winemaker emeritus and roving ambassador of goodwill.

The wine business was always in the back of Tim Mondavi's head, but his father's sibling rivalries gave him pause to consider a different career, perhaps in architecture or marine biology. Eventually, the level of personal expression involved in winemaking overwhelmed him with its appeal. In 1974, he joined his father and brother, Michael, at the winery. After a diverse apprenticeship, he took over the winemaking responsibilities, bringing a younger perspective to the regime. While UC Davis instruction augmented his on-the-job training, there was certainly a lot of both intuitive and practical knowledge handed down from father to son.

Production is reputed to be over half a million cases, including the California appellation, varietal wines made at Woodbridge, the premium wines made at Oakville and Opus One, a joint wine venture of Mondavi and Chateau Mouton Rothschild. No other winery in California offers such a broad scope and style of wines for every taste and price range. Under Tim's guidance, the winery has improved quality in all lines and has gone "back to basics" in making better wines. After nineteen years in the business, Tim Mondavi does not, for a moment, lack enthusiasm for the subject of wine. Those who cross his path cannot help but be optimistic about the future of California wine.

When you decided on a career in the wine business, did you mix formal training with hands-on experience at the winery?

Yes, I went to UC Davis and took enology and some of the viticulture courses, although my emphasis was enology. After completing the course there I felt more could be learned at a winery than in graduate school. But the formal background was something very valuable to me, not only in building confidence but also in developing an ability to hypothesize about how to pursue wine and its improvement. I think it's an important background for a winemaker; however, you can get that inquisitiveness and organization through other means. My father didn't have any formal background in wine, except for what he taught himself. So first and foremost is the orientation and second is the technical background. There's no doubt about that.

So, at some later point, you took charge of production?

Originally, I did some production planning in the winery. After a few years, it was evident my orientation was to be primarily responsible for the wines. That happened quickly. One of the advantages I had coming into the winery was my ability to talk with my father as well as the people who were working for him. My father, I feel, was always the winemaker. Prior to my entry on the scene, there were enologists that worked with him, like Warren Winiarski, Mike Grgich and Zelma Long. I had a good chance to get to know Mike and his feeling for the wines and Zelma for her thorough evaluation of them. But when I came on in 1974, I found I had an ability to communicate between my father, Zelma and the balance of the winemaking team; I was able to contribute immediately to what was going on. Part of that was the result of my ability to taste wines and grow up with them. I understood what my father wanted to say, what he wanted to do. I accepted his palate and he accepted mine. Another important aspect of this was I had great respect for the people I was working with. Over time, I think it became reciprocal and we worked very well together.

Eventually you became the winemaker?

Yes. I became responsible for production and the final decisions. However, I think my formal responsibility came before my exercising of it. I came in early on and within two years became known as the person in charge. Yet I knew people had worked with my father before me and I had a lot to learn. So I worked with those people for some time. Eventually, my confidence grew and their own ability to recognize my potential grew as my abilities developed, and the transition went smoothly.

At this point in time, how do you view your role as winemaker at such a large and diverse number of facilities? What are your responsibilities and priorities?

I see myself not so much as a winemaker but rather as a wine grower. You know, the only person who "made" wine was crucified a number of years ago. The rest of us have to grow it. My role is to insure we maintain and enhance the ability to do two things. One is to do everything the smallest producer can do for his best wine. The other is to be able to see into the future. I think both aspects are extremely important. One speaks of developing the capability of exercising direction through an operational basis. The other paves the future through research and evaluation of what we're looking for. I think both of those roles are extremely important, as are the capabilities to have the commitment and conviction to move forward, to take action, to take risks and to move into that direction. I would say I work with a number of qualified people who are highly motivated toward both of those ends. I see my principal role as being the one who chiefly facilitates that and ultimately develops the direction. And it's a lot of fun.

You have many people working for you who are winemakers in their own right. If you took them out tomorrow and put them in a 30,000 case winery, they would probably be superstars.

Absolutely. In fact, if anything, their technical capabilities are probably well in excess of my own. I don't view myself as a technology whiz, by any means, but I don't believe wine is a technological beverage. It's grown; it's a result of feelings and emotions. Another one of my roles is chief protector against having harm done to the wine; I'm responsible for making sure the wine goes down the right path.

For example, Brad Alderson is our winemaker at the Woodbridge facility. I work closely with him on our "California" varietal wines: California Cabernet Sauvignon, Sauvignon Blanc, White Zinfandel and Gamay Rose. Brad is the winemaker and also manager of the Woodbridge operation. He coordinates the development of those wines very effectively. I think our Woodbridge facility has the capability of developing wines many wineries in Napa Valley don't have. Although that is where we produce our California varietal wines, our goal has been to produce wines of naturalness and character; to be able to handle the wines in just the way we would here in Napa Valley. We do that substantially. I'm very proud of that.

Our Oakville winery in Napa Valley is more complicated. In Oakville, we produce a number of wines and we have a number of vintages in the winery at any one time. By virtue of our desire to dissect the issues that make wine tick, we can have a number of things going on. At any one time, we may have 600 different blend numbers at the winery. In comparison, we produce considerably more wine at Woodbridge, but we have far fewer lots of wine there.

You are producing quite a large quantity of wine. How do you keep things organized? How do you know what's going on?

Legend says wine was first made by accident. It's been around for over 8,000 years and, as a result, it's not difficult to make. It happens by itself. All you have to do is provide a container, bruise the grapes and somehow, over time, you've got it. It may not be good wine; the trick is to duplicate the best Mother Nature can do in the best of years on a consistent basis. Additionally, we have to channel it in the best of ways. I don't mean just for production purposes but for discovery purposes so we can learn more about what it is we do. We have taken a very simple process and complicated it enormously.

If you look at the path of any one wine we have, it's actually rather simple. We have taken great strides to simplify the process for the betterment of the wine. I believe cleanliness and naturalness are perhaps the best things for wine. Robert Parker has given California winemakers a bad name by saying that we tend to overprocess wine and that technology has harmed California wine. In the past, I would agree with his statement in that, on the heels of Prohibition, the young wine industry found it had to clean up its microbial problems. So it focused on caring for wine through repression, that is, repression of fault. This was the technological byword. That continued until relatively recently.

Let me weave through here the fact that we are a young industry in California. We've been in the wine business for as long as it's existed on a formal basis here. But since Prohibition in 1933, there were many years of very little progress. Robert Mondavi Winery was the first new winery to be built in Napa Valley (1966) since repeal. We were the twenty-sixth winery in Napa Valley and now there are over 200. Between the years of 1933 and 1966, I think the focus of wineries, by and large, was on repression of fault. Now, beginning in the mid eighties, I think the focus has been on enhancement of virtue. And that's a major difference. What that says to me is that the simpler the winemaking process in a natural way, the better off the wine will be. We have been forced to correct faults in the vineyard rather than in the winery. Rather than adjusting acid or adjusting pH through acidulation, we now look in the vineyard for canopy management, soil moisture management, crop level care, proper density and proper location. This moves the process to its natural vineyard environment.

The technological approach is appropriate when you can't have anything else; on a last resort basis, it's appropriate. However, our technology is so good now we don't need to use it nearly as often. Technology no longer scares us. In the past, when technology was new, you'd look in a microscope and see things you didn't understand. So the obvious thing you had to do was zap it! That era is gone with the coming of an enlightened wine grower. What we are trying to do now is simplify things. That's basically a broad philosophical way of saying if you draw the path of any of our wines from the grape to the bottle, I think you'll find it a very simple one. The complication comes when you try to vary the path to learn what you can do to improve it. These need to be quite simple. That's to say we'll do experiments in a vineyard or comparisons in the cellar that need to be kept separate. There can be a multiplicity of blends made from a single soil or single vineyard.

The organization we have here is homegrown and it works pretty well but it's very complex. We have a number of good people involved in nurturing it, making sure the system evolves with our changing winemaking. It's a very complex system; we aren't passive wine growers. We are very active in order to make sure the wine is taken care of simply.

Let me get your reaction to the thought that now we know how to make wine in California so the next leap in quality is going to be viticulturally, in the vineyards. That is, learning to plant the right grapes in the right places along with canopy and soil management.

I would agree with that. But I still think there are a number of advances we can make in the winery. I think we know a number of the things, but in the fine-tuned detailing of that, we still have a long way to go.

The substantial growth is clearly in the vineyards. I think Californians made their advancement in the winery by virtue of the fact that we could address it in a controlled fashion. It's very difficult to control vineyard lots. You have to be very patient because of soil and climate variations. Then there's the pragmatic aspect of being able to do a controlled experiment during the pressure of harvest.

So I think we made advancement in the cellar before we did in the vineyard. Also, our environment allowed for a passive approach to viticulture. When you compare our environment to that of Burgundy, Bordeaux or the Mosel, I think you'll find we tend to have a wonderful climate for vineyards. Oftentimes you don't learn things unless you have problems and are motivated to correct them. Moist and cool conditions require an efficient vine. California vines are just the opposite, our environment does not require an efficient vine to give us what it really should. We have bred lazy, vigorous vines that can luxuriate in the environment we have. We have an abundance of sunlight and dry weather, the type of climate people in Burgundy or Bordeaux would love to have. Our problems come from being too warm. Their problems come from being too cool and wet. I'd rather have our problems. But that means we still have lazy vines that give us too large a crop and too high yields. As a result, the potential character is lacking.

Could you single out a couple of ongoing viticultural experiments that you, by virtue of your size, are able to do that smaller wineries can't?

Anybody can do experiments. But our size allows us to do more experiments and do them more thoroughly. This is a real advantage, but as far as I'm concerned, it's not so much a question of size as it is of organization and orientation. The fact is we are a family operation committed to producing the finest wine we possibly can to compete with the finest wines of the world. Smaller wineries can do some experiments and can collaborate with other smaller operators but then consistency of results becomes a question. Our size allows us to have a consistency of result and to do things in a size and scope that gives us greater ability to draw more confidence from the results we get.

Two things we are doing on a viticultural basis are canopy management and leaf removal. These are fairly commonplace at this point but we have done them for a number of years. All our vineyards are taking advantage of them. We are also trying a number of trellising systems, whether it be the Y system, the Geneva double curtain or vertical trellising. There are a number of canopy trials and rootstock trials underway. And we are doing any number of variations.

I don't consider tight spacing an experiment any longer. We are planting our vineyards in Carneros now with the tightest spacing that we can get mechanically. It's seven feet by five feet, which is not all that tight, when you consider all of our new vineyards behind the winery in Oakville are basically four feet by six feet. We are doing some comparisons of various densities between meter by meter and four feet by six feet, which is essentially our adopted norm at this point.

It's something you've evolved over time from the results of your experience?

That's right, we've looked at that. This is still, to a certain extent, a leap of faith. We don't have old vineyards that are tight spaced. What we do have are old vineyards in high vigor and low vigor soil and I would extrapolate density and its match with proper rootstock to be able to superimpose vigor. All the vines we have out there now, as I mentioned before, are a result of taking advantage of a relatively abundant climate. So high vigor was the norm. If you can increase your tonnage and lower your cost, while keeping the same quality levels, which is nothing more than sugar, acid and pH, the enologist turns that over to the viticulturalist and, zap, he's gone. So now I think we're turning those clocks back.

You've acquired the Tepusquet Vineyards in Santa Barbara County. What are you doing with those vineyards viticulturally? Where are those grapes going?

We have made a number of changes. After our first harvest there, we pruned more severely than anyone had ever done before. The vines were spindly and meager. We pruned them way back, which was our only radical change. Also, we cut back the water dramatically. The soils there are sandy and allow water to penetrate quickly; water retention is very low. Frequent irrigations were the norm in the past; we cut way back, maybe by seventy-five percent. We also cut off fertilization and cut back on the method of protection. Previously it was heavy on sulfurs and we changed that to Bayleton late in the season, which I think is clearly the better way to go, especially in a cool environment.

We are going to evaluate the quality of the wines and see what the potential is. But, from my perspective at this point, the Central Coast has the right soils when there is recognition it is not a high yielding area. There are very low yields, even in a good year. You can produce outstanding quality wine there; wines of great suppleness, richness and liveliness.

Do you set the style for any given wine or is that more of an evolution of what's gone on before?

It's an evolution of what has happened. For example, with the Pinot Noir in Oakville, we go through a procedure every year where we methodically evaluate our wines and the wines that are in the marketplace, both foreign and domestic. We see what we like about our wines. We see what's good and bad about other wines. We also evaluate the experiments we have done. These experiments are extremely important to our ability to make progress. So it's not just a passive, external evaluation but it's an inward looking evaluation as well. We collectively evaluate the wines and the directions we want to go. I basically establish the direction for what we ought to be doing and what the normal procedures will be. Then, during harvest, we bring the grapes in at their best. I am very much involved on a day-to-day basis.

Your father has been quoted recently as saying that in the past, we made clean, technically correct wines. You've gotten away from that to a degree; how have you gotten away from that for the better?

In the past, as I mentioned, the focus of technology was on repression. If you use Pinot Noir, for example, and you have a character that you attribute to a microbial problem, then that microbial problem might disallow you to have longer skin contact. You might want to pull the wine off the skins quickly, have malolactic fermentation completed or even repressed. As soon as that was finished you might filter the wine, raise the sulfur and put the wine in older barrels because new barrels would give too much character to a wine that was basically knocked down; then you'd filter prior to bottling. You would have a very clean, repressed, austere but drinkable wine. That was the norm fifteen or twenty years ago.

Grapes used to be something that arrived at the cellar door the day of harvest. Pinot Noir, more than any other variety, has forced us to the vineyard by virtue of its sensitivity. Perhaps because it was the weakest wine in California, it demanded attention. Just as the poor environment in Europe demanded viticultural attention, Pinot Noir did here. The trials we did on yield were extremely responsive. Location again is the age-old story. Light penetration is important, although with Pinot Noir it is not as critical because, by its nature, it's not as vigorous. But still, with better light penetration to the fruit zone, we were able to improve the color and the character.

We did a number of things early on, seeking to avoid the chain of repressive activity. In retrospect, repressive activity took a wine basically weak at the time of harvest and made it weaker. We tried to break that chain by building their resistance. The first thing we did with Pinot Noir was stem retention in 1976. We moved toward longer skin contact; we evaluated whole cluster capabilities. We eliminated the filtrations prior to going into barrel. We eliminated the higher levels of sulfur. With a sturdier wine, we were able to use newer oak barrels. So we began to ratchet this young, failing wine to strengthen it and develop its self-resiliency. We also continued to work in the vineyard, to select the proper sites and lower the yield. By these methods we were able to develop a wine of greatness. Now yields are lower, the sites are proper and irrigation is atypical.

Skin contact is considerably longer; rather than three to four days of skin contact, now it's two to four weeks of skin contact, even for Pinot Noir. Rather than getting the berries to the fermenter with a fairly high level of maceration through an aggressive crusher/stemmer and then an aggressive pump over, we have a very gentle system now where we avoid any pump whatsoever at that stage.

We've come a long way. In place of the filtration and the microscope that scared us, we have a technology that has freed us. Rather than being frightened by what we see in the microscope, we have been able to deal with the knowledge through experiments and understanding microbial activity better than ever before. We now try to live in harmony with it rather than battling it. But that takes a more thorough understanding of the wine than we had fifteen years ago. A little bit of technology can scare you into doing the wrong thing. With greater technology and experience, we'll learn that we can have a gentler hand and still do it safely.

Tell me about your level of involvement with Opus One, the joint winemaking venture between your father and the late Baron Rothschild of Chateau Mouton Rothschild?

The genesis of the project was in 1975 when the Baron contacted my father with the concept; he contacted him about it again in 1978. Basically they came to an agreement in principle contingent upon Lucien Sionneau, the winemaker, coming to California and working with us and our family being in agreement with it. All of us met and finally became enthusiastic about the project. Without knowing the people, I was hesitant about it, but once I met the Baron and Lucien, I became quite enthusiastic.

With Lucien's first visit in 1980, it was our responsibility to establish a style for the wine my father and Baron Philippe had begun. It was up to us, at that point, to talk about what Opus One should be; we did that. We established a style and then we cared for it; we selected the blends. It was very interesting for me to see Lucien's orientation in that his palate, being accustomed to wines from a cooler area, tended to go toward firmer and more structured wines. I would tend to go toward wines of more opulence, suppleness and richness. So we were different in that regard. The area of similarity, however, was that he would orient, in character, directly to the To-Kalon Vineyard of the Oakville bench area, as would we. That's where we were in agreement. It was very interesting for us to develop the blends based on Lucien's orientation, based on tasting Chateau Mouton Rothschild and seeing their evolution over a number of years and based on tasting our wines and seeing our evolution over a number of years. Basically we developed Opus One as a wine that was firmer in structure than the Robert Mondavi Reserve Cabernet would be, yet still a product of our environment, which would indicate greater warmth and richness than that of Pauillac. So in truth, we now have "Oakillac," somewhere between Oakville and Pauillac.

Where do the grapes for Opus One come from? Have you designated a certain vineyard?

Opus One purchased 140 acres of vines in the Oakville bench area. It's across from Robert Mondavi Winery and to the side of us, near Dwyer Road. Those vineyards are still very young because they were never planted to Cabernet. It's a long story, but we had never relied upon them, although our Cabernet Reserves had come from that area for many, many years. Opus One was really a selection of wines Lucien and I would make, and now Patrick Leon, Lucien's successor since the 1985 harvest. We would collectively make a selection of wines from our harvest of Cabernet Sauvignon, Cabernet Franc and Merlot, with the intention of developing the style Lucien and I had established. We will go through all the wines from the harvest, select the wines we feel are most appropriate, try a number of trial blends and then finalize a blend we feel is appropriate.

How have you seen the style of Opus One evolve?

I think Pinot Noir has helped us develop Opus One. Chardonnay has helped us evolve Pinot Noir. As we have understood the sensitivity of Pinot Noir, we have been forced to be gentle with the wine. It's forced us to take care of the vineyards in a better fashion. That includes all the things we have talked about: lower yields, canopy management and everything else. Additionally, we have learned to be gentler with the wines during pump over, to be able to wet the cap as opposed to bash it, to have a much longer skin contact than in the past, to be able to convey the pomace in a gentle fashion and, as a result, being able to incorporate more press wine than in the past. So we now have a far richer wine than in the past, with more layers and more depth. But that's across the board, with all of our wines. I think Pinot Noir has led the way with that recognition. So the wine has evolved and it's very exciting to see. But the basic character and style is the same; it just has more layers there.

What's going to happen in twenty years? Look into your crystal ball. How do you see things changing, as far as the wine drinking public?

I think, over time, the wines we will be making will be even better than they are now. I think the wines will be made in a natural fashion. We will continue the evolution. Our technology will grow to a point where we can be even freer with the art aspect than we are now. I think that the technology historically obliterated the art. Now it's releasing it and allowing for it.

People will begin to recognize the origin of the fruit more so than they do now. The orientation toward appellations is a very strong one and it will continue to grow. Appellations are happening by virtue of what we've been talking about. Twenty years ago, "grapes were grapes" and you produced as much as you could. Then you had relatively short skin contact, macerated aggressively (developing a lot of solids) and used technology with a heavy hand. Thus you obliterated some of the sensitive differences in the soil. But now we have released those differences and we are seeing them strongly. Winemakers know that; wine growers know it even better. And the consumers are beginning to demand that, so over time, there will be a far greater understanding of what people mean when they say, "I'll have a Stag's Leap wine, an Oakville bench wine or a Tokalon wine." In the past, the emphasis was, almost exclusively, on the winemaker. Vintages are of growing importance but soil is the future as to where the consumers are going as well as the winemakers.

People will recognize wine, when moderately consumed, to be a healthy and natural part of the diet. Wine will become more commonplace in the future and people will look for more variation of wine. The variation will come from soil and climate and it will come from varietal differences as well. Twenty years from now, we will begin to put technology into place and develop the art of living as opposed to depressing our activities.

I think many people still have the misconception that California is a hot environment, or that Napa Valley is a warm environment. Relative to some areas, it is; but I will say I'm glad we have the environment we do. It's consistent. The challenge for wine growers in California is to begin to harmonize vines with nature. That is something that will begin to show the world how wonderful our potential really is. Because of Prohibition, we are at a disadvantage to the history of Bordeaux, Burgundy and other fine wine regions. At the end of Prohibition, we took vineyards spaced five feet by five feet and seven feet by seven feet and planted eight feet by twelve and nine feet by twelve feet in their stead; we took lower vigor rootstocks and replaced them with higher vigor rootstocks. The work that had been done by the German and Italian immigrants was essentially wiped out by Prohibition. And all the vineyards planted since that time were planted under a technological, high vigor mentality that took advantage of our climate. It was not in harmony to produce top quality that took advantage of that climate.

Now, as we recognize the virtue of our climate and our orientation toward the best wine, and as our viticulture becomes harmonious with that climate, I think you'll see terrific things. I think it's something that's a challenge and it's a responsibility we have. But it speaks to the future in a very positive way. I don't think you'll see other mature wine regions of the world have the same rapid acceleration of quality that you will see from the New World.

RAVENS WOOD

ZINFANDEL
SONOMA COUNTY
1   9   9   1
MADE AND BOTTLED BY
RAVENSWOOD
SONOMA, CALIFORNIA
CONTAINS SULFITES
ALCOHOL 14.3% BY VOL.

Joel Peterson

RAVENSWOOD

*"I'm familiar with every barrel in the winery and I know
what's going on with each one. I think, in some ways,
that is the way you make great wine."*

When Joel Peterson was growing up, wine was commonplace at the family table. His father, in fact, was head of the San Francisco Wine Club, a group that organized and presented regular, formal tastings of great European wines.

After graduating from Oregon State with an emphasis in biochemistry and microbiology, he bypassed med school and instead went into medical research and immunology. All the while, he pursued a continuing interest in wine by writing about it and by acting as a purchasing consultant to retail wine shops. In his spare time, he began to develop a relationship with the late, legendary winemaker, Joe Swan, helping him at harvest and observing his winemaking style.

In 1976, he crushed a small amount of Zinfandel at Swan's winery and began increasing his production a little every year. By 1981, Peterson had gotten large enough to move into his own winery, just south of Sonoma. To support his winemaking, a self-described labor of love, he worked nights and weekends as a medical technologist to make ends meet. Finally in 1988, with the winery on solid financial ground, he was able to devote all his time to making wine. Production has slowly increased without any loss in quality.

First and foremost, Peterson is one of the world's biggest fans of Zinfandel, a grape seemingly neglected in the industry's rush to fill the demand for Cabernet and Chardonnay. Producing a number of different vineyard designated Zinfandels (Dickerson, Cooke, Old Hill), along with less specific Sonoma County and Vintners Blend bottlings, he has established a reputation for rich, extracted, dense, full-bodied wines.

Despite your father's interest and background in wine, you didn't go off to college to study winemaking?

After Oregon State, I was going to go to medical school but ended up going to Europe for a year instead. On returning I went into medical research and worked as an immunologist. At the same time I was doing consulting for wine stores, advising them what to buy. I was also doing some wine writing. My interest began to switch away from research for a number of reasons, not the least of which was I was in cancer research and had sixty breast and melanoma patients. Some of them died and I wasn't used to that. It was tough. One day I was talking to one of the patients, who was a very intuitive psychiatrist, and he asked if I really liked what I was doing. I told him I was interested in wine but didn't know what I could do outside of consulting and writing. So he asked me if I had ever thought of making wine. I said, "Not really," but that sort of set me on the road and I began looking into it. In those days, as a consultant, I was tasting, on average, five hundred wines a week; so I had a pretty good idea of what was going on in California.

I ran across some wines being made by a guy named Joe Swan; I thought they were the best and most interesting wines I'd tasted from California. His Zinfandels were just unbelievable. So I went and attached myself to Joe Swan. It was good to get involved with Joe because he taught me the nuts and bolts of one-man winemaking and I was able to see how to make wine on a small scale. Joe also had some ideas that coincided with mine about how good wine should be made. I spent all my spare time, including weekends and vacations, with Joe, helping him harvest his grapes and generally being boy Friday whenever possible. During that time, I read a significant amount of French winemaking texts from the turn of the century. A lot of my ideas and a lot of the things I do here at Ravenswood are based on that kind of reading as well as my own sense of what might work.

Winemaking, as I do it, is fairly intuitive, in spite of the fact that I have a very heavy science background. My basic tenet is winemaking should be treated the same way a doctor views medicine. If you have a patient and he's well, you don't treat him. If he's sick, you give him antibiotics if that's what is called for. But you don't keep him on antibiotics all the time in case he might get sick, if there's no indication of that. That's what California wineries do on a routine basis. Industrial winemaking is nothing more than an ability to keep wine from getting sick. They approach every wine as if it were going to be a sick wine. So immediately they refrigerate it, sterilize it and stabilize it, all the things you would do to a wine that was potentially having a problem. That's all fine and good. They have a consistent product and rarely have trouble with it; it tastes okay. But you'll never make great wines that way; in fact, you'll make mediocre wines most of the time. It becomes a standard product. To do anything beyond that, you need to take the risk. You need to believe in the wine, to believe the wine is going to be healthy. If you do get a sick wine, you know you have the technology to take care of it. That's the beauty of being a winemaker at this particular moment in history. In the old days, if the French had a problem wine, they'd sell it right away and hope to get their money out of it. They didn't have the technology to take care of it. Today, we have the technology to take care of any number of problems. Almost every problem, if it's caught early enough, can be handled.

You started your own winery, Ravenswood, in 1976?

Yes, but I was still working with Joe Swan at that time. He was kind enough to allow me to use some of his space. So I went out and bought grapes and made 325 cases of Zinfandel from two old vineyards in Dry Creek. I and others were encouraged by the results and, on the basis of that vintage, I managed to put together a limited partnership. I was able to buy a little more equipment and grapes the following year. Each year I made a little more wine and each year the wine sort of fed on itself. When I knew I was going to jump into winemaking, I got a license as a medical technologist. So until April of 1988, I worked two jobs. Nights and weekends I worked as a medical technologist to support my family, and I made wine as a labor of love. After twelve years, I finally have a full-time salaried position; it's fun and I'm happy making wine.

We are doing fifteen thousand cases, of which nine thousand are super premium wine. The remainder is a vintner's blend of Zinfandel, forty percent of which comes from younger vines and sixty percent from wine we buy in bulk. Most of our Zinfandel, which we make as big and hearty as we can, comes from old vines. Vintner's blend is lighter and fruitier. It's an early drinking blend that has lots of flavor and aging potential but it's lighter than our other Zinfandels.

A lot of your production is less expensive Zinfandel that is good, everyday table wine. It probably helps the cash flow.

It helps the cash flow considerably. In a sense, it takes much less work than everything else we do. The forty percent we make is made like everything else, although we tend to oak it a little heavier. The other sixty percent, we buy. It takes us three days to get the wine put together and bottled and another week to get it out the door. That's moving juice pretty fast and it's gotten us over the hump in terms of allowing us to make the bigger wines and age them longer. It's also the thing that allowed me to be a full-time winemaker.

You're one of the few winemakers that think Zinfandel is still a noble grape, as opposed to Cabernet or Pinot Noir. Why place so much emphasis on Zinfandel?

Well, it is a noble grape. Some of the best California wines I've ever tasted have been Zinfandels. Not only does the grape have the ability to become an incredibly rich, spicy wine that is every bit as good as a Rhone or a Chateauneuf-du-Pape in its best permutations, but it's planted in California in some of the best places you can plant grapes. The guys that planted these grapes knew what they were doing. Most people consider the Zinfandel grapes to be historically lesser than Cabernet or Chardonnay because there's not a European equivalent. There's so much Zinfandel planted in California and it makes such good wine that it's foolish not to look at Zinfandel. It was obvious to me this was not an area over-run with people wanting to make wine. There have been some older Zinfandels I had tasted, like the 1897 Inglenook, that were stunning wines. The 1935 Simi, although it wasn't the biggest wine, had some nice qualities for an aged wine. It was apparent to me that somebody who cared about Zinfandel and wanted to do something serious with it, could make excellent wine. It was an obvious choice for me.

During the seventies, there was a lot of confusion about exactly what a Zinfandel should taste like because it was being made in any number of extreme styles. People didn't know what to expect when they bought a bottle of Zinfandel.

I wouldn't argue with that a bit. And I would say that is also the basic problem with the California wine industry today. Most people don't know how they want to make their wines. So stylistically you get wines all over the map. Now that's interesting. But it's less interesting when you get the same wineries producing wines that are stylistically all over the map from one year to the next. You may get a sweet Chardonnay one year and a dry Chardonnay the next, depending on what they think the market trends are. Most wineries don't work hard in establishing a wine style and identity for themselves.

When I went after Zinfandel, I knew what I wanted to do. I wanted to produce a fairly full-blown, rich, intense, spicy table wine. So that's what I shot for and I think I've achieved it fairly well.

You make several vineyard designated Zinfandels and also a Sonoma appellation Zinfandel. Let's talk a little bit about where they come from and what the differences are.

The Sonoma Zinfandel is a wine I blend using three different vineyards. One is a Dry Creek bench land vineyard that has the typical black cherry/berry-like quality in the nose. It's got a nice flavor but doesn't have a powerful finish. All these vines are sixty-five to one hundred years old. The Cloverdale vineyard is another old vineyard. It's dry-farmed and, as a consequence, the vines have adapted to this by producing grapes that tend to be a little smaller. You get smaller grapes in the clusters and higher skin-to-juice ratio, so the wine tends to be loaded with extract. It has a hard finish, which blends well with the Dry Creek fruit. The third vineyard is in Geyserville and that fruit tends to be a little sweeter in flavor, so it fills out the center of the wine and makes it complete. You'll get those nice black cherry/berry flavors in the front, along with a sweet intensity in the center and a rich, intense, powerful finish.

The other Zinfandels are vineyard designated because they have specific qualities that are all their own. They tend to be pretty complete wines, in their own right, from beginning to end. The Dickerson vineyards is one of the few Napa Valley Zinfandel vineyards I use. It's about eighty years old and a low producer, as are all these vineyards. It produces anywhere from a half a ton to one and half tons an acre. It has a character described as raspberry/eucalyptus/mint. Robert Parker said something to the effect that one vintage smelled like 1959 Mouton, which I thought was a bit of hyperbole, but there is some truth to that. It has those minty, eucalyptus qualities. It's got a long lasting, fruity flavor. Why exactly it does this, I'm not sure but it appears, from my experience, that there are several different clones of Zinfandel running around California. There seem to be two that stand out, even when planted in different areas. One tends to be plummy and peppery, the other this fine-line/cedar/raspberry fruit.

The Old Hill vineyard produces more of black pepper, plummy, rich, intense, almost Rhone-like wine. Tasting it when it's really young, it reminds me of Shiraz; it has that kind of spicy, peppery quality. Part of the reason the Zinfandels have a certain amount of spiced pepper in them is we leave about fifteen percent of the stems that we throw back in when we vinify the lot. But the Old Hill wine has these qualities even without that. It tends to be a dark wine with lots of intensity and flavor. Those two vineyards produce the kind of wines that stand on their own and are individual.

We also do a Merlot that has gotten a lot of attention. The Merlot is a combination of three vineyards: St. Francis, Gundlach-Bundschu and a wonderful vineyard in Knight's Valley. They interact in much the same way as the Zinfandels in Sonoma County: in terms of each other's strengths and deficiencies. The St. Francis has an intense, almost cedar/cigar box-like nose. It's a bit too much on its own but it's a wonderful toner for the wine. The Knight's Valley has a richer, deeper, rounder affect; it's full in the middle and finishes nicely. The Gundlach-Bundschu fruit is plummy; it tends to fill out the center and hold the components together. We vinify it in much the same way we do our Zinfandel, although we don't put in any stems.

All our red wines get long fermentation times, anywhere from three to five weeks. I feel like it intensifies the center of the wine and makes it richer. You also get more of what the grape has to offer. I think Gerald Asher described that as the "onion skin technique." He said something like, "You go for all there is and then you start peeling off the layers, right?" I said, "That's not exactly right but it's something like that." So we do things to give us as much flavor as we can get out of the grape.

Cabernets around here are an ever-changing phenomena. We're finally getting them beat into submission. We're to the point where we're doing a seventy-five percent Cabernet and a twenty-five percent blend of Cabernet Franc and Merlot. It makes the wine much more interesting. It also makes it much less definitive in terms of Cabernet flavor. I've gotten a little tired of green pepper overtones. I've gotten to the point where now I think we should be producing wines that are not necessarily absolutely varietal. I think we're looking for wines with esoteric tones that people can't define necessarily as Cabernet or Zinfandel. You want to be able to say things wine writers get chastised for all the time. For example, "The wine smells like cedar or violets or blackberries." But to be able to define it as the green pepper that is in Cabernet is not a particularly good trait as far as I'm concerned. That's what blending allows you to do. It allows you to give a wine a high-toned nose that is not so closely hung that it's defined as a Cabernet. In our Cabernet, the Cabernet Franc adds a brightness and a lot of spiciness to the wine. The Merlot adds a roundness and depth to the Cabernet that you wouldn't get otherwise. It makes the Cabernet more interesting. I think it's a far better wine than it would be if it were one hundred percent Cabernet.

We are doing one other thing around here and that's our version of the Opus One/Dominus/Trilogy wines, those recent proprietary blends. We have a single vineyard up on Sonoma Mountain called the Pickberry Vineyard that produces phenomenal grapes. The wine is more like a St. Emilion blend than anything else. It's fifty percent Cabernet, forty percent Cabernet Franc and ten percent Merlot. It's a grape blend similar to something like Chateau Figeac. It tends to produce an intense, dark, spicy, somewhat aromatic wine. We've been making the wine for a few years now and the vineyard is fairly young. Each year it gets better.

Since you don't own any vineyards, do you feel in a precarious position in obtaining grapes from year to year?

Sometimes. We tend to have long-term, evergreen contracts with our growers and, in most cases, that works out well. You find that if you work with somebody for a while, they tend to like what you do and you like what they do. There's no reason to change if you're giving each other a fair shake. It's a little harder to keep your wine prices consistent because when one wine is popular, the grape prices necessarily rise. The grapes are a significant portion of what comprises the price of a bottle of wine. For instance, several years ago, I was paying 450 dollars a ton for Zinfandel; now it's anywhere from 850 to 1,000 dollars a ton. So the grape prices doubled but my wine prices haven't. If a winery owns its vineyards, it has much more control over its grape prices. There have been times we've lost good vineyards as a result of not having absolute control over them. I knew I didn't have the money to plant vineyards but I knew I could start a small winery and make it work. Obviously, looking for vineyards is one of the next steps a winery like ours does at this stage.

The flip side is you can choose from a number of contracted vineyards and blend them anyway you want. You're not stuck with a vineyard that's not producing up to your standards.

That's absolutely true. Furthermore, I can't go out and plant eighty-year-old Zinfandel vines. I will always buy grapes. It's nice to have the flexibility to do that, but it's also nice to have something you can actually work on and do exactly in the style that you like. Vineyards are as stylized as wineries, in some ways.

You work closely with the growers to get the kind of fruit you want?

Before we get involved with them, we sit down and have a long discussion about what they're doing in the vineyards. I talk to people who have made wines from these vineyards before. I taste the wines made from the vineyards. I have a pretty good idea what's going on out there before I ever get started. We set certain parameters and work with vineyards that generally have the same ethic about wine and grape growing that we have. That works well for us.

You've long been a proponent of utilizing wild yeast for fermentation?

This is the yeast that comes in with the grapes. I've been doing natural yeast fermentations for fourteen years in spite of the best advice other people gave us which was, "Don't do it; you'll have trouble. You'll get bad odors and stuck fermentations." We've never had a stuck fermentation. We've never had any off odors; certainly there are odors that come through transitorily in the fermentation process but they blow off as the wine continues to ferment. But that happens in a fermentation where you're using known yeast. I think, once again, we're striving for complexity of flavors and a multiple population of yeast, like the ones you get with wild yeast, produce a much more interesting wine than a single yeast. Some people go yeast shopping when they're inoculating their fermentations. They go through the yeast catalog. You look in there and see, "Pasteur red: warm fermenter; produces extremely fruity wines. Assmanhausen: moderately active fermenter, produces more austere, full bodied wines." Well, people go yeast shopping in the catalog depending on what kind of wine they want to make. My feeling is that what you want to produce is a complex, rich wine. If you take all those yeasts in the catalog, mix them all together and throw them into the fermenter, that is, in effect, what we're doing with wild yeast. So you get a much more complex and interesting character in the wine.

What is your percentage of new oak to old oak for aging?

Each wine gets a different quota depending on its weight, what kind of nose accent it has and what I'm looking for. I'd say, on the average, we cycle in about thirty percent new oak in any given year. The old oak is good because it allows you some flexibility if you want to transfer a wine out of new oak but still want to give it some more barrel age. New oak really is for two things. It adds a tone and brightness to the nose that you don't get otherwise. But it also adds more density and more extract to the wine. Overall, oak aging tends to concentrate the wine, so you're really generating a more full-bodied wine.

You do a second year racking of the reds with nitrogen? What's that all about?

It decreases oxygenation of the wine. But more than that, it allows for a more gentle flow of the wine from one barrel to another. If you're putting it through a rotary pump, you're beating it up and whipping it into a fury. Nitrogen racking is more like gravity flow racking. There was an interesting experiment that was done on this subject by Ric Forman when he was at Sterling. He took a wine that he made and split it into two batches. He treated both batches the same in every possible way, except for one thing. One of the batches, he gravity flow racked; the other batch, he racked with a pump. The wines were markedly different when they were finished. The wine that was racked with a pump was somewhat thinner and didn't have as much character as the wine that was gravity racked. So handling the wine more gently kept the wine from being beaten up by being splashed and exposed to oxygen. In the first year, a wine needs a significant amount of oxygen. You need a certain amount of splashing; you need to get rid of some of the early fermentation odors. So, in the first year, we rack with a pump and we're not shy about giving it a lot of air.

How many times do you rack?

Two or three times in the first year. It can be more or less, depending on what's happening with the wine. If a wine starts to get a little hydrogen sulfide in the nose, you rack it more. If a wine has a strong malolactic character, maybe more than we want, we'll rack it a little more. The second year, we rack it three to four times, depending on the wine. Nitrogen racking also probably preserves more of the center and fruit of the wine.

You minimize handling the wine all the way around?

It's the same theory that if it's not broken, don't fix it. If you start with good fruit and a good fermentation, then your job, from that point on, is not to mess it up. You want to make sure it develops the aging components in the barrel that you want and that it's clean when it finally gets into the bottle.

Is it necessarily true that just because you're a small winery that quality is inherent in what you do? Is there any relationship between winery size and quality?

I'm sure that there's a relationship between size and quality. Obviously there are small wineries that produce lousy wines and there are large wineries that produce fine wine on occasion. For me, it's a matter of how much wine I can personally stay in contact with. It's how much wine I personally know barrel by barrel. I'm familiar with every barrel in the winery and I know what's going on with each one. I think, in some ways, that is the way you make great wine. You have to know what's going on in your winery. You can put a protocol together that will make good wine on a large scale. If you're lucky, and if you have perfect grapes, and if your protocol is good, you can make a great wine. On the other hand, that will happen less often in that circumstance than it would if you were smaller and could spend more time with each wine. So that's what being small does for you, if you handle things properly. It's not axiomatic that if you're smaller, you're going to produce great wine.

I think that what I can handle, in terms of knowing what was going on, and in terms of a high quality product like our vineyard designated wine, would probably be fifteen-thousand cases of that and still keep the quality high. At that point, if we were to grow anymore, my concept is a concept that is not that far from what Chalone has done. And that is, you break your winery up into specialty wineries, where one section of the winery would become a Zinfandel winery and another section would become a Cabernet-Merlot winery. That way, you have two individual units working on a scale that would be conducive to producing the highest quality wine without as much risk involved. You would have to have somebody who was very good overseeing the operation. And you would have to have some good individual winemakers with each operation. You'd have to have a tight organization that knew exactly what it was about and what it wanted to do. But that would be the way to do it, rather than getting bigger and bigger. Once you start expanding, then you start leaving more things to chance. Then you start losing control; and then you're really reliant on the California-let's-give-it-medicine technique because you can't afford to lose thirty-thousand tons of grapes. That's a real economic consideration for big wineries. Whereas here, I know what the wine is supposed to be doing. I know if one of the wines has a pH problem it may be causing it to have acetic acid problems. Also, I know things that are going on in the winery before they become a problem and I know what action to take if they do. If I was relying on cellar workers and a few samples taken from barrel periodically and I was making seven times as much wine as I am now, I'd lose something. No question about it.

What is it that attracted you to winemaking?

The reason I got into it was because it's a little bit of everything. It's clearly a science; I know from my science background the things I have to worry about and the things I don't. It's an art in the sense that every wine is a vision. Every wine is an unknown when you start and it develops much like a painting does. You may add a little more of that, take a little bit of that away, etcetera. It's something that pleases the senses, stimulating the nose, the palate and the individual, in some cases, much the same way that art does.

One other thing that needs to be talked about is the whole concept of wines. I don't treat wine as an industrial food product; I'm not producing a manufactured good around here. If I really wanted to make money, I'd make mayonnaise and turn out as much of it as I could. Really what I'm doing is producing something to give people pleasure. It's something for people to enjoy; something that will go well with meals; something which helps them, in some ways, to relate to each other. You know, frequently when you go to a dinner party, you don't know anybody. But usually several people at the table will know something about wine, so you always open a conversation talking about wine and that leads to a whole possibility of things, which is very nice. But what you're doing is producing an element that helps society function in a better way. So I look at myself as doing much the same thing as I did in cancer research. My basic motivation for getting into research and medicine was to help people overcome darkness and misery. Winemaking does some of those same things because it really hooks into the good parts of people's lives. It helps them enjoy life a bit more.

David Ramey
CHALK HILL WINERY

"The central question in making fine wines is how to correctly identify and refine the aesthetic sensibility. What is fine wine? What should it taste like? If you don't know the answer to these questions, you're not going to be using whatever tools you possess on the right problem."

With an undergraduate degree in literature, David Ramey was set to become an english teacher when he began to seriously consider a winemaking career. Without much science background, he suddenly switched gears, enrolled at UC Davis and earned his Masters in three years.

Before he settled down in California, he wanted to augment his academic learning with practical experience in other winemaking regions of the world. He spent a harvest in Bordeaux, working for Christian Moueix at Chateau Petrus and his other vineyard properties in Pomerol. At the other end of the spectrum, he worked a harvest at Lindemans in Australia, where he processed ton after ton of grapes for their wine blends.

In 1980, he put down California roots as assistant to winemaker Zelma Long at Simi Winery, just as they were beginning their cellar expansion program. Four years later, he became winemaker at Mantanzas Creek, where he was instrumental in designing some of the inner workings of the new winery, including a new barrel storage system. He refined and adapted his winemaking philosophy at Mantanzas while producing Sauvignon Blanc, Chardonnay and Merlot. His wines received universal praise, both from wine critics and the buying public.

In 1990, he moved to Chalk Hill Winery where he continues to show an uncanny ability to consistently produce rich, ripe, balanced wines. When people talk about the "elegance" and "finesse" of his wines, what they mean is all the disparate elements of winemaking—the fruit, oak, fermentation, lees contact and extended aging—are brought together in harmony.

At Mantanzas Creek, you purchased the majority of your grapes. Now at Chalk Hill, you're solely working with estate grown grapes. What are the advantages and disadvantages?

There are mostly advantages, assuming one has the resolve and financial backing to make changes in the vineyards when necessary. One of the big advantages of purchasing fruit from a multiple of growers is if you don't like the quality of the fruit, you drop the vineyard. Sometimes estate wineries can be stuck with lousy fruit. The corollary to that is most often where that's the case, it's a situation where you have a relatively small amount of acreage and so you don't have a lot of diversity in the estate grapes.

One of the great things about Chalk Hill is there's a lot of diversity in the fruit; it isn't just a square parcel in front of the winery. There are hillside grapes from all different exposures and little valleys where the gravel has washed down out of the hills, which actually give us some of our best fruit. There's red soil, white soil, heavy clay and loam. There are different exposures and different clones. All this accomplishes the same thing. The percentage of vineyards of the world that can stand alone is very small: like Montrachet, Chassagne or Corton-Charlemagne. In California, you have some people copying the French system but sometimes without understanding the real rationale behind it. Vineyard designating your wine doesn't make it great. Most single vineyards are not complete; few vineyards I've dealt with could stand on their own. You make a balanced wine more often through some form of blending. The biggest advantage, in terms of being estate grown, is the harvest decision. I don't make harvest decisions until four or six p.m. the day before the harvest. That allows us to get up-to-the-minute analysis of the different blocks of the estate. After I get those results, I walk through the vineyard with the vineyard manager and we make the decision right there as to what we're going to pick the next day.

With purchased fruit, you're usually dealing with growers who sell to other wineries. In those situations at Mantanzas, I found I had to schedule harvest several days in advance. I'd look at the maturity graphs, go out to the vineyards and taste everyday. I had to look ahead and make agreements as long as five days in advance to harvest. I had to do that to protect ourselves, because if I didn't another winery would reserve the picking crew for that day.

So it's more optimum?

Yes, optimal harvest is a big advantage. The other advantage, which is just as big or bigger, is the ability to replant. We're replanting various areas because the quality isn't quite what we wanted; or maybe phylloxera is going to come in; or maybe the vines are virused and the yield and quality has gone down. In an estate situation it is our decision, not the grower's, on how to proceed in terms of varietal, rootstock, spacing, trellising, row orientation. and clones.

The other side of the argument is the vineyards at Chalk Hill were already planted when you came there; so how did you, in any sense, control the spacing, clones, etc.?

In any vineyard in the world, the owner or the grower will tell you there are favored and less favored sites. Now with the renewed emphasis on quality at Chalk Hill, the owner is willing to listen and take action. For example, we found the quality from a certain block is not good; we've sold wine from it in bulk for three years; it's got terrible leaf roll virus and is only cropping one and half tons per acre. So we're able to replant that block and that's a real quality decision for the long run.

What is your feeling about phylloxera and how it's affecting the North Coast region?

Well, it's out there. The consensus, and I wouldn't tend to disagree with it, is it's just a matter of time, if you're planted on AxR1 rootstock.

It's not a matter of if, it's a matter of when?

Yes, I believe that's what most people think. The vineyard manager and I are addressing the question right now. At what point do you replant? If you're a grower who sells to others, you can wait until you see the phylloxera before you start replanting. But if you're estate bottled, you need to protect yourself. I think that argues for a more proactive plan. But you hate to tear out producing vineyards before you have to. On the other hand, if you wait until you've got phylloxera and then start replanting, you could end up in a situation where you have all new vines.

But didn't you replant fifteen percent of the vineyards this year?

Well, we ripped out about thirty-five acres in 1991 and replanted in 1992.

So it was something you were eventually going to do anyhow, but with the threat of phylloxera hanging over your head, it makes even more sense and might have hastened your actions.

That's the wisest approach and the best rationalization. If you can afford to go ahead and replant, phylloxera presents an opportunity for even more quality improvement. As a whole, I think phylloxera is going to be good for California because a lot of vines are planted in poor sites and to the wrong varieties. They're just not optimal vineyards. So they're going to be replanted and they're going to be better. The quality of fruit produced twenty years from now will be much better than what we have today. That's really exciting. So I don't see the big picture as some bleak, natural disaster; I see it as a genuine opportunity to continue to propel California quality on the world stage.

You're making Cabernet now, where before the only red wine you made was Merlot. I know you have some ideas about fruit maturity and tannin management that have been evolving.

Let me start by saying that varietal differences are overdone; in terms of whether you're making Merlot or Cabernet, I don't think there's a whole lot of difference. You basically do the same things while the character of the fruit expresses itself. In fact, the character isn't always all that different. It so happens that on this parcel here, the most consistently tannic (analytically) and deepest colored wine is the Merlot. It's not softer than the Cabernet.

I like a story that Jean Claude Barrault from Petrus told me about varieties. The French perspective is Americans place too much emphasis on varieties, whereas in France they're trying to make the best wine for a particular site.

If we're dealing with the Bordeaux complex of grapes, there are some differences between the varieties. Here's how you would use that properly: we know Cabernet is more tannic than Merlot—and this is French experience talking, but I've found it to be true too, once it was pointed out to me and I started paying attention—that gravely soil makes for a less tannic red wine and clay soil makes for a more tannic red wine. If you have a site with clay and a site with gravel, as we do here, you wouldn't put the Cabernet on the clay because it would accentuate the already tannic quality of the fruit. You'd put it on the gravel because it makes a more elegant Cabernet. Same way with the Merlot. If you put the Merlot on the gravel, you can make a lighter wine; if you put Merlot on the clay, you bring up the tannins in the wine and then, if you've properly chosen the site for the grapes, it can be very difficult for even the winemaker who made the wine to tell the varieties apart. That's because each is a proper expression of the soil. So I don't think of Merlot and Cabernet that differently. What we're trying to make is a tasty, delicious, balanced wine with these type of Bordelais flavors.

What does all that mean? What it means to me these days, even more so than when I worked at Mantanzas, is the combination of richness or power with elegance or delicacy. That has sometimes been hard to find in California Cabernets but it's possible. A lot has to do with your harvest decisions, which is something people are only beginning to talk about in California, but is common knowledge in Bordeaux; and that is, the harvest decision is not only one of sugar or of plant physiology—i.e. are the leaves falling off the vine—but of maturity of tannins.

A big concept in Bordeaux is "mature tannins" or "supple tannins," as they call them. Immature tannins are harsh and astringent. Ribereau-Gayon has written a paper where he suggests what happens as the grapes mature; the tannins polymerize on the grape vine, becoming longer. He gives a molecular weight of three thousand as a potential cut off point, below which the tannins are astringent and above which they are soft. Clearly there are probably a lot of other factors and it's probably not exactly right but conceptually what that says is: when in doubt, wait longer to pick, because your tannins are getting softer as the fruit gets more mature. This is why, for example, people in California who have paid attention to alcohol levels should have been paying attention to tannins instead. I know many grape contracts in California specify harvesting at 22.5 brix because they don't want to have an alcohol over 13.3 percent or some arbitrary number. Well, that's fine but if your tannins aren't mature at that point, then they're never going to get mature; they're never going to get as supple as they would if they had been allowed to mature more on the vines. I wasn't so much aware of that while at Mantanzas, although I knew instinctively all the great wines of the world are made by letting the grapes hang longer than normal. But I understand that's part of the rationale for doing so.

But isn't there a downside risk to doing that?

Yes, number one is the rain. Number two would be a porty, pruney, over-ripe character in the wine.

Exactly, so how do you distinguish between the supple tannins level and the level where you start to get overripe qualities?

I would say it's a balance. I happen to think that balance point is a little further along than a lot of people.

But how do you find that point? By taste? By science?

At this point, it's all of the above. You look at the numbers: the sugar, acid and pH. You taste, you look at the vines and you put all that together. You're looking at changes in taste too. We can be tasting a particular Cabernet block and it will be a little veggie, a little less veggie and then, within five days, it goes away. That's an indicator the block has reached some level of maturity. How do you know when you go too far? You start seeing too many raisins. Depending on the season or how dry it is, a few shriveled berries are not out of line. If I don't see some, I'm probably worried I haven't waited long enough. But when you see too many raisins, then you've waited too long.

I know you've recently become more a proponent of utilizing natural yeast for fermentation. Or do you prefer another term?

No, I call it natural, wild, indigenous or native yeast. I was interested in it not only on an experimental basis but also as a means of extending the period of extraction before the fermentation started. That is, extending it to two to four days. I was doing that and, one by one, they all started fermenting without any problems. I kept doing it and, in 1990, we went to one hundred percent wild yeast in the reds. We started then on the whites with experimental lots on a full production scale. In 1992, we've gone to one hundred percent wild yeast for both reds and whites.

In the reds it spreads out the extraction profile of the fermentation. With inoculated yeast fermentations, you get to a point where you will be at twenty-three brix, twenty-two, then twenty and then—boom—you're suddenly at ten degrees brix. It reaches a point where it accelerates and you do half your fermentation in twenty-four hours. That doesn't happen with wild yeast; you see a steady three to five brix decline, at the most, in a day. The fermentation spreads out over a longer period allowing more time for extraction at that elevated temperature. With the reds, I think it's primarily an extraction effect; it impacts the color and tannins in the wines. It's a natural way of prolonging the cuvaison, the skin contact period.

Now in whites—and my conclusions are from about fifteen split comparisons—I note a little more aroma coupled to a slightly higher volatile acidity, with the difference on average between 3.2 and 3.5. There is less pronounced oak in the nose with the natural yeast and, to me, that's a real plus. Because I want the oak to be there but not stand out. On the palate, there is a little more textural roundness in the middle palate and that's also desirable; it may be nothing more than a slightly higher level of residual sugar, below the threshold level, but still texturally important.

Before, with inoculated yeast, our standard was bone dry. And with all the analysis I did on French wines, I never analyzed for residual sugar. Dry was dry. Now that I've started analyzing these Burgundies and Pouilly Fumes, I find a lot of them .15 or .20 residual sugar. That's technically dry; the threshold at which you taste the sweetness is around .40. And the wines are even stable; at .20 you don't have to sterile filter. But .20 residual sugar is going to be texturally different than .05. It's funny because it's so simple and basic; I consider that a significant advance in concept about wine structure.

So you're saying technically the whites don't ferment as dry utilizing the natural yeast?

Exactly. But it's below the threshold level. It's not sweet. But texturally it's important. So those are the advantages to the wild yeast. The wines are more complex and, oh, we also see significantly lower tannins. Why? I don't know. Perhaps because the fermentation stretches out longer, you have more of the yeast-fining effect because the yeast are in suspension for a longer period of time. So we see lower tannins while, at the same time, the wine is rounder and more delicate.

What about the thought that the "natural" yeast is just whatever yeast happens to be the strongest or the most dominant yeast in the winery?

I don't think that's true. This is really nothing new. Many wines of the world have been fermented with their own wild yeast. There have been studies published on this and there are a pretty standard number of yeasts that show up everywhere in the world. It doesn't seem to be that specific to the different sites; they're the same kinds of yeast. When we look at these under the microscope, we do see a lot of different shapes; it's not like the standard, inoculated, pure-culture fermentation. So I'm certain that we are getting a variety of yeasts.

Where do the yeasts come from? I'm not sure it matters. I know we can start the year with a completely clean winery, a sterilized crusher, hopper, press, must pump, tanks, put the wine into brand new barrels and fermentation will start. So I think it is natural flora on the grape berry in the field. They're hard to isolate and identify off of the grape, but as soon as you crush the grapes, they start to multiply. I don't think they are different in any other part of California or Bordeaux.

You have certain positive things to say about allowing brettanomyces in the wine?

Well, let's just say I'm not negative. I think we're at the state about brett in California now where we were on malolactic fermentation in Chardonnay twelve years ago. In the last twelve years we've learned a lot about malolactic in Chardonnay. We've learned the yeast metabolize diacetyl, that buttery-type compound, so it's important you do the malolactic in conjunction with yeast cells instead of on filtered wines so you don't get this one-dimensional butterscotch character. Ten years ago, people would experiment with malolactic, find they didn't like the results and conclude malolactic was bad and they weren't going to use it. When in fact, we find out that it's sort of condition-dependent. Depending on how you do it, under what circumstances and conditions, it will give you different results.

I think brett is kind of the same way. The standard way wine is made in California—if you blend all the Cabernet together just prior to bottling and then you get a brett infection and it happens in the bottle—yes, that can stink and smell bad. Probably all of us have experienced wines that have been spoiled by brett. That's not to say brett can't be a spoilage organism but so is malolactic if it happens in the bottle and so is the primary fermentation if it happens in the bottle. Saccharomyces cerevisiae is a spoilage organism if you're bottling off dry Chenin Blanc. So we get to the perspective that maybe brett isn't black or white; maybe it's condition-dependent. So, yes, we see brett with the wild yeast. Peynaud, in his *Knowing and Making Wine*, lists it as one of the species of useful natural yeasts. In the chapter on fermentation he talks about kinds of yeasts; he lists twenty eight or so species and the first one on the list is brettanomyces intermedius. You start thinking about why brett should be so bad. It turns out empirically then, when the brett is there from the beginning, and you make the blend early and rack and aerate every three months—basically using the Bordelais technique—you never develop the strong kind of barnyard aromas people want to associate with brett. It doesn't happen that way all the time. Another way to look at it is, if that's the case, then brett prevention can be a worse cure than the problem. In other words, what do you have to do to prevent brett? You acidify, lower your pH, raise your free SO_2 and filter. You guarantee you make this sterile, hard wine. Whereas if you move toward all the things that allow the wine to soften and develop—no acidification, high pH, low free SO_2, so that you don't interfere with the polymerization of the tannins—these things are going to make the wine better. So it's almost like, brett's there, so what? In fact you find out, under these conditions, it doesn't smell like brett. It's an analogous situation to people having one set of experiences with brett and then extrapolating that to all sets of conditions; I've found that it's just not true. I'm working on my third vintage of wine that has brett.

So then how does brett manifest itself in your wines? Or does it?

In many cases it doesn't; we confirm it's there through lab analysis. We're making brett counts every three months, when we rack the wine. We're keeping an eye on it but, at this point for us, it's just informational because there's so much interest focused on it.

So the question is: What does brett contribute? What does it add to the wine? Or do you know?

In some cases, I think it adds almost nothing. Our '91 Cabernet has no aroma one would call brett. It seems to develop differently depending on the time. When it's there from the beginning, it doesn't seem to develop the classic brett aromas. When it develops late, then you get the aroma.

So, if it integrates early on in the winemaking process, it becomes just one of a thousand elements that make up the whole? And it's not necessarily as distinctive as most people have noted?

Exactly. Whereas if it happens late it seems this leathery or barnyard character is more pronounced. But on the other hand, I have certainly enjoyed many a Pichon-Lalande and Lynch Bages that had some elements of that.

There are two levels of thinking here. On one level, what's so wrong with wine smelling like that? I think it's great. But I'm not even taking that position because I've found it doesn't even end up smelling like that, if you're using natural yeast and you do the blends early. I'd put it in front of anybody and you wouldn't know that there's brett there. So it's condition-dependent and that's really the position I'm taking; it's not black and white. It doesn't always produce flavor XYZ; under certain conditions, it doesn't do it at all, so where's the problem? It's not that a little bit of it is good necessarily; it's that it's irrelevant.

You're now doing full malolactic with Sauvignon Blanc, where before you weren't doing any, just partial barrel fermentation?

Here again, it's a condition-dependent thing. I had felt I didn't want to do malolactic with Sauvignon Blanc because I wanted to distinguish it stylistically from Chardonnay. It turns out the Sauvignon Blanc doesn't develop the distinctive buttery character that Chardonnay does when it goes through malolactic. Why? I don't know. Maybe partly because, as a variety, Sauvignon Blanc has less malic acid than Chardonnay. So there's less opportunity for the diacetyl to be spit out. But maybe it's basically because Chardonnay is a neutral variety with sort of appley fruit and when you add some buttery characteristics and oak, it really stands out. Whereas Sauvignon Blanc has such assertive fruit that, when you bring in a little butter and oak, it doesn't stand out nearly as much. So what I find with the Sauvignon Blanc is I get a more complex aroma but not necessarily distinctively malolactic. The '91 Sauvignon Blanc is one hundred percent malolactic and no one brings that up to me. You wouldn't know it. It softens the acidity, which is important, while it makes it more complex aromatically and gives it a creamy texture. All barrel fermented, all wild yeast, all malolactic and all sur lies. We grow the Sauvignon Blanc here so we have a strong stake in making a good wine and I think it can be when made seriously.

Have you changed your thoughts about Chardonnay production, other than the use of natural yeast?

No, I continue to work toward as delicate a handling of the wine as possible. At harvest, we're not crushing the fruit; we're not using the rollers and we're not destemming, so we get a significant number of whole berries into the press which helps lower the tannins and make a more delicate wine. Everything is still barrel fermented in Burgundian cooperage, full malolactic and sur lies. We still stir the lees once a week during malolactic and every month or so afterwards. But it's only important while the wine is still microbially active. With the wild yeast, we find we can use less SO_2. The inoculated yeast makes a fair bit of acid aldehyde, which binds up SO_2, and to get a particular free SO_2, you end up with a higher total. Natural yeast doesn't do that, so our total SO_2 is very low. In effect, I can say we're using less SO_2 than before. Although interestingly what we're finding out this year—and the French have talked about this—is natural yeast are more fastidious than inoculated yeast. So we're seeing competition or interference between malolactic bacteria and yeast at the tail end of the fermentation. When the malolactic got a toehold, it stopped the wine at a little higher residual sugar. So I'm actually looking at going back to using a little bit of sulfur before the fermentation just to inhibit the malolactic until after the primary is completed. It's a traditional French concern I have not shared in the last twelve years and now, with my utilization of natural yeast, the circle closes and we go back to the full tradition.

What actually happens when malolactic fermentation starts while the primary fermentation is not yet finished?

Sugar slows down. And it's got to be either one of two mechanisms. It's either nutrient scavenging by the bacteria and not leaving enough for the yeast, or it's the bacteria forming some sort of compound that inhibits the yeast. Which one I don't know but it's a real factor. I never thought I'd go back to adding more SO_2 but now we're going to add thirty or forty parts per million before fermentation.

I tasted your first red wine from Chalk Hill, the '90 Cabernet, and there is a dramatic difference between that and the style of the '89.

That's my first Cab at Chalk Hill and I'm very pleased with it. Everything clicked with that wine; nothing ever went wrong. Natural yeast, no acidification and unfiltered.

What about those who claim that the stability of the wine is threatened because you didn't filter it? That you could have a time bomb in the bottle?

That's the point of the traditional French methods. You know what they call it? They call this period "elevage," as in a child or student. "Elevage" means elevating or bringing up the wine; you're raising the wine, so to speak. That's why it's important to do the blend early; then you have everything in there. You have all your components so you have all your potential substrate for microbially growth together. Then you have this period of eighteen or twenty-two months in barrel. Now think about that. It's not just to give you oak flavor, which seems to be the approach in California. The purpose of that is microbiological and physiological stability. You go through two winters in the barrel; there's your cold stability. You blend early; there's your micro stability. You rack every three months; there's your clarity. So the purpose of all this traditional methodology is to stabilize the wine. At the time you bottle it, you're not introducing any new components, so what's it going to do that it hasn't already done in twenty months in barrel? That's the beauty of it. And that's really important. I don't think it's practiced enough in California. But when you go to that method, when you buy into it, it gives you a lot of advantages. You don't have to worry about this because it takes care of itself during the barrel aging period, which becomes then an active period of raising the wine, not just a passive period of letting it absorb oak extract. There's a fundamental difference in perception on the purpose of this period. You talk about the risks in going to this "Mr. Natural" approach, but there are a lot of advantages too. Oddly enough, it solves many of the problems you're concerned about, when you do it properly and completely. What people have to give up to do this is the late blending of the wine. You need a little more confidence in your palate early on. In California we seem to have this "reserve" concept, where you want to keep all your wine lots separate and, then, just before bottling, you make some presto, magical reserve blend. In Bordeaux, that's not the approach they take. In January or February, they'll be doing assemblage tastings, although it's just a rough cut. They decide what the better lots are and that goes into the first label; the lesser lots go into the second label. It's not some kind of magic blending process. And it's not that hard to do. You take all the lots that taste good, put them together and start making the wine. But that concept of starting to make the wine when you make the blend is one that is not common in California.

From your perspective, everything gets integrated into the wine from the very beginning.

Yes, and I think it makes a difference in the way the wine tastes. The aromatic complexity, the seamless balance of the wine and the silky texture of the wine can be helped along this way.

Do you still use all the scientific tools in the lab available to you?

Yes, we do use them. As I get further along, I get more and more natural with the wines; I do less and less, now I don't even add yeast; I just put the juice in the barrel and let it sit. But I'm still following the wines a lot with numbers, partly to make sure the wines are okay, but also, as an enologist, just out of interest. We observe what's happening and that's how we end up finding out all these different things; it gives rise to theories about what's happening and why things taste the way they do. The technology is great but you can't decide about wine based on numbers; it's got to come from the taste. Wine either tastes good or it doesn't; a lot of times I think people forget that. We have a new motto here: "Great wine doesn't have to taste bad." How many times has some winemaker or retailer tried to tell a customer this particular Cabernet doesn't taste good right now but it will all age out in five years. That's almost never true. Great wine tastes good all the way through, right from the beginning. And if they're not soft and supple now, they're not going to get that way one year or five years from now.

Adam Tolmach
THE OJAI VINEYARD

"If you want to take zero risk, you can have perfectly mediocre wine every year, but if you are trying to produce the best wine in the world, you have to take risks that are inherently somewhat dangerous to the wine. If you're a good winemaker, they work out very well."

Adam Tolmach entered UC Davis with every intention of studying plant science but ended up taking winemaking and viticultural courses as well. After graduation, he did some vegetable farming on his family's property in Ojai and then, in 1979, was hired as the enologist at Zaca Mesa Winery, where his future partner, Jim Clendenen, was assistant winemaker. Two years later, he left to plant his own vineyard in Ojai.

He then went on to Burgundy, meeting up with Clendenen to work the harvest. Returning to California, they teamed up to start Au Bon Climat in a one thousand square foot former dairy shed, utilizing traditional Burgundian techniques to produce Pinot Noir and Chardonnay.

While continuing as co-winemaker at Au Bon Climat, Tolmach's own vineyard plantings were coming to fruition; he began making wine under the Ojai Vineyard label in 1984. Just recently, after nearly ten years at Au Bon Climat, he retired to devote his full attention to his own vineyard. The Ojai Vineyard winery, operated solely by Tolmach and his wife, Helen, is located eight miles from the coast in Ventura County, an area that has recently been the object of renewed viticultural interest. The three thousand case production consists of Syrah, Sauvignon Blanc, Semillon and small amounts of Marsanne and Viognier. Pinot Noir and Chardonnay, purchased from Santa Barbara County sources, have recently been added to their line of handcrafted offerings.

What were your early winemaking experiences that helped form your ideas about winemaking?

When I went to Zaca Mesa Winery, I learned a lot about the basic California technology for processing wines. While I was there, Jim Clendenen and I had an active interest in experimenting and understanding what makes French wines different from California wines, besides the fruit character. In the Burgundian varieties especially, a lot has to do with how the wines are processed. While Cabernet is the variety California seems to do well with, a lot of that has to do with the fact that the famous Bordeaux chateaus are generally large properties producing twenty thousand cases of wine per year. So they process wine like California, a bit like it anyway. I think California had a lot more success with Cabernet because they process wine similarly.

Pinot Noir and Chardonnay are made differently because they were generally produced by small domaines in Burgundy. These are places that make only a few thousand cases a year. The winemaking techniques are completely different. After I quit Zaca Mesa, I planted my vineyard and worked that fall at Edna Valley Vineyards, owned by Chalone. They follow Burgundian techniques; all the Chardonnay is barrel fermented and goes through secondary malolactic fermentation. That taught me a lot because I had learned the traditional California way of processing wines; to see how they did it at Edna Valley was a real eye-opener. Near the end of harvest there, I went to Burgundy. It was fun to see the Burgundian harvest, just to see the similarities and differences from Edna Valley.

One thing I did learn in Burgundy: the techniques are basic, very nontechnological; they don't require a lot of expensive equipment. You don't process the grapes in a complicated fashion; all you need are good French oak barrels. Other than that, the equipment was really minimal. A lot of the people are just farmers with little technical expertise.

What did those experiences confirm for you?

It confirmed for me—at least I believed it at the time and it seems to have worked out that way—that winemaking techniques have a great influence on the final wine. While in France you have French fruit character and in California you have California fruit character. Inherently, there's something to be said about the style of wine. California winemaking techniques impose another style and French winemaking techniques impose a different kind of style. I found I could use traditional French techniques economically because they employ unsophisticated machinery.

In the mid-eighties, when you were co-winemaker at Au Bon Climat, were there already winemakers in California who thought or claimed they were using Burgundian techniques but were bastardizing them and taking shortcuts?

Not exactly. There were some people making wines similar to us. But yes, there were a few doing that; you do things that way and then you veer off in your own direction. But in Burgundy, everybody makes wine in the Burgundian fashion, but everybody makes different wine. You can either like them or dislike them according to their faults or virtues. One thing we found was that grapes grown in a cooler environment really are better suited to making wines using traditional techniques. In Burgundy, it's so cool there that the wines are high in acid and it's necessary to put the wines through the secondary malolactic fermentation, which softens the acidity and makes the wines more drinkable, more complex and interesting. So the primary goal in California was to find grapes naturally high in acid. When you make wines from grapes grown in cool areas like the Santa Maria and Santa Ynez Valleys that don't go through secondary fermentation, they tend to be lean and undrinkable.

There are winemakers who say Chardonnay is too delicate a grape to put through malolactic fermentation.

It all depends on what flavors you happen to like in wine. A lot of people these days claim to want to make wines that are a true expression of the fruit but the meaning of that is a bit nebulous. I don't want to make wines that are just fruity. If you want to do that, you might as well make Beaujolais or Nouveau. If you want to make truly great wines, you need to make wines that are an integration of fruit, character and other complexities like the taste of the soil, the taste of new oak barrels, the taste of contact with the yeast lees and the taste of malolactic fermentation. All those things make up a complex, interesting wine.

You began nurturing vines at the The Ojai Vineyard in the early eighties; how did that evolve?

When I quit Zaca Mesa in 1980, I did so with the intention of going down to Ojai to plant a vineyard. So I spent all my time in 1981 planting the vineyard. It's a five and a half acre vineyard, really tiny. It's planted mostly to Syrah with some Sauvignon Blanc and Semillon and a little Marsanne and Viognier. My intent was to find the grape varieties best suited to the climate, which was one of the useful things UC Davis taught me. One thing stressed there was planting the correct varieties in the correct climate so they divided the state up into hotter and cooler regions. As far as the winemaking goes at UC Davis, I think a lot of the emphasis there, at the time, was to train wine chemists for large wineries. I never had any exposure to the idea of barrel fermentation there. But it's fine to have some formal, background training.

What region is Ojai classified by UC Davis?

Actually Ojai is just like every other coastal valley in that there are both cooler and warmer areas. Where I am is probably around Region II or III, which is actually close to what the Napa Valley is. Nobody is really honest about which region they're in because they always want to be one region cooler than they are.

Chardonnay and Pinot Noir only seem to do well in a cool climate, like Region I. If you get a little warmer, the fruit character of Pinot Noir gets destroyed. With Chardonnay from cooler regions, you have better acidity so you can put them through malolactic fermentation. I assessed the climate in Ojai and I knew it was not good for either of those varieties. I had a real interest in Syrah because I love the wines of the northern Rhone: Cote Rotie, Hermitage, Cornas and St.-Joseph are all primarily Syrah, while southern Rhones are a blend of varieties. Really, as a guess, I planted Syrah. I had tasted some new wines from Estrella River and was excited about the Syrah variety. I felt if you planted it in a slightly cooler area and controlled the yield, then you could produce a wine of great character. As far as Sauvignon Blanc and Semillon, they seem to have a lot of character and seem to do well in slightly warmer areas.

In the sixties, a lot of people planted the wrong varieties all over the place. But they're beginning to recognize that winemakers will pay good money for grapes from the right spot. It makes much more sense to plant the variety that will do the absolute best in that spot than to plant something you know will sell but may only be mediocre.

Is climate or soil more important to you?

They're both important. The thing about soils in California, at least in my view, is they are generally too rich so the vine tends to grow vigorously, not producing as good fruit as it might. There are a few ways to control that. You can trim the vines or avoid watering them too much so they suffer more. In poor soil, the vine suffers more, the yields are lower and almost always the quality is better. That's the way I look at soil.

The soil at The Ojai Vineyard is a little on the rich side. It's pretty poor soil for vegetables but the grapevine doesn't need much. I control the water, prune the vines back and keep the crop small; those things seem to make all the difference in the world as far as grape quality goes. Vineyard practices have a huge amount to do with the quality of the wine. If you don't get greedy and you don't grow your vines like tomato plants, if you grow them so the vines are a bit stressed, then you'll have amazingly better quality.

What kind of yield are you looking at?

Three tons per acre is plenty and if it's a little less than that, that's fine too. Both the white and red varieties seem to do just fine at that level. It's not minuscule, but I'm happy with the quality. The vines could produce more, but at two to three tons per acre, you get a lot more intense flavor concentration.

Is the vineyard close to being organic?

Pretty close, although for the ultimate wine quality I don't know whether it's important or not. For my general philosophy, it is. Because the vineyard is small and so personal, I do most of the work. I'm the one on the tractor and the one who applies any sprays. We don't use any herbicides or insecticides. We use sulfur for the mildew because you have to use something.

Aren't you pioneering a new area in California viticulture with these vineyards in Ojai?

Before Prohibition there were seven vineyards and several wineries in the area. In fairly recent times, there were two wineries here. So it's not really a new viticultural area.

What has your winemaking experience taught you in the last ten years that you now bring to bear on your own vineyards?

We continue to embrace traditional techniques, primarily Burgundian: not intervening in the wines a lot, not using high technology, allowing the wines to evolve by themselves while being attentive to the whole process. Winemaking is both simple and complicated. There are ten or so basic steps that you go through to make a wine but there are a thousand little details that make the wine what it is. In Burgundy, everybody makes wine in the Burgundian fashion and everybody's wines are different. The reason they're different is once you get beyond the ten simple steps to make wine, then there's about a thousand little decisions to make.

A fellow winemaker in the Santa Ynez Valley described it as "the lazy man's way to make wine," but it's not really that simple. By utilizing these traditional techniques, you are putting your wine at more risk. To make the best possible product, you have to take some risk. If you want to take zero risk, you can have perfectly mediocre wine every year, but if you are trying to produce the best wine in the world, you have to take risks that are inherently somewhat dangerous to the wine. If you're a good winemaker, they work out very well.

Examples would be using no pre-fermentation sulfur and using little sulfur dioxide throughout the life of the wine. Utilizing long lees contact time is inherently dangerous; it's much nicer to have real clean wine in an inert container than a dirty wine in an oak barrel.

One thing I've learned going into European cellars over the years is the nicest ones were cold and damp. It seems to be pretty important as far as trying to reproduce traditional techniques. We've done that at Ojai by humidifying and refrigeration. Having the cellar cool is important for me. I think that's an important part of having the wines mature correctly. There's also less evaporation from the barrels. I think when the wines evaporate more slowly they mature more slowly; I think at colder temperatures they also mature more slowly. I think it's a combination of the two things. I think the wines retain some youthfulness and brilliance they don't have otherwise.

Also, another part of using traditional techniques involves not racking the wine a lot and not manipulating the wine through filtration.

Minimal filtration and fining?

I'm a big believer in fining. I'd rather start, in white wines for instance, with grape juice that's not highly settled and or very clear, and then try to get the most out of the grapes in the wine. If there's too much of one element in the wine, I use fining to refine them down. Rather than the other way around, which is more a California technique of highly processing the grape juice before fermentation and then not fining the wine. I'd rather start out with too much and refine the wine at the end. I'm not a big fan of filtration, although it can be useful. That and every other step in the winemaking process can be done well. Not doing it well would be starting with incredibly cloudy wine and filtering it back and forth between tanks several times to get the wine clear for bottling. I think you should use a more natural technique, that is, allowing the wine to settle, using fining agents to help settle the wine and make it clear naturally. Then if you need to filter it, you make one pass through the filter on its way into the bottle. A lot of people don't do it that way because they don't feel an important element in wine quality is minimal handling of the wine.

What about your vinification practices with the Syrah?

We don't use as many stems as we used to so we're using fewer whole clusters in the fermenter. Other than that, we're using pretty traditional techniques. We try to get the grapes picked first thing in the morning so they're cool; we'll destem a portion of the grapes and a portion will go as whole clusters into small, open top, stainless steel fermenters. We try to go through a cold maceration of four or five days. We chill down the room to help prevent the fermentation. After those five days, we go through a normal fermentation and we like to get it pretty hot. It's all punched down by hand. Then we go for a total skin contact time of twenty to twenty-five days. Then it's pressed off and goes directly into barrels; it's not racked off its gross fermentation lees until spring.

What about the whites, the Sauvignon Blanc and Semillon?

They're picked in the morning and directly whole cluster pressed, with no destemming. Having been pressed off, it goes into a stainless steel tank to settle overnight before being put into mostly older French oak for fermentation; they also go through malolactic. The wine basically lives its whole life in barrels. It's racked in the late winter or early spring. It's fined in barrel, racked off, lightly filtered and bottled. So it's only racked once and processed minimally.

You recently started making Chardonnay and Pinot Noir, from purchased grapes. How are you handling the Chardonnay?

I'm not doing anything dramatically different from what I've been doing. The Chardonnay is whole cluster pressed and one hundred percent barrel fermented and one hundred percent malolactic. On the surface, the wine is the same type as Au Bon Climat because we use traditional techniques. But just as in Burgundy, you can have many wonderful white Burgundies that are distinctly different even though they all use the same techniques. They can be different even if the grape source is the same. A lot of that has to do with the subtleties of the winemaking process.

Pinot Noir technique is about the same?

It's a little bit different than what I was doing at Au Bon Climat. The prefermentation maceration goes for five days. I'm also completely destemming so there are no whole clusters. I'm using the same technique I use with the Syrah, which is a much longer total time on the skins, from twenty to twenty-five days. I'm also using lower SO_2 levels than I have in the past.

What does the longer maceration time do for it?

I think you get certain fruit flavors and color extract before the fermentation that you don't get at any other time. I like those components in the wine; it promotes very pretty fruit and nice color. The same thing with leaving it on the skins for an extended time post-fermentation—there are flavors you get there you don't get any other way. Also, the resulting tannins tend to be finer and more tightly knit in an extended fermentation. In a short fermentation, you don't get many tannins at all; in a medium fermentation, you get tannins but they tend to be a little coarser. With a longer time on the skins, the tannins tend to complex with each other and they give a finer textural feel in the mouth.

You're not a big proponent of natural yeast fermentation?

Not particularly. This year we actually did a little bit of experimentation with that in Chardonnay. There may be some differences when the wine is fairly young, but by the time it stays in barrel, gets bottled and ages awhile, the difference between the various lots of yeasts diminishes dramatically. Maybe our winemaking style is more dominating than the yeast types. If you were making Riesling or a wine that was made in stainless steel tanks and spent a short time there before bottling, I could see how yeast types would have a more dramatic difference. Some people believe you get more complexity in the wine by using natural yeasts. I'm not convinced of that theory, although I find it interesting. Actually, the most exciting part of winemaking for me is every year there's tons of new things to learn and new things to see.

There's a lot of intuition in winemaking because there's so many variables in the whole process. It's almost impossible to sort them all out scientifically so intuition is involved; that's part of the fun.

Do you plan on expanding the winery?

Our aim is to stay the same size. The reason is, although it's not fabulously profitable, it's a reasonable size for us and we can make a comfortable living. Helen and I can basically run the whole thing. I like all the various steps in the winemaking process. I don't want to miss out on any of those; that's what I enjoy best—groveling with the grape.

I don't deny you can make pretty great wine at bigger-sized wineries. I was intrigued to find most producers in Burgundy in the one- to five-thousand case winery. I liked the way it worked at that size. For me, winemaking is a lifestyle in that everyday I think, drink, read wine. While I like working hard, I like to have slower times and faster times. At this size, that's possible. At a bigger size I would have to spend more time on the unpleasant task of selling the wine.

Do you think we are moving away from an overblown, over oaked style of wines and moving to stylistic wines more compatible with food?

Yes. The earlier California wines tended to be just that way. They were over extracted, over oaked, too low in acid and they had this tremendous character that wasn't fashioned correctly. They also weren't balanced enough to age properly. One reaction to that is to make more delicate wines. But you can't just make wines that are lighter and don't have as much flavor; you don't want insipid wine. A lot of people haven't known how to go about making wines with tremendous character but that are also in balance. It turns out you don't need incredible ripeness of fruit to make wines with a lot of character. If your wine is based on the theory of expressing only the fruitiness of the wine, then perhaps you can only make the greatest wine if you get incredibly ripe fruit. It would be like the essence of that fruit but then you'd have an unbalanced wine. These days people recognize there are other elements that build up and make a wine—for example, the judicious use of French oak, lees contact and other traditional winemaking techniques give you a wine that evolves instead of falls apart.

Typically, in California, the wine would be way too ripe, with too much alcohol and almost an excess amount of character. It would be pumped around the winery and filtered a lot. It would still have a lot of character but it would fall apart a few years later. There are other ways. For example, if you minimally process the wine, it will show more of its character. If you pick the grapes at a more reasonable ripeness, you can have all the fruit character that you could ever want without having the excess of alcohol.

It seems easy to make wine; the hard part is to make great wine. Is that an oversimplification?

Actually, it is not very complicated, but you do have thousands of choices to make throughout the life of the wine. For example, the white wines are fermented in the barrel, not racked until spring and then only racked once to fine them, put back in barrel and then bottled. It's very simple but it's a lot more complicated than that because you're making a lot of choices all along the way. You're deciding exactly what to do and exactly what effect that has on the wine. Back to Burgundy again: everybody uses Burgundian winemaking techniques, but some people make horrible wine and some people make wonderful wine. It's all those little steps in between. It's also a reaction to each wine too, because every harvest is different and you can't do the same thing every year if you want to make the best wine.

Groth

1985
Napa Valley
Cabernet Sauvignon

GROWN, CELLARED AND BOTTLED BY
GROTH VINEYARDS AND WINERY, NAPA, CALIFORNIA
ALCOHOL 13% BY VOLUME

Nils Venge
GROTH VINEYARDS
AND WINERY

"You can forecast the quality of a vintage right away. . .
You get a gut feeling right off the bat. . ."

Nils Venge has been in the wine business all his life. He's worked twenty-two vintages in the Napa Valley but he's still a relatively young man who maintains a high level of enthusiasm year after year. He had family ties in the wine and beer business growing up in Los Angeles, where his father was an importer and distributor. When it came time for a career choice, his father pointed him toward winemaking at UC Davis.

His first jobs out of school were viticulturally oriented, planting new vines at Charles Krug and then at Sterling. He came to Villa Mt. Eden Winery in 1973 to plant a new vineyard; he stayed on as winemaker until 1982. He developed quite a following for his consistently intense, powerful Cabernet Sauvignons.

When Dennis Groth was starting up Groth Vineyards and Winery, he called on Venge to be the winemaker and general manager, giving him the opportunity to work with excellent vineyards and establish and refine the house styles of Cabernet Sauvignon, Chardonnay and Sauvignon Blanc for the medium-sized winery.

Venge, with help from his family, is also the proprietor of Saddleback Cellars, where he produces fifteen hundred cases of Pinot Blanc, Chardonnay and Cabernet Sauvignon.

Did UC Davis prepare you for the real world of winemaking and viticulture?

Not really. We always made wine in five-gallon lots. You used small presses; you never had anything big to work with. However, I got a bit of crush experience with Fred McCrea's (Stony Hill) Chardonnay before I went back for my final year at Davis. After Davis, I was really able to see all the aspects of the winemaking process through Bill Bonetti of Krug and Ric Forman at Sterling. Then the offer from Villa Mt. Eden was tempting; it was an opportunity to be in charge of all aspects of production. After I planted the vineyards in 1973, I completed the renovation of the old facility and started making wine there the next year.

Looking back, Sterling was good for me and I think I came fairly well prepared to Villa Mt. Eden. I'd never renovated an old building like that before. We insulated this old winery, got the barrel racks situated and got the right tank sizes for the building. By hook or by crook, it all worked out.

UC Davis centers mostly on the theoretical and analytical. We were actually trained to become employees for E & J Gallo. For a lot of classmates, at the time, Gallo was the employer in the industry. Walt Schug and several other California winemakers worked at Gallo first before they went on to other jobs.

You were at Villa Mt. Eden from 1974 through 1982. Were you working with estate fruit?

Yes, the wines were all estate bottled. It was a challenge to see what the fruit character was going to be like in the wine. It was good to experience another area; as you know, the soils and microclimate of Calistoga are quite different from Oakville. I adapted fairly quickly and figured out the correct pH and acid levels to work with. Our first crop years were really great. We were getting good reviews right off the bat, although we were mostly using fruit from three-year-old vines. The soil was magnificent and we had plenty of water to keep them healthy. They grew nicely and we got good fruit development.

Now here at Groth, I am working with mature grapevines such as our Sauvignon Blanc vines, which are sixteen years old, in their prime of life. We're consistently picking five to six tons per acre. We don't have to drip-irrigate much, although this year we started in March because we were worried we wouldn't have enough ground moisture to carry the crop to harvest.

You made some good Cabernets at Villa Mt. Eden. I came across something Ric Forman said after a vertical tasting of those Cabernets: "The Cabernets were remarkably consistent in quality, showing intense Cabernet flavors with good balance and more power than finesse, more intensity than complexity." Is that a fair assessment of your winemaking style when you were there?

That's correct. They're intense wines that should be laid down before drinking. During my tenure, I was also in charge of sales in Southern California due to my background. Most of my sales were made to retailers who were supplying people with wine cellars. They were cellaring the wines. After two or three years of cellaring, these wines came around beautifully. Even in a drought year like 1976, the wine is still holding up and doing well, even though it was one of my lighter years in terms of structure.

With the Cabernets at Villa Mt. Eden, how did you maintain that consistency from year to year?

Stylistically I'm handling the grape and the young wine in the same manner from year to year. That sets the pace. It's really up to grape development, rain or shine. Harvesting them at the right maturity level is most important. I work harder the day before the decision to go ahead and pick, than the actual day of picking. I just want to make sure the grapes are ready by constantly testing for sugar/acid balance. Obviously, with a new vineyard, you're getting more uniformity of fruit, which is a direct advantage. If you have an older vineyard dying from disease and a new vineyard healthy and strong, then perhaps you'll have an uncomplimentary combination of underripe and overripe fruit.

With the new vineyards at Villa Mt. Eden, the fruit was regular and consistent; it all came off with no surprises. I tried using a new German-made field crushing system. That provided a quality control aspect because as we were receiving fruit for crushing, the operator was able to throw out any unsuitable fruit right then and there. A lot of wineries don't have that option since once the fruit is in their receiving hopper, it gets crushed and that's it. With a field crusher, you're right there with the pickers and, if you get into an area you're not happy about picking, you're there to make harvesting decisions on the spot. So you have total control over quality right off the bat, in the vineyards, where it counts.

How and why did you go from Villa Mt. Eden to Groth Vineyards and Winery?

Justin Meyer asked me if I wanted to meet with our neighbors, Dennis and Judy Groth. Dennis had a mini-model of the new winery he was getting ready to build; it had already been approved by the county. We met in the summer of 1982 and I looked over his plans, which appeared sound and exciting. He is close to my age and has a good business background. He liked the way I made wine, especially the Cabernets I was making at Villa Mt. Eden, and he offered me a job. He told me he wasn't going to persuade me to change my winemaking style and he also offered me a percent of the business as well.

Are you in a totally estate grown situation at Groth?

We are now. We developed Chardonnay vineyards in 1983 on a twenty-three acre parcel around the winery site. It wasn't until 1985 that we collected some fruit off those vines. By 1987 we were utilizing all our own fruit. Sometimes when you buy fruit from prime vineyards in the neighborhood and begin using more and more of your own fruit, you wonder if you're going to get a noticeable difference in wine character. But I believe the Oakville area is a good area for growing Chardonnay as well as Cabernet. When you think about it, a few decades ago, the UC Davis people had some brilliant people on staff and they chose Oakville as a location for their sub-station. They picked a prime area of the Napa Valley where most varieties can mature properly and do well. It was here that they had all their experimental varietal plots and worked out their trellising systems.

We have deep soil and fairly good drainage. Some spots have heavier soil types, but most of that is actually in the topsoil profile. We don't have much standing water and, if we do, it comes from the underground springs.

And what kind of soil and climate area do you have here?

Before I answer that, let me tell you about an experimental, four-row plot of Merlot I had at Villa Mt. Eden. It never amounted to more than two percent of the blend, which wasn't much of an influence on the Villa Mt. Eden Cabernet. But I'd keep the wine barreled separately and I always loved the kind of cof-fee-bean characteristic we would get out of those grapes. I was happy with the Merlot flavors we extracted there. But here at Groth, the Merlot has different characteristics. It's more of a black currant/cassis type flavor. Here we have a cooler climate with well-drained soil in a little rockier part of the property. I think it's ideal and it's much sought after by other wineries. Over time we've supplied Merlot for blending to Duckhorn and Newton. We currently supply a bit to Shafer and Burgess, but eventually we plan to use all the Merlot our-selves.

Do you keep the free-run separate from the press lots?

At Villa Mt. Eden, besides Cabernet and Chardonnay, I had Chenin Blanc, Gewurztraminer and Pinot Noir. There, we had our different press lots and we kept them all separate. If we didn't like a particular wine, we sold it in bulk to other wineries. Here at Groth, we don't keep our press lots separate because we have an hour-long pressing using our Bucher membrane press and it is put together in one lot. Therefore, there's no free-run versus press-run juice. With the invention of the membrane press and the knowledge of how to use that tool, there's really no reason to keep the press-run juice separate anymore. A gentle pressing works just fine.

With the Cabernet, what type of numbers are you looking for as far as sugar and pH?

I think ripeness starts between 22.5 and 23.5 brix. A special lot over 24.0 brix goes into our reserve label. That stems from my experience of the 1974 Villa Mt. Eden Cabernet. We would always hold out for that higher sugar level before picking the Cabernet, even if it looked like some rain was coming. I don't worry much about rot because Cabernet can hold up to a bit of rain and I have a large picking crew on hand as security. Our Cabernet harvest at Groth can be up to 280 tons in a good year, part of which goes off to Inglenook, Sequoia Grove and Cuvaison. I may pick a little for Cuvaison and Inglenook, for instance, get a basic idea of what numbers are showing up in their tanks and then start picking for myself. We have selected areas we designate for each of these wineries.

The acid levels and pH levels in Oakville are pretty consistent. Sometimes the pH level goes up a bit higher than you'd like, especially after malolactic. Normally we need a little acid adjustment after the Cabernet goes through malolactic fermentation. Overall acid levels are usually in the .6 to .75 TA range. Fermentation-wise I do the standard pumping-over twice a day. I haven't gone for anything extended; I just ferment to dryness and press. When we press out, we can empty two twelve-ton tanks a day. As I mentioned, because we have a mix of gravelly and heavier soils, it spreads out the crush nicely for me. Our Cabernet crush can extend over a two to two-and-a-half week period. I can figure on using my tanks twice for the Cabernet. I like using small 3,000 gallon tanks. I've got involved with custom machine harvesting some Cabernet. I fermented those lots in 6,000 gallon fermenters. I got good extraction from them and overall it made fine wine. I'm looking forward to doing more of that as long as it's economical.

How long do you leave the Cabernet grapes on the skins?

Usually for seven days. Then they're pressed and I always rack within a week to eliminate any H$_2$S problems. We'll inoculate for malolactic fermentation the third or fourth day, and if it finishes, fine. Otherwise, it'll finish out in the barrel. I use one hundred percent French oak for my aging. I enjoy the Nevers oak character and flavor from Demptos. That's what I used at Villa Mt. Eden and I just don't mess with success. I've used other oaks, such as Allier and Troncais. I'm on a rotating program in the cellar where I'm using a third new oak each year.

We normally keep to eighteen months in barrels for the regular Cabernet and twenty-four months for the Cabernet Reserve. I don't do any filtration of the wine prior to pumping into barrels. One of the fining or winemaking practices I'm adamant about is I want to make sure clarification occurs naturally in the barrel through slow settling and the racking process.

How often do you rack the Cabernet?

At Villa Mt. Eden, I consistently racked the Cabernet every three months. But now I'm cutting back on rackings and only doing a couple rackings for each vintage over that eighteen month period. As far as fining the wine, right now we've gone through the exercise of fining trials on the Cabernet. At this point, we're using a little gelatin and egg white. At Villa Mt. Eden, I was always using egg white. But here it's just hit or miss if I want to use fining agents. I keep wine movements to a minimum. I think the wines are turning out to be consistently good without necessarily going through all those extra winemaking practices.

At Villa Mt. Eden, we did have a bit more tannin structure to the wines, while at Groth the Cabernet has a lot of fruit, but not a great amount of tannin. We get more tannin from the addition of the Merlot but the most we've ever added was twenty percent in the 1985 Cabernet. We usually blend in about fifteen to seventeen percent Merlot. It generally adds a little extra color plus tannin backbone to the wine. I want to hold onto that fruit character of the Cabernet and once I see the Merlot impinging on that, I don't blend in any more. We have T-budded some vines to Cabernet Franc and someday we may add as much as five percent to the blend. Dennis Groth's taste and sensitivity is close to my own, so if Dennis and I are consistent on a taste, then that's the way it will be. We do a lot of tasting together prior to making our final blending decision.

The 1984 Groth Cabernet is indicative of your style. It was released in early 1988 and it was very drinkable then.

We like the wine to be fairly drinkable at the time of release. But it still has some good aging potential. That was the earliest harvest I've ever experienced, 1984; we were all wrapped up by September 26th or so. The grapes were not on the vine long enough in 1984 to become complex. So this vintage will come around early. It's a very approachable wine right now. But I would hope it would stay on a good plateau for a number of years because the acid, pH and tannins were all in balance. The numbers say the wine should hold up with cellaring.

So the 1984 Cabernet was atypical as far as your style because of the early harvest?

Not really. I think the black cherriness we like is still there. That's what I'm always looking for and want to hold on to. I prefer the 1983 Cabernet a bit more because of its structure and rich mouth feel. The hallmarks for a Groth Cabernet are basically in the taste, on the palate. They're not real perfumey wines. They all have a black cherry nose but it's on the palate where they follow through and shine. And the 1985 Cabernet is a classic from a great vintage. You can forecast the quality of a vintage right away. From pump-over, you can tell from the amount of color extraction and the amount of flavor from your tank samples. You get a gut feeling right off the bat and, if the numbers show up well in the lab, then you know you've got yourself a good wine.

What about the style of your white wines?

As far as the other wines I make, the style for the Sauvignon Blanc is to keep its natural citric crispness. I think the consumer wants a good, clean, crisp Sauvignon Blanc with youthful character. Then you can have the experience of a richer, fuller and more complex wine in the Chardonnay. I like to have them presentable to the restaurant trade early; they usually can't store wine, they want to sell it as soon as it arrives.

Tell me about the fermentation practices for your white wines.

I want a good cold settling down at the 45F or 46F degree level after pressing. This all occurs in stainless steel. We lees filter the cold settlings and throw all that back into the primary fermenter. It's good, clear juice. You have to be right on top of it though, as it can start to ferment within a day or two. I let the tank warm up to get fermentation rolling. I like a good 51F or 52F degree fermentation with cultured yeasts. I've yet to have a stuck fermentation. I love using the Montrachet yeast although you have to watch it for H_2S production. You need to get your rackings done quickly to clean up the wine.

Both this and last year, because we had the physical space, we barrel fermented Chardonnay in Troncais and Limousin oak. I've always tended to like the more crisp, lemony, vanilla extract out of the French oak. My ideal Chardonnay, on a consistent basis, is Chateau Montelena's Chardonnay. That's my benchmark. They are not overly oaked and they live a long time. They have a butterscotch character that becomes prominent as it ages in the bottle. I rely on bottle age to give my Chardonnays roundness instead of relying on malolactic fermentation to bring the wines around quickly. I had a good experience with barrel fermenting in 1987, although they fermented out much too quickly even when we brought the cellar temperature down to 58F degrees. They fermented in the mid-60F degree range and it was complete within four days. But for me, I typically like to capture the apple-fruit character over a long period of time and that's usually three weeks of fermentation.

So the 1987 Chardonnay wasn't totally barrel fermented?

No, one-third barrel fermented in brand new oak. We use the barrel fermented Chardonnay to condition our new barrels before we use them for long term storage. All of the wine ends up in one hundred percent French oak. I don't order overly toasted barrels and that's part of the fine-tuning of winemaking. That's why I have my barrels only constructed here in the Napa Valley. I'm able to go in at the time they're making my barrels and can determine the right amount of toast.

Do you find new challenges every year so you don't get bored?

That reminds me of the 1986 harvest, when all my fermenters were full but I still had three tons of Sauvignon Blanc left in the vineyards. I always wanted to make a sweet wine. So we went ahead and let the grapes hang. They didn't get much botrytis; it was pretty clean fruit. But we got some shriveling which concentrated the ripeness. We harvested the grapes at 32 brix, right where I wanted it. The acid was a bit low but we made an acid adjustment prior to fermentation. That's when I like to make adjustments: early on, right there at the fermenting stage to assist clean fermentations and proper settlings. Your acids and tannins accomplish that for you. The sweet Sauvignon Blanc was barrel fermented over three months time and I now have a sweet wine to pour at winemaker dinners. We didn't really make enough to market. That was a fun thing to do and I've had something fun to experiment with every year in one aspect or another.

You are also the owner/winemaker of Saddleback Cellars.

Yes, my father-in-law and I are partners. When we bought the place in 1976, we were growers of Cabernet and now it's turned out to be a vineyard where I'm growing Pinot Blanc, Chardonnay and older Cabernet vines I'm having to replant. We're not thrilled with the production of the two tons of grapes to the acre I get there, but I like the concentrated fruitiness and the berry structure. Usually I have to pick late, after I get through harvesting at Groth. I only pick up to eighteen tons of Cabernet at Saddleback. It's totally different in style than Groth because the Cabernet is unblended and I haven't personally been able to afford the 500 new French barrels. What I'm doing is buying three or four year old barrels from other wineries, shaving those barrels and retoasting them to the level I like. I'm augmenting that with new American oak barrels. I like the flavors. They're a bit more aggressive but when you take into account I'm using older French barrels, the marriage is pretty good. In recent vintages, I've gone to more French barrels cooperage.

Saddleback Cellars is a serious commercial venture; it's not just a hobby?

It's a project that brings the family together a few times a year. We all get together at planting, harvest and bottling, etc. I'm a weekend warrior there. You'll usually find me somewhere in the vineyards or winery at Saddleback on the weekends. It's basically a one-man operation. I'm producing about fifteen hundred cases now. The Pinot Blanc is coming on strong in the marketplace. At Saddleback, we bottle three hundred cases of both Pinot Blanc and Chardonnay and five hundred cases of Cabernet. It pretty much sells itself. Conveniently, our seventeen acres of vineyards are just to the west of the Groth Vineyards in Oakville.

What do you like about Pinot Blanc?

The reason I got into Pinot Blanc is the vineyard is situated in a low spot, which is an area that could get hit hard by frost. Chardonnay buds out early and is very sensitive to frost. But Pinot Blanc is a mid-season varietal and is not as frost sensitive. It also has consistently been the second highest paid white varietal. It doesn't get overcropped, you get medium-sized canopies and you can narrow your vine spacings and your row spacings. Viticulturally, it's a nice varietal to work with. You probably get more ground suckering and second crop than you'd like out of that varietal but you live with that. Pinot Blanc is a clonal offshoot of Pinot Noir. It mutated from a black to a white grape. So European viticulturalists propagated this white varietal and called it Pinot Blanc or Blanco. In the old days at UC Davis, you wanted to shy away from the varietal because it had browning problems. But if you harvest the grape cool and keep the SO_2 up, you really don't have a problem. Pinot Blancs can age wonderfully. They develop just as good as Chardonnay when they're bottle aged. There is a little extra astringency and spiciness that makes them special.

GLOSSARY OF WINEMAKING TERMS

ACID—a principal component of wine that shows up as a sharpness or tartness, giving wine a freshness and snap.

ACIDULATION—adding acid to wine made from grapes that were deficient in natural acid in order to bring the wine into balance. Legal in California, illegal in France.

AMERICAN VITICULTURAL AREA (also AVA)—grape growing region recognized as distinct by the U.S. Bureau of Alcohol, Tobacco and Firearms (also BATF), the official federal regulatory agency. To use an AVA on a wine label, eighty-five percent of the grapes must come from that appellation.

APPELLATION—geographic origin of a wine.

AROMA—the smell of the wine acquired from the grapes and the fermentation process.

ASTRINGENCY—the mouth puckering quality found in many young red wines.

BALANCED—all the components of the wine contribute to a harmonious whole.

BARREL FERMENTED—wine that is fermented in oak barrels as opposed to stainless steel tanks.

BODY—the weight of the wine in the mouth; usually manifested by a richness or fullness.

BOUQUET—the smell that develops from the process of the wine aging in the bottle.

BRETTANOMYCES—type of yeast that imparts a distinctive aroma and taste to wine.

BLENDING—combining the same or different grapes varietals, possibly from different regions, to achieve a whole that is greater than the sum of its parts.

BRIX—a measurement of the sugar content of grapes; critical component in determining ripeness. Wine grapes are normally harvested in the range of 20 to 26 degrees brix, depending on the grape and intentions of the winemaker.

BUTTERY—a component that gives white wines a full, rich, roundness that resembles the taste of butter.

CARBONIC MACERATION—fermentation method that utilizes whole grape clusters rather than crushed ones; results in a lighter, fruitier wine.

CHAPTALIZATION—practice of adding sugar to fermenting wines to increase the alcohol content; legal in France, illegal in California.

CLONE—vine reproduced from vine cuttings in order to resemble the same characteristics of the parent vine.

COLD FERMENTATION—temperature-controlled fermentation in closed stainless steel tanks in order to retain fresh, fruity character of the wine.

COLD STABILIZATION—method of clarifying wine by lowering the temperature of wine to thirty-two degrees F for a short period, allowing the suspending particulate matter to drop out.

COMPLEX—a wine that has many different levels of flavors.

CONCENTRATED—a wine that is rich, intense and full of flavors.

COOPERAGE—barrels for holding wine; by extention any vessel that serves the same purpose in the winery.

CRUSH—physical act of crushing the grapes; also a general term referring to the harvest season

DOSAGE—the process of adding a small amount of sugar in solution to sparkling wine.

DRY—a wine with no apparent residual sugar.

EARTHY—positive characteristics of loamy topsoil, mushrooms or truffles sometimes found in red wines; in French, "gout de terroir" (i.e., taste of the earth).

EXTENDED MACERATION—allowing the red wine must to remain in contact with the grape skins for an extended period, after fermentation is completed.

FERMENTATION—the process in which grapes sugars are converted into alcohol and carbon dioxide (CO_2) to make wine.

FERMENTER—any vessel that ferments the wine (e.g., barrel, bin, tank, etc.).

FILTERING—method of clarifying wine by passing it through a filter, thereby removing any suspended particulate matter in the liquid.

FINING—method of clarifying wine by introducing a clarifying agent (egg whites, bentonite, isinglass, casein, etc.) into the wine; the agent then drags suspended particulate matter to the bottom of the wine barrel or tank.

FLORAL—flowery aromas and tastes, associated with white wines.

FREE RUN—the juice that comes when the grapes are crushed, before pressing begins.

FRUIT—what wine is made from, i.e., grapes.

FRUITY—the taste of the fruit of the grapes themselves, often manifested as other fruit flavors, i.e., apples, strawberries or black currants.

GRASSY—aromas and flavors resembling new mown grass, negative when dominate.

HERBACEOUS—aromas and flavors displaying various type of herbs, negative when extreme.

JAMMY—in red wines, ripe fruitiness, combined with natural berry-like flavors.

LEES-spent yeast cells that fall to the bottom of the barrel during the process of fermentation.

MALOLACTIC FERMENTATION—secondary fermentation that converts the tarter malic acid into a softer lactic acid.

MICRO CLIMATE—an area where soil, combined with other environmental factors, produce a distinctive wine.

MUST—unfermented crushed grapes or juice of same.

NATIVE YEAST—natural yeast attached to the skins of the grapes, sometimes solely utilized to do the fermentation.

NOSE—all elements detected by the sense of smell, including aroma and bouquet.

OAKY—flavors of oak, in which the wine is fermented and/or aged.

OVERCROPPING—practice of allowing vines to produce more fruit than they can physiologically ripen.

PH—a chemical measurement of hydrogen ions in solution used in determining acidity.

PHYLLOXERA—root louse that attacks and kills grape vines.

RACKING—a method of aerating and clarifying wine by moving it from one container to another, leaving the lees and sediment behind in the first container.

REGIONS I THRU V—a U.C. Davis classification of grape growing regions based on climatic heat conditions.

RESIDUAL SUGAR (also RS)—level of sugar that remains in wine after fermentation.

RIPENESS—a measurement of acid, ph and sugar in the grapes; also important in conjunction with these empirical measures is how the grapes "taste" to the winemaker.

SKIN CONTACT—allowing the grape skins in contact with the must, in order to extract more color and flavor, generally utilized with red wines.

SMOKY—roasted or toasted characteristic attributable to aging in oak barrels.

SPICY—spice like flavor elements found in wine, such as pepper, cardamom, clove and cinnamon.

SUGAR—an important component of physiological grape ripeness, expressed as brix.

SULFUR DIOXIDE (also SO_2)—chemical often used to retard oxidation in wine making process.

SUR LIE (French)—allowing the wine to be aged in contact with the lees, the expired yeast cells from fermentation.

SUPPLE—a wine that tastes soft and smooth; easy to drink.

TANNIN—mouth puckering astringency often found in young, red wines.

TERROIR (French)—an all encompassing French term referring to the particular characteristics of a specific piece of vineyard land, including but not limited to the sum total of soil, exposure, drainage, climate, trellising, varietal and clone.

U.C. DAVIS (also University of California at Davis)—the California university branch that has the most extensive concentration of viticultural and vinicultural courses.

VARIETAL—the primary grape variety from which a wine takes its name (e.g., Chardonnay). The varietal name on the label indicates that at least seventy-five percent comes from grapes of that varietal.

VEGETAL—unattractive component in wine, often resembling bell peppers, cabbage or asparagus.

WHOLE CLUSTER PRESSING—a grape processing method that avoids crushing and maceration. Generally utilized with white wine grapes, entire clusters are gently pressed, minimizing skin contact time.

YEAST—cellular organism that does the work of fermenting grape juice into wine.